Tl

Jon Stallworthy is a poet who has
Literature at Oxford University and Acting President of
Wolfson College. He is a now a Fellow of the British
Academy and a Senior Research Fellow at Wolfson College.
He is the author of many distinguished works of poetry,
criticism, and translation. Among his books are critical
studies of Yeats's poetry, and prize-winning biographies of
Louis MacNiece and Wilfred Owen (hailed by Graham
Greene as 'one of the finest biographies of our time'). He
is an editor of *The Norton Anthology of English Literature*
and of the definitive edition of Wilfred Owen's poetry. His
most recent publications are *Anthem for Doomed Youth:
Soldier Poets of the First World War* and *Survivors' Songs
from Maldon to the Somme*.

The Oxford Book of War Poetry

Chosen and Edited by

Jon Stallworthy

OXFORD
UNIVERSITY PRESS

OXFORD
UNIVERSITY PRESS

Great Clarendon Street, Oxford OX2 6DP

Oxford University Press is a department of the University of Oxford.
It furthers the University's objective of excellence in research, scholarship,
and education by publishing worldwide in

Oxford New York

Auckland Cape Town Dar es Salaam Hong Kong Karachi
Kuala Lumpur Madrid Melbourne Mexico City Nairobi
New Delhi Shanghai Taipei Toronto

With offices in

Argentina Austria Brazil Chile Czech Republic France Greece
Guatemala Hungary Italy Japan Poland Portugal Singapore
South Korea Switzerland Thailand Turkey Ukraine Vietnam

Oxford is a registered trade mark of Oxford University Press
in the UK and in certain other countries

Published in the United States
by Oxford University Press Inc., New York

First published by Oxford University Press 1984
First issued as an Oxford University Press paperback 1988
Reissued 2003, 2008

British Library Cataloguing in Publication Data
Data available

Library of Congress Cataloging in Publication Data
Data available

Typeset by SPI Publisher Services, Pondicherry, India
Printed in Great Britain by
Clays Ltd, St. Ives plc

ISBN 978–0–19–955453–9

6

CONTENTS

CONTENTS

CONTENTS

CONTENTS

CONTENTS

CONTENTS

CONTENTS

CONTENTS

CONTENTS

CONTENTS

CONTENTS

CONTENTS

CONTENTS

INTRODUCTION

'POETRY', Wordsworth reminds us, 'is the spontaneous overflow of powerful feelings', and there can be no area of human experience that has generated a wider range of powerful feelings than war: hope and fear; exhilaration and humiliation; hatred—not only for the enemy, but also for generals, politicians, and war-profiteers; love—for fellow soldiers, for women and children left behind, for country (often) and cause (occasionally).

Man's early war-songs and love-songs were generally exhortations to action, or celebrations of action, in one or other field, but no such similarity exists between what we now more broadly define as love poetry and war poetry. Whereas most love poems have been in favour of love, much—and most recent—war poetry has been implicitly, if not explicitly, anti-war. So long as warrior met warrior in equal combat with sword or lance, poets could celebrate their courage and chivalry, but as technology put ever-increasing distance between combatants and, then, ceased to distinguish between combatant and civilian, poets more and more responded to 'man's inhumanity to man'. Not that heroic societies were oblivious to the domestic consequences of their heroes' 'brain-spattering, windpipe-slitting art'. *The Iliad* (3)[1] ends with Andromache watching from the walls of Troy, as her husband's broken body is dragged away behind his killer's chariot: 'she mourned, and the women wailed in answer'. Similarly, as the hero's funeral pyre is lit at the close of the Old English epic, written 1,500 years later,

> his ancient wife with braided hair,
> Grief-stricken raised a song of lamentation
> For Beowulf; repeatedly she said
> That sore she dreaded evil days would come,
> Much carnage, war's alarms, captivity
> And ignominy. Heaven swallowed up the smoke.[2]

Hers, however, is not the last word. That is spoken by Beowulf's warriors, 'his hearth-companions':

> It was their part to mourn, bewail their king,
> Recite an elegy and acclaim the man;
> They praised his prowess, and his mighty deeds
> They fittingly extolled, as right it is
> A man should honour his kind lord in words. . . .

[1] Numbers in brackets refer to poems in this anthology.
[2] Mary E. Waterhouse, trans., *Beowulf in Modern English*, 1949, p. 108.

> They said that of all earthly kings he was
> Gentlest of men and kindest unto all,
> To men most gracious and most keen for praise.[3]

Such societies recognized the cost of warfare, but the code to which they subscribed counted it a necessary price for the pursuit of 'praise', honour, renown. This was to be acquired by generosity in peace, mighty deeds in war, loyalty to the living and loyalty to the dead.

That heroic tradition died, and another was transplanted to English soil, when King Harold's foot-soldiers were cut down on a ridge above Hastings by the cavalry of William, Duke of Normandy. Less than a hundred years before, one of the last Old English poets had chanted or declaimed in a Saxon hall the poem we know as 'The Battle of Maldon' (12). And three hundred years after Harold and his housecarls had gone the way of Byrtnoth and his thanes, the first new English poet introduced to a more cultivated audience

> A knight . . . a worthy man
> That fro the time that he first bigan
> To riden out, he lovèd chivalry. . . .

The intervening years had seen Duke William's son Henry, in the words of the Anglo-Saxon Chronicle, 'dubbed a rider', married to a Saxon girl, and the two people and the two languages fused and intermingled. Under the influence of the troubadours, the Church, and the new learning out of Italy, *chivalry* had come to mean more than *cavalry*, that other derivative of the Latin *caballarius*, a horseman. The descendant of Duke William's superbly efficient but hardly sophisticated *chevalier* could, like Chaucer's Squire,

> Wel . . . sitte on hors, and fairè ride;
> He coudè songès make, and wel endite,
> Juste and eek daunce, and wel portraye and write.

The Universities of Oxford and Cambridge had been founded before Chaucer was born, and in his lifetime the first of the so-called 'public schools', Winchester, opened its doors to the sons of noblemen and gentlemen. By 1440, when Eton was founded, the word *gentleman* had come to denote a clearly defined social status, inferior to nobility and superior to the yeomanry, but not necessarily dependent on ancestry. These schools and those others later modelled on them grafted the 'classical learning of the monastic schools upon the chivalric training in honour, in sport, in military exercise, in social intercourse, in courtesy

---

[3] Ibid., p. 109.

and generosity, in reverence and devotion, of the schools of Christian knighthood'.[4]

Chaucer had seen military service—had been captured and ransomed—in France, where two centuries later fought and was wounded Henry Howard, Earl of Surrey, who returned to translate Books III and IV of the *Aeneid* into blank verse. Raleigh served in the Huguenot army at Jarnac and Moncoutour; Gascoigne saw military service in Holland; Donne took part in the Earl of Essex's two expeditions to Cadiz; Davenant was knighted by Charles I at the siege of Gloucester; Lovelace served in the Scottish expeditions of 1639; and the Earl of Rochester showed conspicuous courage in the Second Dutch War of 1665–6.

The chivalric tradition, transmuted into the courtly tradition of the High Renaissance, required proficiency in the arts of war as well as in such peaceable arts as music and poetry. The courtier-poet was expected to serve his king in much the same way as the Anglo-Saxon *scop* took his place in the shield-wall with his lord. The Earl of Surrey left a moving elegy to his Squire (19); Gascoigne, a rueful account of his capture and ransom (20); and Donne condensed his experience of Cadiz into an epigram (22). Considering how many courtier-poets had experience of battle, however, the reader in a later century—when war poems are commonly written by those who have never seen a battlefield—may be surprised by how rarely Renaissance poets write of war. Conventions had changed. Love had become the subject proper to a poet. On the rare occasion when the blast of war blows through a poem, it is likely to be the carefully orchestrated overture to a protestation of devotion, such as Lovelace, the dashing Cavalier, offers 'To Lucasta, Going to the Wars' (24). Paradoxically, the convention that proclaimed the subject of warfare too gross for the polite art of poetry sanctioned, and indeed required, a select use of military terminology in the imagery of the love lyric. Cupid is an archer. The besieging lover, having no shield proof against his darts, can only hope that his Beloved in a spirit of Christian compassion will surrender.

During the eighteenth century, soldiering reached the low place in British society that it was to hold until the Great War; an occupation despised by the middle and working classes as a disgrace hardly less than prison. If an eighteenth-century poet wrote of war—which he seldom did—it was as a remote phenomenon. So John Scott of Amwell declares (35):

> I hate that drum's discordant sound,
> Parading round, and round, and round:

[4] F. J. C. Hearnshaw, 'Chivalry and its place in History', *Chivalry*, ed. Edgar Prestage, 1928, p. 22.

> To me it talks of ravaged plains,
> And burning towns, and ruined swains,
> And mangled limbs, and dying groans,
> And widows' tears, and orphans' moans;
> And all that Misery's hand bestows,
> To fill the catalogue of human woes.

As the French Revolution made its contribution to that catalogue, warfare once more became a subject of interest to British poets. The Napoleonic wars moved Sir Walter Scott and Thomas Campbell to patriotic outpourings (36). Coleridge and Wordsworth, on the other hand, 'hailed the rising orb of liberty'. Both were subsequently disillusioned, and in Book 4 of *The Prelude* Wordsworth writes movingly of his meeting with a battered veteran of Wellington's armies. No poet of the Romantic period, however, was more alive to the horrors of war than Byron; alive not only to the sufferings of the combatants but to the domestic consequences. The eyes of the dying Gladiator in *Childe Harold* are

> with his heart and that was far away;
> He recked not of the life he lost nor prize,
> But where his rude hut by the Danube lay,
> *There* were his young barbarians all at play,
> *There* was their Dacian mother—he, their sire,
> Butchered to make a Roman holiday. . . .

Byron, as a schoolboy at Harrow, had been steeped in the classics. He visited Greece in 1809 and 1810 and the first two cantos of *Childe Harold*, based on his experiences, launched a tidal wave of literary philhellenism.

By the time of the Greek Revolution in 1821, the educated public in Europe had been deeply immersed in three attractive ideas – that Ancient Greece had been a paradise inhabited by supermen; that the Modern Greeks were the true descendants of the Ancient Greeks; and that a war against the Turks could somehow 'regenerate' the Modern Greeks and restore the former glories.[5]

Invoking the example of Leonidas and his 300 Spartans, commemorated in Simonides' epigram (4), Byron sounded the call to arms:

> Must *we* but weep o'er days more blest?
> Must *we* but blush?—Our fathers bled.
> Earth! render back from out thy breast
> A remnant of our Spartan dead!
> Of the three hundred grant but three,
> To make a new Thermopylae.

[5] William St Clair, *That Greece might Still be Free*, 1972, p. 19.

His love for the land of Pericles and Homer proving stronger than his hatred of war, he set off for Greece with half a dozen military uniforms and a couple of helmets, gilded, crested, and bearing the family motto: 'Crede Byron'.

Like every other philhellene who took that road, he was to learn how unrelated were the reality and the dream. Those more fortunate, who returned with their lives, brought tales of betrayal and brutality, squalor and needless suffering, that anticipate the war correspondents' revelations from the Crimea thirty years later. The philanthropic spirit of the age that urged Florence Nightingale to the hospitals of Scutari found expression in anti-war poems by Thackeray (61) and others, but these were counterbalanced by many sounding a savage note, and the one poem from the Crimean War to have survived in the popular memory celebrates a heroic exploit. Significantly, since Tennyson's imagination had long been engaged with the chivalric world of King Arthur and his knights, it was the *cavalry* charge of the Light Brigade in 1854 that spurred him into song (59).

It is one thing to 'Honour the charge' of professional cavalrymen of one's own country against foreign gunners thousands of miles away; but quite another to watch one's own countrymen—many of them boy civilians in uniform—killing and maiming each other. Walt Whitman was drawn into the American Civil War by a brother, wounded in the battle of Fredericksburg, who was in need of nursing. He remained, long after his brother was better, a non-combatant witness to the horrors of war, tending the wounded (66):

> Bearing the bandages, water and sponge,
> Straight and swift to my wounded I go . . .

He regards them as '*my* wounded', seeing the results of cavalry action from a markedly *un*-Tennysonian perspective:

The neck of the cavalry-man with the bullet through and through I examine,
Hard the breathing rattles, quite glazed already the eye, yet life struggles hard,
(Come sweet death! be persuaded O beautiful death!
In mercy come quickly.)

His eyes unclouded by the chivalric vision, his tongue untrammelled by the chivalric diction and rhetoric, he perceives 'in camp in the daybreak grey and dim' what Siegfried Sassoon and Wilfred Owen were to perceive in the trenches of the Western Front:

Young man I think I know you—I think this face is the face of the Christ himself,
Dead and divine and brother of all, and here again he lies.

While America was forging a new society in the fires of Civil War, Britain was making one of those cautious adjustments to the old society by which she had avoided civil strife for three hundred years. Thomas Arnold, as headmaster of Rugby from 1827 to 1842, had revitalized the public school system. Perceiving that the country and the empire needed more—and more efficient—civil servants and managers than the aristocracy and landed gentry could supply, he and the headmasters of the many Anglican boarding schools that opened their gates in the 1850s sought to make 'Christian gentlemen' of the sons of the middle classes. The ethos of these schools was essentially chivalric. As readers of *Tom Brown's Schooldays* will remember, schoolboy fights were elevated into gentlemanly duels, and on the playing fields the same code of etiquette called for 'fair play' and 'the team spirit'. Each school was dominated by its chapel, which suited the philistine respectability of the devout bourgeois, and the curriculum was dominated by Latin, and to a lesser extent, Greek. In 1884 there were twenty-eight classics masters at Eton, six mathematics masters, one historian, no modern language teachers, and no scientists. As late as 1905, classics masters still formed more than half the teaching staff.

The poet-spokesman for the public schools at the end of the nineteenth century was Henry Newbolt. The title of his poem 'Clifton Chapel' acknowledges a debt to Matthew Arnold's 'Rugby Chapel', but whereas the headmaster's son addresses his father and 'the noble and great who are gone', Newbolt exhorts a new generation of imperialists:

> To set the cause above renown,
>   To love the game beyond the prize,
> To honour, while you strike him down,
>   The foe that comes with fearless eyes;
> To count the life of battle good,
>   And dear the land that gave you birth,
>   And dearer yet the brotherhood
>   That binds the brave of all the earth.

> * * *

> God send you fortune: yet be sure,
>   Among the lights that gleam and pass,
> You'll live to follow none more pure
>   Than that which glows on yonder brass:
> '*Qui procul hinc,*' the legend's writ,—
>   The frontier-grave is far away—
> '*Qui ante diem periit:*
>   *Sed miles, sed pro patria.*'[6]

In a more famous or notorious poem, 'Vitaï Lampada' (83)—a title taken

---

[6] 'He who lies far from this place . . . died before daybreak: but he was a soldier and he died for his country.'

from Lucretius, meaning '[They pass on] the Torch of Life'—he envisaged the public-school ethic at work on a frontier far away:

> The river of death has brimmed his banks,
> And England's far, and Honour a name,
> But the voice of a schoolboy rallies the ranks:
> 'Play up! play up! and play the game!'

Newbolt's repeated celebration of the imperialist officer and gentleman, carrying to his country's battlefields a sporting code acquired on the playing fields of his public school, parallels a poetic reappraisal of the private soldier initiated by Kipling's *Barrack-room Ballads* (81) and sustained by Housman's *A Shropshire Lad* (90).

Requirements for a commission in the army had altered radically since the 1850s. 'In place of the old patronage system came, first, limited competition—examination for the select few whom the authorities had personally nominated—and then, in 1870, open competition.'[7] The year 1870, of course, saw the outbreak of the Franco-Prussian War that inaugurated the era of violence in international politics, precipitating further army reforms, the rapid mechanization of warfare, and the growth of imperialist ideologies. Malvern van Wyk Smith has shown how in Britain, at the start of the Boer War, militarist and pacifist doctrines were clearly defined and opposed; and how, because the Education Acts of 1870 and 1876 had made the army that sailed for South Africa the first literate army in history, the British Tommy sent home letters and poems that anticipate those his sons were to send back from the Western Front.[8]

These factual and often bitter accounts of combat, to say nothing of the greater poems by Thomas Hardy (84), had been forgotten by 1914 when that War we still—many wars later—know by the adjective Great was greeted in some quarters with a curious gaiety and exhilaration. Rupert Brooke captured the mood of that moment in a sonnet to which he gave the paradoxical title of 'Peace' (101). His first line 'Now, God be thanked Who has matched us with His hour'—and the 'hand' and the 'hearts' that follow reveal one of his sources: the hymn, and ironically it is a hymn translated from the German, beginning

> Now thank we all our God
> With heart, and hands, and voices. . . .

Shortly before Brooke's death, the Dean of St Paul's read aloud in a sermon from the Cathedral pulpit another of his 'war sonnets', 'The

---

[7] Rupert Wilkinson, *Gentlemanly Power: British Leadership and the Public School Tradition*, 1964, p. 10.

[8] *Drummer Hodge: The Poetry of the Anglo-Boer War*, 1978.

Soldier' (103). So the soldier poet was canonized by the Church, and many other poets—civilians and soldiers alike—found inspiration for their battle-hymns, elegies, exhortations, in the well-thumbed pages of *Hymns Ancient and Modern.*

Most of the British poets we associate with the years 1914 and 1915 had a public-school education and this, more than any other factor, distinguishes them from those we associate with the later phases of the war. The early poems return again and again to the appallingly anachronistic concept of war as a game; a concept most clearly articulated by E. B. Osborn, in the introduction to his best-selling anthology *The Muse in Arms*, published in 1917. He wrote:

Modern battles are so vast and so extended in both space and time that composed battle-pieces, such as have come down to us from the far-off centuries of archery and ballad-making, may no longer be looked for. The thread on which all such pictures are strung—the new impressions such as 'The Assault' [a poem by Robert Nichols] and old ballads such as 'Agincourt, or the English Bowman's Glory'—is the insular conception of fighting as the greatest of all great games, that which is the most shrewdly spiced with deadly danger. The Germans, and even our allies, cannot understand why this stout old nation persists in thinking of war as a sport; they do not know that sportsmanship is our new homely name, derived from a racial predilection for comparing great things with small, for the *chevalerie* of the Middle Ages. In 'The English Bowman's Glory', written before any of our co-operative pastimes were thought of, the fine idea is veiled in this homely term:

> Agincourt, Agincourt!
> Know ye not Agincourt?
> Oh, it was noble sport!
>   Then did we owe men;
> Men, who a victory won us
> 'Gainst any odds among us:
>   Such were our bowmen.

Light is thrown on this phase of the British Soldier's mentality by the verse . . . he writes in honour of the games and the field-sports in which he acquired the basal elements of all true discipline—confidence in his companions and readiness to sacrifice the desire for personal distinction to the common interest of his team, which is, of course, a mimic army in being.

The legacy of the public-school classroom was as significant for the poets as that of the playing field. Paul Fussell rightly points out in his stimulating book, *The Great War and Modern Memory*, that the British soldier tended to look at the war through literary spectacles. He evidences the popularity of Quiller-Couch's *Oxford Book of English Verse*, but surprisingly overlooks the extent to which the public-school poets' attitude to war was conditioned by their years of immersion in the works of Caesar, Virgil, Horace, and Homer. A reading of these authors would leave no intelligent boy in any doubt that war was a brutal business, but by setting 'The Kaiser's War' in a long, and dare one say a time-honoured tradition, the classics encouraged a detached perspective—quite apart from offering the soldier, by analogy, the intoxicating prospect of a place in history and literature. In the poems of 1914 and the first half of 1915, there are countless references to sword and legion, not a few to chariot and oriflamme, but almost none to gun and platoon. Siegfried Sassoon writes, in a poem of 1916, 'We are the happy legion'; while Herbert Asquith begins his elegy, 'The Volunteer' (104),

> Here lies a clerk who half his life had spent
> Toiling at ledgers in a city grey,
> Thinking that so his days would drift away
> With no lance broken in life's tournament.
> Yet ever 'twixt the books and his bright eyes
> The gleaming eagles of the legions came,
> And horsemen, charging under phantom skies,
> Went thundering past beneath the oriflamme.

A similar vision prompted Rupert Brooke, under orders for the Dardanelles, to write to Asquith's sister, Violet:

> Do you *think* perhaps the fort on the Asiatic corner will want *quelling*, and we'll land and come at it from behind and they'll make a sortie and meet us on the plains of Troy? . . .
>
> I've never been quite so happy in my life, I think. Not quite so *pervasively* happy; like a stream flowing entirely to one end. I suddenly realize that the ambition of my life has been—since I was two—to go on a military expedition against Constantinople.[9]

On the troopship, he and his friends read Homer to each other, and in a verse-letter from the trenches, Charles Hamilton Sorley remembers how Homer sung

> Tales of great war and strong hearts wrung,
> Of clash of arms, of council's brawl,
> Of beauty that must early fall,
> Of battle hate and battle joy
> By the old windy walls of Troy. . . .
> And now the fight begins again,
> The old war-joy, the old war-pain.
> Sons of one school across the sea
> We have no fear to fight. . . .[10]

The poems of these young men move us, as human documents, more than many better poems. They illustrate the hypnotic power of a long

---

[9] Geoffrey Keynes, ed., *The Letters of Rupert Brooke*, 1968, pp. 662–3.
[10] *Marlborough and Other Poems*, 1919, pp. 82–3.

cultural tradition; the tragic outcome of educating a generation to face not the future but the past. By the end of 1915, Brooke, Sorley, and many lesser public-school poets were dead. Sassoon, it is true, survived to follow Sorley's lead and break the code of his upbringing—and all honour to him. By publicly protesting in 1917 against the continuance of the war, and by lashing the leaders of Church and State and the Armed Forces in his poems, he rejected the obedience to authority that is one of the prime tenets of the public-school system. The poets who followed him—Owen, Rosenberg, Gurney—had no such conventions to reject. They went to war, as Whitman had done, with no Homeric expectations, and set themselves to expose what Owen called

> The old Lie: Dulce et decorum est
> Pro patria mori.

One, indeed, had Whitman in mind. 'When I think of *Drum Taps*,' wrote Rosenberg three months before he was killed, '[*my* poems] are absurd.'

It is often assumed that chivalry died with the cavalry, scythed by machine guns, in the Battle of the Somme. Auden, characterizing the past in his poem 'Spain 1937' (179) wrote:

> Yesterday the belief in the absolute value of Greek;
> The fall of the curtain upon the death of a hero . . .

The curtain may have fallen, but it was to rise and fall again. It is a commonplace that traditions die hard, and none die harder than military ones. Leaving Oxford in 1940 to join a cavalry regiment, Keith Douglas embellished a photograph of himself in uniform—humorously, it must be said—with the scrolled caption 'Dulce et decorum est pro patria mori'. Two years later, chafing at his enforced inactivity behind the lines while his regiment was engaging Rommel's tanks in the Western Desert, Douglas drove off—in a two-ton truck and direct disobedience of orders—to join them; earning thereby his batman's commendation: 'I like you, sir. You're shit or bust!' His subsequent achievement as a poet was to celebrate the last stand of the chivalric hero (201),

> the doomed boy, the fool
> whose perfectly mannered flesh fell
> in opening the door for a shell
> as he had learnt to do at school.

In 1915, on the Western Front, Julian Grenfell had written of the cavalryman (105) that

> In dreary, doubtful waiting hours,
> Before the brazen frenzy starts,
> The horses show him nobler powers;
> O patient eyes, courageous hearts!

So Douglas, in his fine elegy, 'Aristocrats' (203), takes the horse as the natural symbol for his anachronistic hero, and in its last line we seem to hear the last echo from the Pass at Roncesvalles: 'It is not gunfire I hear but a hunting horn.' The poem succeeds where most poems of 1914 and 1915 fail. It is sharply focused, acknowledging both the stupidity and the chivalry, the folly and the glamour of cavalrymen on mechanical mounts duelling in the desert. Douglas's language, finely responsive to his theme, fuses ancient and modern: his heroes are 'gentle'—like Chaucer's 'verray parfit gentil knight'—and at the same time 'obsolescent'.

Sidney Keyes was killed on his first patrol in North Africa, but in such poems of 1942 as 'Orestes and the Furies' and 'Rome Remember' he sees the Gorgon-head reflected in the classical shield he had acquired at a public school. He wrote:

> I am the man who groped for words and found
> An arrow in my hand.

Not a rifle, but an arrow. Henry Reed celebrated the rifle in the first of his 'Lessons of the War' (193), but the ironic detachment of these superb meditations on war and peace owes something to the poet whose lines, saucily emended, stand as epigraph to the sequence:

> *Vixi puellis nuper idoneus*
> *Et militavi non sine gloria.*

wrote Horace (*Odes*, iii. 26), which may be roughly rendered:

> Lately, I have lived among girls, creditably enough,
> and have soldiered, not without glory.

By changing *puellis*, to *duellis*, exchanging girls for battles, Reed cunningly announces and encapsulates the theme of his Lessons.

By no means all British poets of the Second World War came from public schools, and many more spoke a language that had more in common with Owen and Rosenberg. None, however, offers so sharp a contrast to the work of Douglas and Keyes as the American infantryman-poets, Louis Simpson and Lincoln Kirstein. Simpson tells us that after the war he suffered from amnesia, eventually broken by dreams of battle that—as with Owen—released his poems. He has, indeed, other resemblances to Owen—admiration for the soldier's endurance, compassion for his suffering, of which he writes with something of the same reverberant simplicity (217):

> Most clearly of that battle I remember
> The tiredness in eyes, how hands looked thin
> Around a cigarette, and the bright ember
> Would pulse with all the life there was within.

In his long poem 'The Runner', Simpson's college-boy anti-hero Dodd is humiliated by the rest of his platoon for a momentary act of cowardice; although like the Youth in *The Red Badge of Courage* he redeems himself subsequently. Cowardice, a taboo subject to poets in the chivalric tradition, is a theme of Kirstein's *Rhymes of a PFC*, the first poem of which ends:

> The rage of armies is the shame of boys;
> A hero's panic or a coward's whim
> Is triggered by nerve or nervousness.
> We wish to sink. We do not choose to swim.

Where Douglas had asked, in 'Gallantry' (201), 'Was George fond of little boys?' and had answered

> . . . who will say: since George was hit
> we never mention our surmise.

Kirstein writes openly and tenderly of homosexual love. Similarly, he and Simpson share—and show in their poems—what Simpson has described as 'the dog-face's suspicion of the officer class, with their abstract language and indifference to individual, human suffering'. It is interesting that he identifies the general infantryman with the animal that used to run beside the huntsman-cavalryman's horse. Simpson and Kirstein speak for the civilian stuffed into uniform not very tidily and against his will. They write of a wider range of military experience—not excluding cowardice and homosexuality—because they write as men rather than as soldiers conscious of soldierly tradition.

What may be termed the anti-heroic tradition is at least as old as Falstaff. It makes sporadic appearances in eighteenth-century English poetry, but does not oust its older rival until transplanted to America in the next century. A civil war fought by large numbers of conscripted civilians, a high proportion of them literate (but few versed in classical literature), was a new kind of conflict, and America's produced a new kind of poetry. Its principal poets, Whitman and Melville, were civilians and they established a perspective and a tone that would be adopted by those that followed them, combatant and civilian alike: so James Dickey, veteran of a hundred combat missions, begins 'The Firebombing' (225): 'Homeowners unite'. That, surely, is the one hope for the human race. Only if the poets' perception that we are all civilians gains universal acceptance will we be spared the fulfilment of Peter Porter's dark prophecy, 'Your Attention Please' (259).

The poems in this anthology have, with few exceptions, been arranged chronologically by conflict. Thus, Tate's 1928 'Ode to the Confederate Dead' (77), appearing with other poems of the American

Civil War, comes before earlier evocations of the Franco-Prussian War by Rilke (78) and Rimbaud (79). The exceptions to this arrangement are mainly such nineteenth-century versions of heroic epic as Arnold's 'Sohrab and Rustum' (57), that tell us more about the period of their composition than that of their historical origin.

Long poems pose a special problem in an anthology of this kind, and I have preferred to print extracts than to omit them altogether as, for reasons of space, I felt obliged to omit dramatic poetry. It would have been unthinkable to exclude, for example, representative passages from the Greek and Latin epics that have so influenced war poetry in English. Translations from other literatures have been admitted when—but only when—they seem to me English poems in their own right.

The resulting selection necessarily includes many more 'horse-face' poems than 'dog-face' ones, and I am aware that the latter category could have been swelled by the addition of popular ballads such as appear in the 'Soldiers and Sailors' section of Frederick Woods's excellent *Oxford Book of English Traditional Verse*. I decided, however, that they show to better advantage in that context than they would in this.

Many friends helped in the preparation of the anthology, and I am particularly indebted to Miss Jacqueline Doyle, Professor Steven Fix, Professor Ephim Fogel, Professor Anthony Hecht, Professor Alan Heuser, Dr Dominic Hibberd, Professor Mary Jacobus, Professor Gwyn Jones, Mrs Judith Luna, Professor Kevin McManus, Professor Stephen Parrish, Mrs Jacqueline Simms, and Mr Charles Tomlinson. I am also grateful to the Royal Society of Literature, in whose transactions, *Essays by Divers Hands* (new series, vol. xli, edited by Brian Fothergill, 1980), a version of this essay appeared.

JON STALLWORTHY

Cornell University, 1984

THE BIBLE

I   from *The Book of Exodus*

Then sang Moses and the children of Israel this song unto the Lord, and spake, saying, I will sing unto the Lord, for he hath triumphed gloriously: the horse and his rider hath he thrown into the sea.

The Lord is my strength and song, and he is become my salvation: he is my God, and I will prepare him an habitation: my father's God, and I will exalt him.

The Lord is a man of war: the Lord is his name.

Pharaoh's chariots and his host hath he cast into the sea: his chosen captains also are drowned in the Red sea.

The depths have covered them: they sank into the bottom as a stone.

Thy right hand, O Lord, is become glorious in power: thy right hand, O Lord, hath dashed in pieces the enemy.

And in the greatness of thine excellency thou hast overthrown them that rose up against thee: thou sentest forth thy wrath, which consumed them as stubble.

And with the blast of thy nostrils the waters were gathered together, the floods stood upright as an heap and the depths were congealed in the heart of the sea.

The enemy said, I will pursue, I will overtake, I will divide the spoil; my lust shall be satisfied upon them; I will draw my sword, my hand shall destroy them.

Thou didst blow with thy wind, the sea covered them: they sank as lead in the mighty waters.

Who is like unto thee, O Lord, among the Gods? who is like thee, glorious in holiness, fearful in praises, doing wonders?

Thou stretchedst out thy right hand, the earth swallowed them.

Thou in thy mercy hast led forth the people which thou hast redeemed: thou hast guided them in thy strength unto thy holy habitation.

The people shall hear, and be afraid: sorrow shall take hold on the inhabitants of Palestina.

Then the dukes of Edon shall be amazed; the mighty men of Moab, trembling shall take hold upon them; all the inhabitants of Canaan shall melt away.

Fear and dread shall fall upon them; by the greatness of thine arm they shall be as still as a stone; till thy people pass over, O Lord, till the people pass over, which thou hast purchased.

Thou shalt bring them in, and plant them in the mountain of thine inheritance, in the place, O Lord, which thou hast made for thee to dwell in, in the Sanctuary, O Lord, which thy hands have established.

The Lord shall reign for ever and ever.

Translated from the Hebrew by William Tyndale

2   from *The Second Book of Samuel*

The beauty of Israel is slain upon thy high places: how are the mighty fallen!

Tell it not in Gath, publish it not in the streets of Askelon; lest the daughters of the Philistines rejoice, lest the daughters of the uncircumcised triumph.

Ye mountains of Gilboa, let there be no dew, neither let there be rain, upon you, nor fields of offerings: for there the shield of the mighty is vilely cast away, the shield of Saul, as though he had not been anointed with oil.

From the blood of the slain, from the fat of the mighty, the bow of Jonathan turned not back, and the sword of Saul returned not empty.

Saul and Jonathan were lovely and pleasant in their lives, and in their death they were not divided: they were swifter than eagles, they were stronger than lions.

Ye daughters of Israel, weep over Saul, who clothed you in scarlet, with other delights, who put on ornaments of gold upon your apparel.

How are the mighty fallen in the midst of the battle! O Jonathan, thou wast slain in thine high places.

I am distressed for thee, my brother Jonathan: very pleasant hast thou been unto me: thy love to me was wonderful, passing the love of women.

How are the mighty fallen, and the weapons of war perished!

Translated from the Hebrew by William Tyndale

HOMER

*c.*900 BC

3   from *The Iliad*

Achilles with wild fury in his heart
pulled in upon his chest his beautiful shield—
his helmet with four burnished metal ridges
nodding above it, and the golden crest
Hephaestus locked there tossing in the wind.
Conspicuous as the evening star that comes,
amid the first in heaven, at fall of night,
and stands most lovely in the west, so shone
in sunlight the fine-pointed spear
Achilles poised in his right hand, with deadly
aim at Hector, at the skin where most
it lay exposed. But nearly all was covered
by the bronze gear he took from slain Patroclus,
showing only, where his collarbones
divided neck and shoulders, the bare throat
where the destruction of a life is quickest.
Here, then, as the Trojan charged, Achilles
drove his point straight through the tender neck,
but did not cut the windpipe, leaving Hector
able to speak and to respond. He fell
aside into the dust. And Prince Achilles
now exulted:

'Hector, had you thought
that you could kill Patroclus and be safe?
Nothing to dread from me; I was not there.
All childishness. Though distant then, Patroclus,
comrade in arms was greater far than he—
and it is I who had been left behind
that day beside the deepsea ships who now
have made your knees give way. The dogs and kites
will rip your body. His will lie in honour
when the Achaeans give him funeral.'

Hector, barely whispering, replied:

'I beg you by your soul and by your parents,
do not let the dogs feed on me
in your encampment by the ships. Accept
the bronze and gold my father will provide
as gifts, my father and her ladyship
my mother. Let them have my body back,
so that our men and women may accord me
decency of fire when I am dead.'

Achilles the great runner scowled and said:

'Beg me no beggary by soul or parents,
whining dog! Would god my passion drove me
to slaughter you and eat you raw, you've caused
such agony to me! No man exists
who could defend you from the carrion pack—
not if they spread for me ten times your ransom,
twenty times, and promise more as well;
aye, not if Priam, son of Dardanus,
tells them to buy you for your weight in gold!
You'll have no bed of death, nor will you be
laid out and mourned by her who gave you birth.
Dogs and birds will have you, every scrap.'

Then at the point of death Lord Hector said:

'I see you now for what you are. No chance
to win you over. Iron in your breast
your heart is. Think a bit, though: this may be
a thing the gods in anger hold against you
on that day when Paris and Apollo
destroy you at the Gates, great as you are.'

Even as he spoke, the end came, and death hid him;
spirit from body fluttered to undergloom,
bewailing fate that made him leave his youth
and manhood in the world. And as he died
Achilles spoke again. He said:

'Die, make an end. I shall accept my own
whenever Zeus and the other gods desire.'

At this he pulled his spearhead from the body,
laying it aside, and stripped
the bloodstained shield and cuirass from his shoulders.
Other Achaeans hastened round to see
Hector's fine body and his comely face,
and no one came who did not stab the body.
Glancing at one another they would say:

'Now Hector has turned vulnerable, softer
than when he put the torches to the ships!'

And he who said this would inflict a wound.
When the great master of pursuit, Achilles,
had the body stripped, he stood among them,
saying swiftly:
       'Friends, my lords and captains
of Argives, now that the gods at last have let me
bring to earth this man who wrought
havoc among us—more than all the rest—
come, we'll offer battle around the city,
to learn the intentions of the Trojans now.
Will they give up their strongpoint at this loss?
Can they fight on, though Hector's dead?
                        But wait:
why do I ponder, why take up these questions?
Down by the ships Patroclus' body lies
unwept, unburied. I shall not forget him
while I can keep my feet among the living.
If in the dead world they forget the dead,
I say there, too, I shall remember him,
my friend. Men of Achaea, lift a song!
Down to the ships we go, and take this body,
our glory. We have beaten Hector down,
to whom as to a god the Trojans prayed.'

Indeed, he had in mind for Hector's body
outrage and shame. Behind both feet he pierced
the tendons, heel to ankle. Rawhide cords
he drew through both and lashed them to his chariot,
letting the man's head trail. Stepping aboard,
bearing the great trophy of the arms,
he shook the reins, and whipped the team ahead
into a willing run. A dustcloud rose
above the furrowing body; the dark tresses
flowed behind, and the head so princely once
lay back in dust. Zeus gave him to his enemies
to be defiled in his own fatherland.
So his whole head was blackened. Looking down,
his mother tore her braids, threw off her veil,
and wailed, heartbroken to behold her son.
Piteously his father groaned, and round him
lamentation spread throughout the town,
most like the clamour to be heard if Ilium's
towers, top to bottom, seethed in flames.
They barely stayed the old man, mad with grief,
from passing through the gates. Then in the mire
he rolled, and begged them all, each man by name:

'Relent, friends. It is hard; but let me go
out of the city to the Achaean ships.
I'll make my plea to that demonic heart.
He may feel shame before his peers, or pity
my old age. His father, too, is old,
Peleus, who brought him up to be a scourge
to Trojans, cruel to all, but most to me,
so many of my sons in flower of youth
he cut away. And, though I grieve, I cannot
mourn them all as much as I do one,
for whom my grief will take me to the grave—
and that is Hector. Why could he not have died
where I might hold him? In our weeping, then,
his mother, now so destitute, and I
might have had surfeit and relief of tears.'

These were the words of Priam as he wept,
and all his people groaned. Then in her turn
Hecabe led the women in lamentation:

'Child, I am lost now. Can I bear my life
after the death of suffering your death?
You were my pride in all my nights and days,
pride of the city, pillar to the Trojans
and Trojan women. Everyone looked to you
as though you were a god, and rightly so.
You were their greatest glory while you lived.
Now your doom and death have come upon you.'

These were her mournful words. But Hector's lady
still knew nothing; no one came to tell her
of Hector's stand outside the gates. She wove
upon her loom, deep in the lofty house,
a double purple web with rose design.
Calling her maids in waiting,
she ordered a big cauldron on a tripod
set on the hearthfire, to provide a bath
for Hector when he came home from the fight.
Poor wife, how far removed from baths he was
she could not know, as at Achilles' hands
Athena brought him down.

                  Then from the tower
she heard a wailing and a distant moan.
Her knees shook, and she let her shuttle fall,
and called out to her maids again:

                      'Come here.
Two must follow me, to see this action.
I heard my husband's queenly mother cry.
I feel my heart rise, throbbing in my throat.
My knees are like stone under me. Some blow
is coming home to Priam's sons and daughters.
Ah, could it never reach my ears! I die
of dread that Achilles may have cut off Hector,
blocked my bold husband from the city wall,
to drive him down the plain alone! By now
he may have ended Hector's deathly pride.
He never kept his place amid the chariots
but drove ahead. He would not be outdone
by anyone in courage.'

                Saying this, she ran
like a madwoman through the megaron,
her heart convulsed. Her maids kept at her side.

On reaching the great tower and the soldiers,
Andromache stood gazing from the wall
and saw him being dragged before the city.
Chariot horses at a brutal gallop
pulled the torn body toward the decked ships.
Blackness of night covered her eyes; she fell
backward swooning, sighing out her life,
and let her shining headdress fall, her hood
and diadem, her plaited band and veil
that Aphrodite once had given her,
on that day when, from Eetion's house,
for a thousand bridal gifts, Lord Hector led her.
Now, at her side, kinswomen of her lord
supported her among them, dazed and faint
to the point of death. But when she breathed again
and her stunned heart recovered, in a burst
of sobbing she called out among the women:

'Hector! Here is my desolation. Both
had this in store from birth—from yours in Troy
in Priam's palace, mine by wooded Placus
at Thebe in the home of Eetion,
my father, who took care of me in childhood,
a man cursed by fate, a fated daughter.
How I could wish I never had been born!
Now under earth's roof to the house of Death
you go your way and leave me here, bereft,
lonely, in anguish without end. The child
we wretches had is still in infancy;
you cannot be a pillar to him, Hector,
now you are dead, nor he to you. And should
this boy escape the misery of the war,
there will be toil and sorrow for him later,
as when strangers move his boundary stones.
The day that orphans him will leave him lonely,
downcast in everything, cheeks wet with tears,
in hunger going to his father's friends
to tug at one man's cloak, another's khiton.
Some will be kindly: one may lift a cup
to wet his lips at least, though not his throat;
but from the board some child with living parents
gives him a push, a slap, with biting words:
"Outside, you there! Your father is not with us

8

here at our feast!" And the boy Astyanax
will run to his forlorn mother. Once he fed
on marrow only and the fat of lamb,
high on his father's knees. And when sleep came
to end his play, he slept in a nurse's arms,
brimful of happiness, in a soft bed.
But now he'll know sad days and many of them,
missing his father. "Lord of the lower town"
the Trojans call him. They know, you alone,
Lord Hector, kept their gates and their long walls.
Beside the beaked ships now, far from your kin,
the blowflies' maggots in a swarm will eat you
naked, after the dogs have had their fill.
Ah, there are folded garments in your chambers,
delicate and fine, of women's weaving.
These, by heaven, I'll burn to the last thread
in blazing fire! They are no good to you,
they cannot cover you in death. So let them
go, let them be burnt as an offering
from Trojans and their women in your honour.'

Thus she mourned, and the women wailed in answer.

Translated from the Greek by Robert Fitzgerald

SIMONIDES

c.556–c.468 BC

4   *Thermopylae**

Go tell the Spartans, thou that passest by,
That here, obedient to their laws, we lie.

Translated from the Greek by William Lisle Bowles

* At Thermopylae, a narrow pass between mountain and sea, 6,000 Greeks including
300 Spartans fought off a vast army of invading Persians in 480 BC.

ANONYMOUS

4th century BC

5   *Hymn to the Fallen*

'We hold our flat shields, we wear our jerkins of hide;
The axles of our chariots touch, our short swords meet.
Standards darken the sun, the foe roll on like clouds;
Arrows fall thick, the warriors press forward.
They have overrun our ranks, they have crossed our line;
The trace-horse on the left is dead, the one on the right is wounded.
The fallen horses block our wheels, our chariot is held fast;
We grasp our jade drum-sticks, we beat the rolling drums.'

Heaven decrees their fall, the dread Powers are angry;
The warriors are all dead, they lie in the open fields.
They set out, but shall not enter; they went but shall not come back.
The plains are empty and wide, the way home is long.
Their tall swords are at their waist, their bows are under their arm;
Though their heads were severed their spirit could not be subdued.
They that fought so well—in death are warriors still;
Stubborn and steadfast to the end, they could not be dishonoured.
Their bodies perished in the fight; but the magic of their souls is
    strong—
Captains among the ghosts, heroes among the Dead!

Translated from the Chinese by Arthur Waley

VIRGIL

70–19 BC

6   from *The Aeneid*

And now Aeneas charges straight at Turnus.
He brandishes a shaft huge as a tree,
and from his savage breast he shouts: 'Now what
delay is there? Why, Turnus, do you still

draw back from battle? It is not for us
to race against each other, but to meet
with cruel weapons, hand to hand. Go, change
yourself into all shapes; by courage and
by craft collect whatever help you can;
take wing, if you so would, toward the steep stars
or hide yourself within the hollow earth.'
But Turnus shakes his head: 'Your burning words,
ferocious Trojan, do not frighten me;
it is the gods alone who terrify me,
and Jupiter, my enemy.' He says
no more, but as he looks about he sees
a giant stone, an ancient giant stone
that lay at hand, by chance, upon the plain,
set there as boundary mark between the fields
to keep the farmers free from border quarrels.
And twice-six chosen men with bodies such
as earth produces now could scarcely lift
that stone upon their shoulders. But the hero,
anxious and running headlong, snatched the boulder;
reaching full height, he hurled it at the Trojan.
But Turnus does not know if it is he
himself who runs or goes or lifts or throws
that massive rock; his knees are weak; his blood
congeals with cold. The stone itself whirls through
the empty void but does not cross all of
the space between; it does not strike a blow.
Just as in dreams of night, when languid rest
has closed our eyes, we seem in vain to wish
to press on down a path, but as we strain,
we falter, weak; our tongues can say nothing,
the body loses its familiar force,
no voice, no word, can follow: so whatever
courage he calls upon to find a way,
the cursed goddess keeps success from Turnus.
The shifting feelings overtake his heart;
he looks in longing at the Latin ranks
and at the city, and he hesitates,
afraid; he trembles at the coming spear.
He does not know how he can save himself,
what power he has to charge his enemy;
he cannot see his chariot anywhere;
he cannot see the charioteer, his sister.

In Turnus' wavering Aeneas sees
his fortune; he holds high the fatal shaft;
he hurls it far with all his body's force.
No boulder ever catapulted from
siege engine sounded so, no thunderbolt
had ever burst with such a roar. The spear
flies on like a black whirlwind, carrying
its dread destruction, ripping through the border
of Turnus' corselet and the outer rim
of Turnus' seven-plated shield; hissing,
it penetrates his thigh. The giant Turnus,
struck, falls to earth; his knees bend under him.
All the Rutulians leap up with a groan,
and all the mountain slopes around re-echo;
tall forests, far and near, return that voice.
Then humble, suppliant, he lifts his eyes
and, stretching out his hand, entreating, cries:
'I have indeed deserved this; I do not
appeal against it; use your chance. But if
there is a thought of a dear parent's grief
that now can touch you, then I beg you, pity
old Daunus—in Anchises you had such
a father—send me back or, if you wish,
send back my lifeless body to my kin.
For you have won, and the Ausonians
have seen me, beaten, stretch my hands; Lavinia
is yours; then do not press your hatred further.'

Aeneas stood, ferocious in his armour;
his eyes were restless and he stayed his hand;
and as he hesitated, Turnus' words
began to move him more and more—until
high on the Latin's shoulder he made out
the luckless belt of Pallas, of the boy
whom Turnus had defeated, wounded, stretched
upon the battlefield, from whom he took
this fatal sign to wear upon his back,
this girdle glittering with familiar studs.
And when his eyes drank in this plunder, this
memorial of brutal grief, Aeneas,
aflame with rage—his wrath was terrible—
cried: 'How can you who wear the spoils of my
dear comrade now escape me? It is Pallas

who strikes, who sacrifices you, who takes
this payment from your shameless blood.' Relentless,
he sinks his sword into the chest of Turnus.
His limbs fell slack with chill; and with a moan
his life, resentful, fled to Shades below.

Translated from the Latin by Allen Mandelbaum

HORACE

65–8 BC

7

from *The Odes*

(i)

Disciplined in the school of hard campaigning,
Let the young Roman study how to bear
Rigorous difficulties without complaining,
And camp with danger in the open air,

And with his horse and lance become the scourge of
Wild Parthians. From the ramparts of the town
Of the warring king, the princess on the verge of
Womanhood with her mother shall look down

And sigh, 'Ah, royal lover, still a stranger
To battle, do not recklessly excite
That lion, savage to touch, whom murderous anger
Drives headlong through the thickest of the fight.'

The glorious and the decent way of dying
Is for one's country. Run, and death will seize
You no less surely. The young coward, flying,
Gets his quietus in the back and knees.

Unconscious of mere loss of votes and shining
With honours that the mob's breath cannot dim,
True worth is not found raising or resigning
The fasces at the wind of popular whim.

To those who do not merit death, exploring
Ways barred to ordinary men, true worth
Opens a path to heaven and spurns on soaring
Pinions the trite crowds and the clogging earth.

Trusty discretion too shall be rewarded
Duly. I will not suffer a tell-tale
Of Ceres' sacred mysteries to be boarded
Under my roof or let my frail boat sail

With him; for, slighted, often God confuses
The innocent with the evil-doer's fate.
Yet Vengeance, with one lame foot, seldom loses
Track of the outlaw, though she sets off late.

(ii)

Pompeius, chief of all my friends, with whom
I often ventured to the edge of doom
    When Brutus led our line,
    With whom, aided by wine

And garlands and Arabian spikenard,
I killed those afternoons that died so hard—
    Who has new-made you, then,
    A Roman citizen

And given you back your native gods and weather?
We two once beat a swift retreat together
    Upon Philippi's field,
    When I dumped my poor shield,

And courage cracked, and the strong men who frowned
Fiercest were felled, chins to the miry ground.
    But I, half-dead with fear,
    Was wafted, airborne, clear

Of the enemy lines, wrapped in a misty blur
By Mercury, not sucked back, as you were,
    From safety and the shore
    By the wild tide of war.

Pay Jove his feast, then. In my laurel's shade
Stretch out the bones that long campaigns have made
    Weary. Your wine's been waiting
    For years: no hesitating!

Fill up the polished goblets to the top
With memory-drowning Massic! Slave, unstop
    The deep-mouthed shells that store
    Sweet-smelling oil and pour!

Who'll run to fit us out with wreaths and find
Myrtle and parsley, damp and easily twined?
    Who'll win the right to be
    Lord of the revelry

By dicing highest? I propose to go
As mad as a Thracian. It's sheer joy to throw
    Sanity overboard
    When a dear friend's restored.

Translated from the Latin by James Michie

ANEIRIN

6th century

8   from *The Gododdin**

Men went to Gododdin, laughter-loving,
Bitter in battle, each blade in line.
A brief year they were quiet, in peace.
Bodgad's son with his hand took revenge.
Though they went to churches for shriving,
Old men and young, noble and lowly,
True is the tale, death confronted them.

* Sometime around 600 AD, Mynyddawg Mwynfawr, a king of the North British people known as the Gododdin, assembled 300 Celtic warriors and feasted them for a year at his court in Edinburgh, before leading them south. At Catterick in Yorkshire they encountered the English hosts and in the ensuing battle all, or all but a handful, were killed.

Men went to Gododdin, laughing warriors,
Assailants in a savage war-band
They slaughtered with swords in short order,
War-column of kind-hearted Rhaithfyw.

Men went to Catraeth, keen their war-band.
Pale mead their portion, it was poison.
Three hundred under orders to fight.
And after celebration, silence.
Though they went to churches for shriving,
True is the tale, death confronted them.

Men went to Catraeth, mead-nourished band,
Great the disgrace should I not praise them.
With huge dark-socketed crimson spears,
Stern and steadfast the battle-hounds fought.
Of Brennych's band I'd hardly bear it
Should I leave a single man alive.
A comrade I lost, faithful I was,
Keen in combat, leaving him grieves me.
No desire had he for a dowry,
Y Cian's young son, of Maen Gwyngwn.

Men went to Catraeth at dawn:
All their fears had been put to flight.
Three hundred clashed with ten thousand.
They stained their spears ruddy with blood.
He held firm, bravest in battle,
Before Mynyddawg Mwynfawr's men.

Men went to Catraeth at dawn:
Their high spirits lessened their life-spans.
They drank mead, gold and sweet, ensnaring;
For a year the minstrels were merry.
Red their swords, let the blades remain
Uncleansed, white shields and four-sided spearheads,
Before Mynyddawg Mwynfawr's men.

.   .   .   .

Men went to Catraeth, they were renowned.
Wine and mead from gold cups was their drink,
A year in noble ceremonial,
Three hundred and sixty-three gold-torqued men.

Of all those who charged, after too much drink,
But three won free through courage in strife,
Aeron's two war-hounds and tough Cynon,
And myself, soaked in blood, for my song's sake.

Translated from the Welsh by Joseph P. Clancy

RIHAKU

8th century

9   *Lament of the Frontier Guard*

By the North Gate, the wind blows full of sand,
Lonely from the beginning of time until now!
Trees fall, the grass goes yellow with autumn.
I climb the towers and towers
      to watch out the barbarous land:
Desolate castle, the sky, the wide desert.
There is no wall left to this village.
Bones white with a thousand frosts,
High heaps, covered with trees and grass;
Who brought this to pass?
Who has brought the flaming imperial anger?
Who has brought the army with drums and with kettle-drums?
Barbarous kings.
A gracious spring, turned to blood-ravenous autumn,
A turmoil of wars-men, spread over the middle kingdom,
Three hundred and sixty thousand,
And sorrow, sorrow like rain.
Sorrow to go, and sorrow, sorrow returning.
Desolate, desolate fields,
And no children of warfare upon them,
      No longer the men for offence and defence.
Ah, how shall you know the dreary sorrow at the North Gate,
With Rihaku's name forgotten,
And we guardsmen fed to the tigers.

Translated from the Chinese by Ezra Pound

ANONYMOUS

8th century

10   *The Finnesburh Fragment**

'. . . the gables are not burning.'
Then the young king spoke, a novice in battle:
'This light is not the light of dawn; no fiery dragon flies overhead;
The gables of this hall are not lit up with licking flames;
But men draw near with shining weapons. The birds of battle screech,
The grey wolf howls, the spear rattles,
Shield answers shaft. The pale moon wanders
On her way below the clouds, gleaming; evil deeds will now be done
Provoking pitched battle.
Wake up now, my warriors!
Grasp your shields, steel yourselves,
Step forward and be brave!'
So many a thane, ornamented in gold, buckled his sword-belt.
Then the stout warriors, Sigeferth and Eaha
Strode to one door and unsheathed their swords;
Ordlaf and Guthlaf went to guard the other,
And Hengest himself followed in their footsteps.
When he saw this, Guthere said to Garulf
That he would be unwise to go to the hall doors
In the first fury of the onslaught, risking his precious life,
For Sigeferth the strong was set upon his death.
But Garulf, a hero of great heart,
Shouted out, 'Who holds the door?'
'I am Sigeferth, a warrior of the Secgan
And a well-known campaigner; I've lived through many conflicts,
Many stern trials. Here, in strife with me,
You'll discover your fate, victory or defeat.'
Then the din of battle broke out in the hall;
The hollow shield, defender of the body, was doomed to disintegrate
In the hero's hand; the hall floor boomed.
Then Garulf, the son of Guthlaf, gave his life
In the fight, first of all the warriors
Living in that land, and many heroes lay prostrate beside him.
A crowd of pale faces fell to the earth. The raven wheeled,

* The Finnesburh fragment recounts a portion of the tale of Finn and Hildeburh sung
by the minstrel in the Old English epic *Beowulf*.

18

Dusky, dark brown. The gleaming swords so shone
It seemed as if all Finnesburh were in flames.
I have never heard, before or since, of sixty triumphant warriors
Who bore themselves more bravely in the thick of battle.
And never did retainers repay their prince more handsomely
For his gift of glowing mead than did those men repay Hnæf.
They fought five days and not one of the followers
Fell, but they held the doors firmly.
Then Guthere retired, worn out and wounded;
He said that his armour was almost useless,
His corselet broken, his helmet burst open.
The guardian of those people asked him at once
How well the warriors had survived their wounds
Or which of the young men. . . .

Translated from the Anglo-Saxon by Kevin Crossley-Holland

ANONYMOUS

10th century

11

*The Battle of Brunanburh**

I

Athelstan King,
Lord among Earls,
Bracelet-bestower and
Baron of Barons,
He with his brother,
Edmund Atheling,
Gaining a lifelong
Glory in battle,
Slew with the sword-edge
There by Brunanburh,
Brake the shield-wall,
Hewed the lindenwood,
Hacked the battleshield,
Sons of Edward with hammered brands.

* At the Battle of Brunanburh in 937, King Athelstan's English army defeated the Vikings, supported by the forces of Scotland and Wales.

II

Theirs was a greatness
Got from their Grandsires—
Theirs that so often in
Strife with their enemies
Struck for their hoards and their hearths and their homes.

III

Bowed the spoiler,
Bent the Scotsman,
Fell the shipcrews
Doomed to the death.
All the field with blood of the fighters
Flowed, from when first the great
Sun-star of morningtide,
Lamp of the Lord God
Lord everlasting,
Glode over earth till the glorious creature
Sank to his setting.

IV

There lay many a man
Marred by the javelin,
Men of the Northland
Shot over shield.
There was the Scotsman
Weary of war.

V

We the West-Saxons,
Long as the daylight
Lasted, in companies
Troubled the track of the host that we hated.
Grimly with swords that were sharp from the grindstone,
Fiercely we hacked at the flyers before us.

VI

Mighty the Mercian,
Hard was his hand-play,
Sparing not any of
Those that with Anlaf,

Warriors over the
Weltering waters
Borne in the bark's-bosom,
Drew to this island:
Doomed to the death.

VII

Five young kings put asleep by the sword-stroke,
Seven strong Earls of the army of Anlaf
Fell on the war-field, numberless numbers,
Shipmen and Scotsmen.

VIII

Then the Norse leader,
Dire was his need of it,
Few were his following,
Fled to his warship:
Fleeted his vessel to sea with the king in it,
Saving his life on the fallow flood.

IX

Also the crafty one,
Constantinus,
Crept to his North again,
Hoar-headed hero!

X

Slender warrant had
He to be proud of
The welcome of war-knives—
He that was reft of his
Folk and his friends that had
Fallen in conflict,
Leaving his son too
Lost in the carnage,
Mangled to morsels,
A youngster in war!

XI

Slender reason had
He to be glad of
The clash of the war-glaive—

Traitor and trickster
And spurner of treaties—
He nor had Anlaf
With armies so broken
A reason for bragging
That they had the better
In perils of battle
On places of slaughter—
The struggle of standards,
The rush of the javelins,
The crash of the charges,
The wielding of weapons—
The play that they played with
The children of Edward.

XII

Then with their nailed prows
Parted the Norsemen, a
Blood-reddened relic of
Javelins over
The jarring breaker, the deep-sea billow,
Shaping their way toward Dyflen again,
Shamed in their souls.

XIII

Also the brethren,
King and Atheling,
Each in his glory,
Went to his own in his own West-Saxonland,
Glad of the war.

XIV

Many a carcase they left to be carrion,
Many a livid one, many a sallow-skin—
Left for the white tailed eagle to tear it, and
Left for the horny-nibbed raven to rend it, and
Gave to the garbaging war-hawk to gorge it, and
That gray beast, the wolf of the weald.

XV

Never had huger
Slaughter of heroes
Slain by the sword-edge—

ANONYMOUS

Such as old writers
Have writ of in histories—
Hapt in this isle, since
Up from the East hither
Saxon and Angle from
Over the broad billow
Broke into Britain with
Haughty war-workers who
Harried the Welshmen, when
Earls that were lured by the
Hunger of glory gat
Hold of the land.

Translated from the Anglo-Saxon by Alfred, Lord Tennyson

ANONYMOUS

11th century

12 *The Battle of Maldon**

. . . it was shattered.
Then Byrhtnoth ordered every warrior to dismount,
Let loose his horse and go forward into battle
With faith in his own skills and bravery.
Thus Offa's young son could see for himself
That the earl was no man to suffer slackness.
He sent his best falcon flying from his wrist
To the safety of the forest and strode into the fight;
The boy's behaviour was a testament
That he would not be weak in the turmoil of battle.
Eadric too was firmly resolved to follow his leader
Into the fight. At once he hurried forward
With his spear. He feared no foe
For as long as he could lift his shield
And wield a sword: he kept his word
That he would pierce and parry before his prince.

* At Maldon in Essex, a small force of East Saxons was cut down by Viking invaders in 991.

Then Byrhtnoth began to martial his men.
He rode about, issuing instructions
As to how they should stand firm, not yielding an inch,
And how they should tightly grip their shields
Forgetting their qualms and pangs of fear.
And when he had arrayed the warriors' ranks
He dismounted with his escort at a carefully chosen place
Where his finest troops stood prepared for the fight.
Then a spokesman for the Vikings stood on the river bank
And aggressively shouted
A message from the seafarers
To Byrhtnoth, the earl, on the opposite bank.
'The brave seafarers have sent me to say to you
That they will be so good as to let you give gold rings
In return for peace. It is better for you
To buy off our raid with gold
Than that we, renowned for cruelty, should cut you down in battle.
Why destroy one another? If you're good for a certain sum,
We'll settle for peace in exchange for gold.
If you, most powerful over there, agree to this
And wisely decide to disband your men,
Giving gold to the seafarers on their own terms
In return for a truce,
We'll take to the sea with the tribute you pay
And keep our promise of peace.'
Then Byrhtnoth spoke. He grasped his shield
And brandished his slender ashen spear,
Resentful and resolute he shouted his reply:
'Can you hear, you pirate, what these people say?
They will pay you a tribute of whistling spears,
Of deadly darts and proven swords,
Weapons to pay you, pierce, slit and slay you in storming battle.
Listen, messenger! Take back this reply:
Tell your people the unpleasant tidings
That over here there stands a noble earl with his troop—
Guardians of the people and of the country,
The home of Ethelred, my prince—who'll defend this land
To the last ditch. We'll sever the heathens' heads
From their shoulders. It would be much to our shame
If you took our tribute and embarked without battle
Since you've intruded so far
And so rudely into this country.
No! You'll not get your treasure so easily.

The spear's point and the sword's edge, savage battle-play,
Must teach us first that we have to yield tribute.'
Then Byrhtnoth gave word that all his warriors should walk
With their shields to the river bank.
The troops on either side could not get at one another,
For there the flood flowed after the turn of the tide;
The water streams ran together. Waiting seemed like passing years,
Waiting to cross and clash their spears.
The East-Saxons and the Ship-army
Stood beside the River Panta in proud array.
But no warrior could work harm on another
Except by the flight of a feathered arrow.
The tide ebbed; the pirates stood prepared,
Many bold Vikings ready for battle.
Then Byrhtnoth, brave protector of his men, ordered
A warrior, Wulfstan by name, to defend the ford.
He was Ceola's son, outstanding for his courage amongst courageous
    men.
He struck the first seafarer with his spear
Who stepped intrepidly on to the ford.
Two experienced warriors stood with Wulfstan,
Ælfere and Maccus, both brave men.
Nothing could have made them take flight at the ford.
They would have defended it
For as long as they could wield their weapons.
But as it was, the Danes found the dauntless guardians
Of the ford too fierce for their liking. . . .
The hateful strangers began to use guile
And asked if they could cross,
Leading their warriors over the water.
Then, in foolhardy pride, the earl permitted
Those hateful strangers to have access to the ford.
The son of Byrhthelm began to call out
Across the cold water (the warriors listened):
'Now the way is clear for you. Come over to us quickly,
Come to the slaughter. God alone can say
Who of us that fight today will live to fight again.'

Then the wolvish Vikings, avid for slaughter,
Waded to the west across the River Panta;
The seafarers hoisted their shields on high
And carried them over the gleaming water.
Byrhtnoth and his warriors awaited them,

Ready for battle: he ordered his men
To form a phalanx with their shields, and to stand firm
Against the onslaught of the enemy. Then was the battle,
With its chance of glory, about to begin. The time had come
For all the doomed men to fall in the fight.
The clamour began; the ravens wheeled and the eagle
Circled overhead, craving for carrion; there was shouting on earth.
They hurled their spears, hard as files,
And sent sharp darts flying from their hands.
Bow strings were busy, shield parried point,
Bitter was the battle. Brave men fell
On both sides, youths choking in the dust.
Byrhtnoth's sister's son, Wulfmær, was wounded;
Slashed by the sword, he decided
To sleep on the bed of death.
This was violently requited, the Vikings were repaid in kind.
I was told that Eadweard swung his sword
So savagely—a full-blooded blow—
That a fated warrior fell lifeless at his feet.
Byrhtnoth shouted out his thanks to him,
His chamberlain, as soon as he had a chance to do so.
The brave men stood resolute, rock firm.
Each of them eagerly hunted for a way
To be first in with his spear,
Winning with his weapons the life
Of a doomed warrior; the dead sank down to the earth.
But the rest stood unshaken and Byrhtnoth spurred them on,
Inciting each man to fight ferociously
Who wished to gain glory against the Danes.
Then a brave seafarer raised up his spear,
Gripped his shield and advanced towards Byrhtnoth.
The resolute earl advanced towards the churl;
Each had evil designs on the other.
The Viking was the quicker—he hurled his foreign spear
Wounding the lord of the warriors.
Byrhtnoth broke the shaft with the edge of his shield;
The imbedded spear-head sprang out of his wound.
Then he flung his spear in fury
At the proud Viking who dared inflict such pain.
His aim was skilful. The spear
Slit open the warrior's neck.
Thus Byrhtnoth put paid to his enemy's life.
Then, for safety's sake, he swiftly hurled another

Which burst the Viking's breastplate, cruelly wounding him
In the chest; the deadly spear pierced his heart.
The brave earl, Byrhtnoth, was delighted at this;
He laughed out loud and gave thanks to the Lord
That such good fortune had been granted to him.
But one of the seafarers sent a sharp javelin
Speeding from his hand
That pierced Byrhtnoth's body, the noble thane of Ethelred.
By his side stood a young warrior,
Wulfmær by name, Wulfstan's son,
Who without a moment's hesitation
Drew out the blood-red javelin from Byrhtnoth's side
And hurled it back as hard as he could
At the man who had grievously injured his prince.
The sharp point struck home; the Viking sagged, and sank into the dust.
Another seafarer advanced on the earl, meaning to make
Short work of him and snatch away his treasures—
His armour and his rings and his ornamented sword.

Byrhtnoth drew out his sword from its sheath,
Broad-faced and gleaming, and made to slash at the seafarer's corselet,
But his enemy stopped him all too soon,
Savagely striking Byrhtnoth's arm.
The golden-hilted sword dropped from his hand.
He could hold it no longer
Nor wield a weapon of any kind. Then the old warrior
Raised his men's morale with bold words,
Called on his brave companions to do battle again.
He no longer stood firmly on his feet
But swayed, and raised his eyes to heaven:
'O Guardian of the people, let me praise and thank you
For all the real joys I received in this world.
Now, gracious Lord, as never before,
I need Your grace,
That my soul may set out on its journey to You,
O Prince of Angels, that my soul may depart
Into Your power in peace. I pray
That the devils may never destroy it.'
Then the heathens hewed him down
And the two men who stood there supporting him;
Ælfnoth and Wulfmær fell to the dust,
Both gave their lives in defence of their lord.
Then certain cowards beat a hasty retreat:

The sons of Odda were the first to take flight;
Godric fled from the battle, forsaking Byrhtnoth.
Forgetting that his lord had given him often the gift of a horse,
He leapt into the saddle
Of his lord's own horse, most unlawfully,
And both his brothers, Godwine and Godwig,
Galloped beside him; forgetting their duty
They fled from the fight
And saved their lives in the silent wood.
And more men followed than was at all fitting
Had they remembered the former rewards
That the prince had given them, generous presents.
It was just as Offa once said to Byrhtnoth
At an open council in the meeting place,
That many spoke proudly of their prowess
Who would prove unworthy of their words under battle-stress.

So Ethelred's earl, the prince of those people,
Fell; all his hearth-companions
Could see for themselves that their lord lay low.
Then the proud thanes, with the utmost bravery,
Threw themselves once more into the thick of the battle.
They all, without exception, strove to one of two ends—
To avenge their lord or to leave this world.
Ælfwine the son of Ælfric, still a young man,
Shouted encouragement, urging them on.
He rallied them with valiant words:
'Think of all the times we boasted
At the mead-bench, heroes in the hall
Predicting our own bravery in battle.
Now we shall see who meant what he said.
Let me announce my ancestry to one and all:
I come from a mighty family of Mercian stock;
My grandfather was Ealhelm,
A wise ealdorman, well endowed with worldly riches.
No thane shall ever have reason to reproach me
With any desire to desert this troop
And hurry home, now that my prince has been hewn down
In battle. This is the most bitter sorrow of all.
He was my kinsman and my lord.'
Then he went forward into the fight
And pierced a pirate's body with his spear.
The man keeled over, dead,

Killed by Ælfwine's weapon. Again he urged
His friends and companions
To follow him into the fray.
Then Offa spoke and brandished his ash-spear:
'Ælfwine, you've encouraged all the thanes
At exactly the right time. Now that our prince
Is slain, the earl on the earth,
We must all encourage each other
To fight, for as long as we can wield
Our weapons, pierce with our spears,
And lunge and parry with our swords.
Godric, the cowardly son of Odda, has betrayed us all.
When he hurried off towards the woods on our lord's fine horse
He misled many men into believing it was Byrhtnoth himself;
And so they followed him, and here on the field
The phalanx was broken: may fortune frown on him
Whose cowardice has caused this catastrophe.'
Then Leofsunu spoke. He raised his shield
For protection, and replied to Offa:
'I give you my word that I will not retreat
One inch; I shall forge on
And avenge my lord in battle.
Now that he has fallen in the fight
No loyal warrior living at Sturmere
Need reproach me for returning home lordless
In unworthy retreat, for the weapon shall take me,
The iron sword.' He strode forward angrily,
Fighting furiously; he spurned escape.
Then Dunnere spoke and shook his spear;
A lowly churl, he cried out loud
And asked every man to avenge Byrhtnoth's death:
'Whoever intends to avenge our prince
Must not flinch, nor care for his own life.'
Then they hurried forward, heedless of their lives;
The brave followers, fiercely carrying spears,
Fought with great courage, and prayed to God
That they should be allowed to avenge their lord
By killing all his enemies.
The hostage helped them with all his might—
His name was Æscferth, the son of Ecglaf;
He came from a family renowned in Northumbria.
In the fire of battle he did not flinch,
Notching arrow after arrow as quick as he could.

Sometimes he hit a shield, sometimes he pierced a man,
Again and again he inflicted wounds
For as long as he could hold a bow in his hands.

Eadweard the tall, eager and impetuous,
Did not stray from the line of battle. He boasted that he
Would not shrink so much as a footstep,
Or seek safety by flight, now that his lord lay dead.
He smashed the wall of shields, and attacked the seafarers
Worthily avenging his ring-giver's death.
He sold his life dearly in the storm of battle.
And so too did Ætheric, a stalwart companion. . . .
He grappled aggressively and without delay.
The brother of Sibyrht, both he and many others
Split the hollow shields and warded off the seafarers.
The corner of the shield broke and the corselet sang
A terrible song. Then in the turmoil
Offa struck a seafarer; he fell dead at his feet.
But the kinsman of Gadd was killed there too,
Offa was quickly brought down in the battle.
Yet he had kept his promise to his prince;
He fulfilled his former boast to Byrhtnoth, the ring-giver,
That they should either return unhurt, riding to the stronghold
In victory together, or together surrender their lives,
Bleeding from wounds on the battlefield.
He lay near his lord as befits a thane.
Then shields were shattered; the seafarers surged forward,
Embittered by bloodshed. Often a spear
Sank into the body of a fated warrior. Then Wistan advanced,
The son of Thurstan; he fought with the Vikings,
Slew three in the struggling throng
Before he, Wigelm's brave son, was himself brought down.
That was a savage fight; the warriors stood firm
In the struggle. Strong men fell,
Utterly worn out by wounds; the dead dropped to the earth.
The brothers Oswold and Eadweard
Continuously encouraged the companions;
They urged their kinsmen to use
Their weapons without slackening
And endure the stress to the best of their strength.
Byrhtwold grasped his shield and spoke.
He was an old companion. He brandished his ash-spear
And with wonderful courage exhorted the warriors:

'Mind must be the firmer, heart the more fierce,
Courage the greater, as our strength diminishes.
Here lies our leader, dead,
An heroic man in the dust.
He who now longs to escape will lament for ever.
I am old. I will not go from here,
But I mean to lie by the side of my lord,
Lie in the dust with the man I loved so dearly.'
Godric, too, the son of Æthelgar, gave them courage
To continue the fight. Often he let fly his spear,
His deadly javelin, at the Vikings
As he advanced at the head of the host.
He humbled and hewed down until at last he fell himself. . . .

Translated from the Anglo-Saxon by Kevin Crossley-Holland

ANONYMOUS

12th century

13   from *The Song of Roland**

In wrath and grief away the Paynims fly;
Backward to Spain with headlong haste they hie.
The County Roland cannot pursue their flight,
Veillantif's lost, he has no steed to ride;
Will he or nill he, he must on foot abide,
He's turned to aid Archbishop Turpin's plight,
And from his head the gilded helm untied,
Stripped off the hauberk of subtle rings and bright,
And all to pieces has cut the bliaut fine
Wherewith to bandage his wounds that gape so wide.
Then to his breast he clasps and lifts him light
And gently lays him upon the green hill-side,
With fair soft speech entreating on this wise:
'Ah, noble sir, pray give me leave awhile;
These friends of ours, we loved so well in life,
We must not leave them thus lying where they died.

* Together with his comrade Oliver and Archbishop Turpin, Roland commanded Emperor Charlemagne's retreating rearguard in the Pyrenees in 778. Far outnumbered by the attacking Saracens, Roland and the valiant Franks were all killed, in a battle at the mountain pass of Roncesvalles.

I will go seek them, find, and identify,
And lay them here together in your sight.'
'Go and return,' the Bishop makes reply;
'Thanks be to God, this field is yours and mine.'

Roland departs and through the field is gone;
Alone he searches the valleys and high rocks.
[And there he finds Ivor, and there Ivon],
Gerier and Gerin, the good companions,
[And Engelier whom Gascony begot];
And he has found Berenger and Oton,
And after finds Anseïs and Samson,
And finds Gerard the Old, of Roussillon.
He lifts them up, brave baron, one by one,
To the Archbishop he carries them anon,
And by his knees ranges them all along.
The Bishop weeps, he cannot stint thereof;
He lifts his hand and gives them benison,
And after saith: 'Alack, brave champions!
May your souls rest with the all-glorious God
In Paradise, amid the rose-blossoms.
I too am dying and sorrow for my lot,
Who the great Emperor no more may look upon.'

Roland once more unto the field repairs,
And has sought out his comrade Oliver.
Close to his breast he lifts him, and with care
As best he may to the Archbishop bears
And on his shield lays with the others there;
The Bishop signs and shrives them all with prayer.
With tears renewed their sorrow is declared,
And Roland saith: 'Fair fellow Oliver,
You were own son unto Duke Renier
That held the marches of the Vale of Runers.
To shatter shield or break lance anywhere,
And from their seat proud men to overbear,
And cheer the brave with words of counsel fair,
And bring the cruel to ruin and despair,
No knight on earth was valiant as you were.'

Translated from the French by Dorothy L. Sayers

ANONYMOUS

12th century

14   *The Lament of Maev Leith-Dherg*

Raise the Cromlech high!
  MacMoghcorb is slain,
And other men's renown
  Has leave to live again.

Cold at last he lies
  Neath the burial-stone;
All the blood he shed
  Could not save his own.

Stately-strong he went,
  Through his nobles all
When we paced together
  Up the banquet-hall.

Dazzling white as lime
  Was his body fair,
Cherry-red his cheeks,
  Raven-black his hair.

Razor-sharp his spear,
  And the shield he bore,
High as champion's head—
  His arm was like an oar.

Never aught but truth
  Spake my noble king;
Valour all his trust
  In all his warfaring.

As the forkèd pole
  Holds the roof-tree's weight,
So my hero's arm
  Held the battle straight.

33

Terror went before him,
　　Death behind his back;
Well the wolves of Erinn
　　Knew his chariot's track.

Seven bloody battles
　　He broke upon his foes;
In each a hundred heroes
　　Fell beneath his blows.

Once he fought at Fossud
　　Thrice at Ath-finn-Fail
'Twas my king that conquered
　　At bloody Ath-an-Scail.

At the boundary Stream
　　Fought the Royal Hound,
And for Bernas battle
　　Stands his name renowned.

Here he fought with Leinster—
　　Last of all his frays—
On the Hill of Cucorb's Fate
　　High his Cromlech raise.

Translated from the Irish by T. W. Rolleston

GEOFFREY CHAUCER

1343–1400

15　　from *The Knight's Tale*

But in the dome of mighty Mars the red
With different figures all the sides were spread;
This temple, less in form, with equal grace,
Was imitative of the first in Thrace:
For that cold region was the loved abode
And sovereign mansion of the warrior god.
The landscape was a forest wide and bare,
Where neither beast nor humankind repair;

The fowl that scent afar the borders fly,
And shun the bitter blast, and wheel about the sky.
A cake of scurf lies baking on the ground,
And prickly stubs, instead of trees, are found;
Or woods with knots and knares deformed and old;
Headless the most, and hideous to behold:
A rattling tempest through the branches went,
That stripped 'em bare, and one sole way they bent.
Heaven froze above, severe; the clouds congeal,
And through the crystal vault appeared the standing hail.
Such was the face without: a mountain stood
Threatening from high, and overlooked the wood;
Beneath the lowering brow, and on a bent,
The temple stood of Mars armipotent:
The frame of burnished steel, that cast a glare
From far, and seemed to thaw the freezing air.
A strait, long entry to the temple led,
Blind with high walls, and horror overhead:
Thence issued such a blast and hollow roar,
As threatened from the hinge to heave the door.
In through that door, a northern light there shone;
'Twas all it had, for windows there were none.
The gate was adamant; eternal frame!
Which, hewed by Mars himself, from Indian quarries came,
The labour of a god; and all along
Tough iron plates were clenched to make it strong.
A tun about was every pillar there;
A polished mirror shone not half so clear.
There saw I how the secret felon wrought,
And treason labouring in the traitor's thought,
And midwife Time the ripened plot to murder brought.
There the red Anger dared the pallid Fear;
Next stood Hypocrisy, with holy leer;
Soft smiling, and demurely looking down,
But hid the dagger underneath the gown:
Th' assassinating wife, the household fiend;
And, far the blackest there, the traitor-friend.
On t'other side there stood Destruction bare;
Unpunished Rapine, and a waste of war;
Contest, with sharpened knives, in cloisters drawn,
And all with blood bespread the holy lawn.
Loud menaces were heard, and foul disgrace,
And bawling infamy, in language base;

Till sense was lost in sound, and silence fled the place.
The slayer of himself yet saw I there;
The gore congealed was clottered in his hair:
With eyes half closed and gaping mouth he lay,
And grim, as when he breathed his sullen soul away.
In midst of all the dome Misfortune sat,
And gloomy Discontent, and fell Debate,
And Madness laughing in his ireful mood,
And armed complaint on theft, and cries of blood.
There was the murdered corpse, in covert laid,
And violent death in thousand shapes displayed;
The city to the soldier's rage resigned;
Successless wars, and poverty behind;
Ships burnt in fight, or forced on rocky shores,
And the rash hunter strangled by the boars;
The newborn babe by nurses overlaid;
And the cook caught within the raging fire he made.
All ills of Mars his nature, flame, and steel;
The gasping charioteer, beneath the wheel
Of his own car, the ruined house that falls
And intercepts her lord betwixt the walls;
The whole division that to Mars pertains,
All trades of death that deal in steel for gains,
Were there: the butcher, armourer, and smith,
Who forges sharpened fauchions, or the scythe.
The scarlet conquest on a tower was placed,
With shouts and soldiers' acclamations graced;
A pointed sword hung threatening o'er his head,
Sustained but by a slender twine of thread.
There saw I Mars his ides, the Capitol,
The seer in vain foretelling Caesar's fall;
The last triumvirs, and the wars they move,
And Antony, who lost the world for love.
These, and a thousand more, the fane adorn;
Their fates were painted ere the men were born,
All copied from the heavens, and ruling force
Of the red star, in his revolving course.

Translated from the Middle English by John Dryden

MICHAEL DRAYTON

1563–1631

16   *To the Cambro-Britons, and their harp,*
*his Ballad of Agincourt**

Fair stood the wind for France,
When we our sails advance,
Nor now to prove our chance,
   Longer will tarry;
But putting to the main,
At Caux, the mouth of Seine,
With all his martial train,
   Landed King Harry.

And taking many a fort,
Furnished in warlike sort,
Marcheth towards Agincourt,
   In happy hour;
Skirmishing day by day,
With those that stopped his way,
Where the French General lay,
   With all his power.

Which in his height of pride,
King Henry to deride,
His ransom to provide
   To the King sending.
Which he neglects the while,
As from a nation vile,
Yet with an angry smile,
   Their fall portending.

And turning to his men,
Quoth our brave Henry then,
Though they to one be ten,
   Be not amazed.

* In 1415, Henry V renewed the Hundred Years War with France, laying successful
siege to Harfleur. On 25 October 1415, with an army of only 14,000 men, he defeated a
French force numbering 50,000 in a famous battle at Agincourt.

Yet have we well begun,
Battles so bravely won,
Have ever to the sun,
    By fame been raised.

And for my self (quoth he,)
This my full rest shall be,
England ne'er mourn for me,
    Nor more esteem me.
Victor I will remain,
Or on this earth lie slain,
Never shall she sustain,
    Loss to redeem me.

Poitiers and Cressy tell,
When most their pride did swell,
Under our swords they fell,
    No less our skill is,
Than when our grandsire great,
Claiming the regal seat,
By many a warlike feat,
    Lopped the French lilies.

The Duke of York so dread,
The eager vaward led;
With the main, Henry sped,
    Amongst his henchmen.
Exeter had the rear,
A braver man not there,
O Lord, how hot they were,
    On the false Frenchmen!

They now to fight are gone,
Armour on armour shone,
Drum now to drum did groan,
    To hear, was wonder;
That with cries they make,
The very earth did shake,
Trumpet to trumpet spake,
    Thunder to thunder.

Well it thine age became,
O noble Erpingham,
Which didst the signal aim,
　　To our hid forces;
When from a meadow by,
Like a storm suddenly,
The English archery
　　Struck the French horses,

With Spanish yew so strong,
Arrows a cloth-yard long,
That like to serpents stung,
　　Piercing the weather;
None from his fellow starts,
But playing manly parts,
And like true English hearts,
　　Stuck close together.

When down their bows they threw,
And forth their bilboes drew,
And on the French they flew,
　　Not one was tardy;
Arms were from shoulders sent,
Scalps to the teeth were rent,
Down the French peasants went,
　　Our men were hardy.

This while our noble King,
His broad sword brandishing,
Down the French host did ding,
　　As to o'erwhelm it;
And many a deep wound lent,
His arms with blood besprent,
And many a cruel dent
　　Bruisèd his helmet.

Gloucester, that Duke so good,
Next of the royal blood,
For famous England stood,
　　With his brave brother;

Clarence, in steel so bright,
Though but a maiden knight,
Yet in that furious fight,
    Scarce such another.

Warwick in blood did wade,
Oxford the foe invade,
And cruel slaughter made,
    Still as they ran up;
Suffolk his axe did ply,
Beaumont and Willoughby
Bare them right doughtily,
    Ferrers and Fanhope.

Upon Saint Crispin's day
Fought was this noble fray,
Which fame did not delay,
    To England to carry;
O, when shall English men
With such acts fill a pen,
Or England breed again,
    Such a King Harry?

EDMUND SPENSER

1552–1599

17

from *Astrophel*

A Pastorall Elegie

Upon the Death of the Most Noble and Valorous Knight,
*Sir Philip Sidney**

Such skill, matcht with such courage as he had,
Did prick him foorth with proud desire of praise
To seek abroad, of daunger nought ydrad,
His mistresse name, and his owne fame, to raise.
What needeth perill to be sought abroad,
Since, round about us, it doth make aboad!

* In 1586, the Earl of Leicester unsuccessfully attempted to wrest the city of Zutphen
in the Netherlands from the Spanish. Sir Philip Sidney, his thirty-two year old nephew,
was killed in the skirmish.

It fortunèd as he that perilous game
In forreine soyle pursuèd far away;
Into a forest wide and waste he came,
Where store he heard to be of salvage pray.
So wide a forest and so waste as this,
Nor famous Ardeyn, nor fowle Arlo, is.

There his welwoven toyles, and subtil traines,
He laid the brutish nation to enwrap:
So well he wrought with practice and with paines,
That he of them great troups did soone entrap.
Full happie man (misweening much) was hee,
So rich a spoile within his power to see.

Eftsoones, all heedlesse of his dearest hale,
Full greedily into the heard he thrust,
To slaughter them, and worke their finall bale,
Least that his toyle should of their troups be brust.
Wide wounds emongst them many one he made,
Now with his sharp borespear, now with his blade.

His care was all how he them all might kill,
That none might scape, (so partiall unto none:)
Ill mynd so much to mynd anothers ill,
As to become unmyndfull of his owne.
But pardon that unto the cruell skies,
That from himselfe to them withdrew his eies.

So as he rag'd emongst that beastly rout,
A cruell beast of most accursèd brood
Upon him turnd, (despeyre makes cowards stout,)
And, with fell tooth accustomèd to blood,
Launchèd his thigh with so mischievous might,
That it both bone and muscles ryvèd quight.

So deadly was the dint and deep the wound,
And so huge streames of blood thereout did flow,
That he endurèd not the direfull stound,
But on the cold deare earth himselfe did throw;
The whiles the captive heard his nets did rend,
And, having none to let, to wood did wend.

Ah! where were ye this while his shepheard peares,
To whom alive was nought so deare as hee:
And ye faire Mayds, the matches of his yeares,
Which in his grace did boast you most to bee!
Ah! where were ye, when he of you had need,
To stop his wound that wondrously did bleed!

Ah! wretched boy, the shape of dreryhead,
And sad ensample of mans suddein end:
Full litle faileth but thou shalt be dead,
Unpitièd, unplaynd, of foe or frend!
Whilest none is nigh, thine eyelids up to close,
And kisse thy lips like faded leaves of rose.

SAMUEL DANIEL

1562–1619

18   from *The Civil Wars between the Two Houses of
Lancaster and York**

It was upon the twilight of that day
(That peaceful day) when the religious bear
The olive-branches as they go to pray,
(And we, in lieu, the blooming palm use here)
When both the armies, ready in array
For th'early sacrifice of blood, appear
Prepared for mischief, ere they had full light
To see to do it, and to do it right.

Th'advantage of the time, and of the wind
(Which, both, with York seem as retained in pay)
Brave Falconbridge takes hold-on, and assigned
The archers their flight-shafts to shoot away:
Which, th'adverse side (with sleet and dimness, blind,
Mistaken in the distance of the way)
Answer with their sheaf-arrows; that come short
Of their intended aim, and did no hurt;

---

* In 1461, Edward IV was proclaimed King in London, and went on to defeat the
Lancastrians and Henry VI at Towton Field in Yorkshire. 'In this battle of Towton, on
King Henry's side were slain Henry Percy Earl of Northumberland, the Earls of
Shrewsbury and Devonshire ... The whole number slain were accounted, by some,
33,000; by others, 35,091.' [SD]

But, gathered by th'on-marching enemy,
Returnèd were, like clouds of steel; which pour
Destruction down, and did new-night the sky:
As if the day had failed to keep his hour.
Whereat, the rangèd horse break-out, deny
Obedience to the riders, scorn their power,
Disrank the troops, set all in disarray,
To make th'assailant owner of the day.

Thus, thou peculiar engine of our land
(Weapon of conquest, master of the field)
Renownèd Bow (that mad'st this Crown command
The towers of France, and all their powers to yield)
Art made at home to have th'especial hand
In our dissensions, by thy work upheld:
Thou first didst conquer us; then raised our skill
To vanquish others; here ourselves to spill.

And now how com'st thou to be out of date,
And all neglected leav'st us, and art gone?
And with thee, th'ancient strength, the manly state
Of valour, and of worth, that glory won?
Or else stay'st thou, till new prized shot abate?
(That never shall effect what thou hast done)
And only but attend'st some blessèd Reign,
When thou and Virtue shalt be graced again.

But this sharp tempest drave Northumberland,
(Who led the vanguard of King Henry's side)
With eager heat join battle, out of hand;
And this disorder, with their swords to hide.
Where, twice five hours, these furious armies stand;
And Fortune's Balance weighed on neither side;
Nor either did but equal bloodshed gain,
Till Henry's chiefest leaders all were slain.

Then, lo, those spirits, which from these heads derive
Their motions gave off working; and, in haste,
Turn all their backs to Death, and mainly strive
Who from themselves shall run away most fast.
The after-flyers on the former drive:
And they again, by the pursuers chased
Make bridges of their fellows' backs, to pass
The brooks and rivers, where-as danger was.

Witness O clear-streamed Cock: within whose banks,
So many thousand, crawling, helpless lay,
With wounds and weariness; who in their ranks
Had valiantly behaved themselves that day:
And might have had more honour, and more thanks
By standing to their work, and by their stay,
'But men, at once, life seem to love and loath;
Running to lose it, and to save it both.'

Unhappy Henry, from a little hill,
Placed not far off (whence he might view the fight)
Had all th'entire full prospect of this ill,
With all the scattered slaughter, in his sight:
Saw how the victor raged, and spoiled at will,
And left not off when all was in his might:
Saw, with how great ado himself was won;
And with what store of blood kings are undone.

HENRY HOWARD, EARL OF SURREY*

1517-1547

19   Norfolk sprang thee, Lambeth holds thee dead,
Clere of the County of Cleremont though hight;
Within the womb of Ormond's race thou bred,
And saw'st thy cousin crownèd in thy sight.
Shelton for love, Surrey for Lord thou chase:
Ay me, while life did last that league was tender;
Tracing whose steps thou saw'st Kelsal blaze,
Laundersey burnt, and battered Bullen render.
At Muttrell gates, hopeless of all recure,
Thine Earl half dead gave in thy hand his Will;
Which cause did thee this pining death procure,
Ere summers four times seven thou could'st fulfil.
   Ah Clere, if love had booted, care, or cost,
   Heaven had not won, nor Earth so timely lost.

---

* Henry Howard, Earl of Surrey, and Thomas Clere, his squire and companion, fought together in expeditions to Kelsal in Scotland, Landrecy in the Netherlands, and Boulogne in France. At the siege of Montreuil, on 19 September 1544, Clere received wounds while protecting Surrey, from which he died the following spring. He was buried at Lambeth, in the chapel assigned to the Howards.

GEORGE GASCOIGNE

?1525–1577

20   from *The Fruits of War*

A conference among ourselves we called,
Of officers and captains all yfere,
For truth (to tell) the soldiers were appalled,
And when we asked, 'Now mates, what merry cheer?'
Their answer was: 'It is no biding here.'
So that perforce we must from thence be gone,
Unless we meant to keep the place alone.

Herewith we thought that if in time we went,
Before all straits were stopped and taken up,
We might perhaps our enemies prevent,
And teach them eke to taste of sorrow's cup:
At Maesland Sluyse, we hopèd for to sup,
A place whereas we might good service do,
To keep them out which took it after too.

Whiles thus we talk, a messenger behold,
From Alphen came, and told us heavy news.
'Captains,' quoth he, 'Hereof you may be bold,
Not one poor soul of all your fellows' crews
Can scape alive, they have no choice to choose:
They sent me thus to bid you shift in time,
Else look like them to stick in Spanish lime.'

This tale once told, none other speech prevailed,
But pack and trudge, all leisure was too long,
To mend the mart, our watch (which never failed)
Descried our foes which marchèd all along,
And towards us began in haste to throng,
So that before our last could pass the port,
The foremost foes were now within the Fort.

I promised once and did perform it too,
To bide therein as long as any would,
What booted that? or what could captains do,

45

When common sort would tarry for no good?
To speak a truth, the good did what they could,
To keep the bad in ranks and good array,
But labour lost to hold that will away.

It needless were to tell what deeds were done,
Nor who did best, nor who did worst that day,
Nor who made head, nor who began to run,
Nor in retreat what chief was last alway,
But soldier-like we held our enemies' play:
And every captain strove to do his best,
To stay his own and so to stay the rest.

In this retire three English miles we trod,
With face to foes and shot as thick as hail,
Of whose choice men full fifty souls and odd,
We laid on ground, this is withouten fail,
Yet of our own, we lost but three by tale:
Our foes themselves confessed they bought full dear
The hot pursuit which they attempted there.

Thus came we late at last to Leyden walls,
Too late, too soon, and so may we well say,
For notwithstanding all our cries and calls,
They shut their gates and turned their ears away:
In fine they did forsake us every way,
And bade us shift to save ourselves apace,
For unto them were fond to trust for grace.

They neither gave us meat to feed upon,
Nor drink, nor powder, pickaxe, tool, nor spade,
So might we starve, like misers woebegone,
And fend our foes, with blows of English blade,
For shot was shrunk, and shift could none be made:
Yea more than this, we stood in open field,
Without defence from shot ourselves to shield.

This thus well weighed, when weary night was past,
And day gan peep, we heard the Spanish drums,
Which struck a march about us round to cast,
And forth withall their ensigns quickly comes,
At sight whereof, our soldiers bit their thumbs:
For well they wist it was no boot to fly,
And biding there, there was no boot but die.

So that we sent a drum to summon talk,
And came to parley middle way between.
Monsieur de Licques and Mario did walk
From foemen's side, and from our side were seen
Myself, that match for Mario might been,
And Captain Sheffield born of noble race,
To match de Licques, which there was chief in place.

Thus met we talked, and stood upon our toes,
With great demands whom little might content,
We craved not only freedom from our foes,
But shipping eke with sails and all full bent,
To come again from whence we first were went:
I mean to come, into our English coast,
Which soil was sure, and might content us most.

An old-said saw, and oft seen, that whereas
Thou comest to crave, and doubts for to obtain,
Iniquum pete (then) *ut æquum feras,*
This had I heard, and sure I was full fain
To prove what profit we thereby might gain:
But at the last when time was stolen away,
We were full glad to play another play.

We rendered then with safety for our lives,
Our ensigns 'splayed, and managing our arms,
With further faith, that from all kinds of gives,
Our soldiers should remain withouten harms:
And sooth to say, these were no false alarms,
For why? they were within twelve days discharged,
And sent away from prison quite enlarged.

They were sent home, and we remainèd still,
In prison pent, but yet right gently used,
To take our lives, it was not Licques' will,
(That noble blood, which never man abused,)
Nor ever yet was for his faith accused.
Would God I had the skill to write his praise,
Which lent me comfort in my doleful days.

We bode behind, four months or little less,
But whereupon that God he knows not I,
Yet if I might be bold to give a guess,

Then would I say it was for to espy
What ransom we would pay contentedly;
Or else to know how much we were esteemed,
In England here, and for what men ydeemed.

Howso it were, at last we were despatched,
And home we came as children come from school,
As glad as fish which were but lately catched,
And straight again were cast into the pool;
For by my fay I count him but a fool,
Which would not rather poorly live at large,
Than rest in prison fed with costly charge.

Now I have told a tedious tale in rhyme,
Of my mishaps, and what ill luck I had,
Yet some may say, that all too loud I chime,
Since that in wars my fortune was not bad,
And many a man in prison would be glad
To fare no worse, and lodge no worse than we,
And eke at last to scape and go so free.

GEORGE PEELE

?1558–1596

21   *Farewell to Arms*

To Queen Elizabeth

His golden locks time hath to silver turned;
    O time too swift, O swiftness never ceasing!
His youth 'gainst time and age hath ever spurned,
    But spurned in vain; youth waneth by increasing:
Beauty, strength, youth, are flowers but fading seen;
Duty, faith, love, are roots, and ever green.

His helmet now shall make a hive for bees;
    And, lovers' sonnets turned to holy psalms,
A man-at-arms must now serve on his knees,
    And feed on prayers, which are age's alms:
But though from court to cottage he depart,
His saint is sure of his unspotted heart.

And when he saddest sits in homely cell,
  He'll teach his swains this carol for a song:
'Blest be the hearts that wish my sovereign well,
  Curst be the souls that think her any wrong.'
Goddess, allow this agèd man his right,
To be your beadsman now, that was your knight.

JOHN DONNE

1572–1631

22 *A Burnt Ship**

Out of a fired ship, which, by no way
But drowning, could be rescued from the flame,
Some men leaped forth, and ever as they came
Near the foe's ships, did by their shot decay;
So all were lost, which in the ship were found,
  They in the sea being burnt, they in the burnt ship drowned.

SIR WILLIAM DAVENANT

1606–1668

23 *The Soldier Going to the Field*

Preserve thy sighs, unthrifty girl,
  To purify the air;
Thy tears to thread instead of pearl
  On bracelets of thy hair.

The trumpet makes the echo hoarse
  And wakes the louder drum;
Expense of grief gains no remorse
  When sorrow should be dumb.

---

* John Donne took part in the naval expeditions against Cadiz in June to August 1596 (under the Earl of Essex and Sir Walter Ralegh) and against the Azores in July to October 1597.

For I must go where lazy Peace
　　Will hide her drowsy head,
And, for the sport of Kings, increase
　　The number of the dead.

But first I'll chide thy cruel theft:
　　Can I in war delight,
Who being of my heart bereft
　　Can have no heart to fight?

Thou know'st the sacred Laws of old
　　Ordained a thief should pay,
To quit him of his theft, sevenfold
　　What he had stolen away.

Thy payment shall but double be;
　　O then with speed resign
My own seducèd heart to me,
　　Accompanied with thine.

RICHARD LOVELACE
1618–1658

24　　*To Lucasta, Going to the Wars*

Tell me not, sweet, I am unkind,
　　That from the nunnery
Of thy chaste breast and quiet mind
　　To war and arms I fly.

True, a new mistress now I chase,
　　The first foe in the field;
And with a stronger faith embrace
　　A sword, a horse, a shield.

Yet this inconstancy is such
　　As you too shall adore;
I could not love thee, dear, so much,
　　Loved I not honour more.

ANDREW MARVELL
1621–1678

25

An Horatian Ode
upon Cromwell's Return from Ireland, 1650

The forward youth that would appear
Must now forsake his Muses dear,
    Nor in the shadows sing
    His numbers languishing.

'Tis time to leave the books in dust.
And oil the unusèd armour's rust,
    Removing from the wall
    The corslet of the hall.

So restless Cromwell could not cease
In the inglorious arts of peace,
    But through adventurous war
    Urgèd his active star:

And like the three-forked lightning, first
Breaking the clouds where it was nurst,
    Did thorough his own side
    His fiery way divide:

For 'tis all one to courage high,
The emulous, or enemy;
    And with such, to enclose
    Is more than to oppose.

Then burning through the air he went
And palaces and temples rent;
    And Caesar's head at last
    Did through his laurels blast.

'Tis madness to resist or blame
The force of angry Heaven's flame;
    And if we would speak true,
    Much to the man is due,

Who, from his private gardens, where
He lived reservèd and austere
  (As if his highest plot
  To plant the bergamot),

Could by industrious valour climb
To ruin the great work of time,
  And cast the Kingdom old
  Into another mould.

Though Justice against Fate complain,
And plead the ancient rights in vain—
  But those do hold or break
  As men are strong or weak—

Nature, that hateth emptiness,
Allows of penetration less,
  And therefore must make room
  Where greater spirits come.

What field of all the civil wars
Where his were not the deepest scars?
  And Hampton shows what part
  He had of wiser art;

Where, twining subtle fears with hope,
He wove a net of such a scope
  That Charles himself might chase
  To Car'sbrook's narrow case;

That thence the Royal Actor borne
The tragic scaffold might adorn:
  While round the armèd bands
  Did clap their bloody hands.

He nothing common did or mean
Upon that memorable scene,
  But with his keener eye
  The axe's edge did try;

Nor called the Gods, with vulgar spite,
To vindicate his helpless right;
  But bowed his comely head
  Down, as upon a bed.

This was that memorable hour
Which first assured the forcèd power:
    So when they did design
    The Capitol's first line,

A bleeding head, where they begun,
Did fright the architects to run;
    And yet in that the State
    Foresaw its happy fate!

And now the Irish are ashamed
To see themselves in one year tamed:
    So much one man can do
    That does both act and know.

They can affirm his praises best,
And have, though overcome, confest
    How good he is, how just
    And fit for highest trust;

Nor yet grown stiffer with command,
But still in the Republic's hand—
    How fit he is to sway
    That can so well obey!

He to the Commons' feet presents
A Kingdom for his first year's rents,
    And, what he may, forbears
    His fame, to make it theirs:

And has his sword and spoils ungirt
To lay them at the public's skirt.
    So when the falcon high
    Falls heavy from the sky,

She, having killed, no more does search
But on the next green bough to perch,
    Where, when he first does lure,
    The falconer has her sure.

What may not then our Isle presume
While victory his crest does plume?
    What may not others fear,
    If thus he crown each year?

As Caesar he, ere long, to Gaul,
To Italy an Hannibal,
    And to all States not free
    Shall climacteric be.

The Pict no shelter now shall find
Within his particoloured mind,
    But from this valour sad
    Shrinks underneath the plaid,

Happy, if in the tufted brake
The English hunter him mistake,
    Nor lay his hounds in near
    The Caledonian deer.

But thou, the War's and Fortune's son,
March indefatigably on;
    And for the last effect,
    Still keep thy sword erect:

Besides the force it has to fright
The spirits of the shady night,
    The same arts that did gain
    A power, must it maintain.

JOHN MILTON
1608–1674

26   *On the Late Massacre in Piedmont**

Avenge, O Lord, thy slaughtered saints, whose bones
    Lie scattered on the Alpine mountains cold,
    Even them who kept thy truth so pure of old
    When all our fathers worshipped stocks and stones,
Forget not; in thy book record their groans
    Who were thy sheep and in their ancient fold
    Slain by the bloody Piedmontese that rolled

* The heretical Waldensian sect, which inhabited northern Italy (Piedmont) and southern France, held beliefs compatible with Protestant doctrine. Their massacre by Catholics in 1655 was widely protested by Protestant powers, including Oliver Cromwell and his Latin secretary, John Milton.

JOHN MILTON

Mother with infant down the rocks. Their moans
The vales redoubled to the hills, and they
To Heaven. Their martyred blood and ashes sow
O'er all th' Italian fields where still doth sway
The triple tyrant, that from these may grow
A hundredfold, who having learnt thy way,
Early may fly the Babylonian woe.

27   from *Paradise Lost*

They ended parle, and both addressed for fight
Unspeakable; for who, though with the tongue
Of angels, can relate, or to what things
Liken on earth conspicuous, that may lift
Human imagination to such heighth
Of godlike power: for likest gods they seemed,
Stood they or moved, in stature, motion, arms
Fit to decide the Empire of great Heaven.
Now waved their fiery swords, and in the air
Made horrid circles; two broad suns their shields
Blazed opposite, while expectation stood
In horror; from each hand with speed retired
Where erst was thickest fight, th' angelic throng,
And left large field, unsafe within the wind
Of such commotion, such as to set forth
Great things by small, if Nature's concord broke,
Among the constellations war were sprung,
Two planets rushing from aspect malign
Of fiercest opposition in mid sky,
Should combat, and their jarring spheres confound.
Together both with next to almighty arm,
Uplifted imminent one stroke they aimed
That might determine, and not need repeat,
As not of power, at once; nor odds appeared
In might or swift prevention; but the sword
Of Michael from the armoury of God
Was given him tempered so, that neither keen
Nor solid might resist that edge: it met
The sword of Satan with steep force to smite
Descending, and in half cut sheer, nor stayed
But with swift wheel reverse, deep entering sheared
All his right side; then Satan first knew pain,

And writhed him to and fro convolved; so sore
The griding sword with discontinuous wound
Passed through him, but th' ethereal substance closed
Not long divisible, and from the gash
A stream of nectarous humour issuing flowed
Sanguine, such as celestial spirits may bleed,
And all his armour stained ere while so bright.
Forthwith on all sides to his aid was run
By angels many and strong, who interposed
Defence, while others bore him on their shields
Back to his chariot, where it stood retired
From off the files of war; there they him laid
Gnashing for anguish and despite and shame
To find himself not matchless, and his pride
Humbled by such rebuke, so far beneath
His confidence to equal God in power.
Yet soon he healed; for spirits that live throughout
Vital in every part, not as frail man
In entrails, heart or head, liver or reins,
Cannot but by annihilating die;
Nor in their liquid texture mortal wound
Receive, no more than can the fluid air:
All heart they live, all head, all eye, all ear,
All intellect, all sense, and as they please,
They limb themselves, and colour, shape or size
Assume, as likes them best, condense or rare.

CHARLES SACKVILLE,
EARL OF DORSET

1638–1706

28   *Song*

Written at Sea in the First Dutch War (1665),
the night before an Engagement

To all you ladies now at land
    We men at sea indite;
But first would have you understand
    How hard it is to write:

The Muses now, and Neptune too,
We must implore to write to you—
    With a fa, la, la, la, la.

For though the Muses should prove kind,
    And fill our empty brain,
Yet if rough Neptune rouse the wind
    To wave the azure main,
Our paper, pen, and ink and we,
Roll up and down our ships at sea—
    With a fa, la, la, la, la.

Then if we write not by each post,
    Think not we are unkind;
Nor yet conclude our ships are lost
    By Dutchmen or by wind:
Our tears we'll send a speedier way,
The tide shall bring them twice a day—
    With a fa, la, la, la, la.

The King with wonder and surprise
    Will swear the seas grow bold,
Because the tides will higher rise
    Than e'er they did of old:
But let him know it is our tears
Bring floods of grief to Whitehall stairs—
    With a fa, la, la, la, la.

Should foggy Opdam chance to know
    Our sad and dismal story,
The Dutch would scorn so weak a foe,
    And quit their fort at Goree:
For what resistance can they find
From men who've left their hearts behind?—
    With a fa, la, la, la, la.

Let wind and weather do its worst,
    Be you to us but kind;
Let Dutchmen vapour, Spaniards curse,
    No sorrow we shall find:
'Tis then no matter how things go,
Or who's our friend, or who's our foe—
    With a fa, la, la, la, la.

To pass our tedious hours away
  We throw a merry main,
Or else at serious ombre play;
  But why should we in vain
Each other's ruin thus pursue?
We were undone when we left you—
    With a fa, la, la, la, la.

But now our fears tempestuous grow
  And cast our hopes away;
Whilst you, regardless of our woe,
  Sit careless at a play:
Perhaps permit some happier man
To kiss your hand, or flirt your fan—
    With a fa, la, la, la, la.

When any mournful tune you hear,
  That dies in every note
As if it sighed with each man's care
  For being so remote,
Think then how often love we've made
To you, when all those tunes were played—
    With a fa, la, la, la, la.

In justice you cannot refuse
  To think of our distress,
When we for hopes of honour lose
  Our certain happiness:
All those designs are but to prove
Ourselves more worthy of your love—
    With a fa, la, la, la, la.

And now we've told you all our loves,
  And likewise all our fears,
In hopes this declaration moves
  Some pity for our tears:
Let's hear of no inconstancy—
We have too much of that at sea—
    With a fa, la, la, la, la.

JOHN DRYDEN

1631–1700

29   from *Annus Mirabilis**

Now van to van the foremost squadrons meet,
    The midmost battles hasting up behind,
Who view, far off, the storm of falling sleet,
    And hear their thunder rattling in the wind.

At length the adverse admirals appear:
    (The two bold champions of each country's right)
Their eyes describe the lists as they come near,
    And draw the lines of death before they fight.

The distance judged for shot of every size,
    The linstocks touch, the pond'rous ball expires:
The vig'rous seaman every port-hole plies,
    And adds his heart to every gun he fires.

Fierce was the fight on the proud Belgians' side,
    For honour, which they seldom sought before:
But now they by their own vain boasts were tied,
    And forced, at least in show, to prize it more.

But sharp remembrance on the English part,
    And shame of being matched by such a foe:
Rouse conscious virtue up in every heart,
    And seeming to be stronger makes them so.

Nor long the Belgians could that fleet sustain,
    Which did two gen'rals' fates, and Caesar's bear.
Each several ship a victory did gain,
    As Rupert or as Albemarl were there.

---

* The second of the Dutch Wars erupted in 1664; in March 1665, Charles II officially
declared war on the Netherlands. The English victory at sea described here took place off
the coast of Holland at North Foreland on 25 July 1666.

Their battered admiral too soon withdrew,
    Unthanked by ours for his unfinished fight:
But he the minds of his Dutch masters knew,
    Who called that providence which we called flight.

Never did men more joyfully obey,
    Or sooner understand the sign to fly:
With such alacrity they bore away,
    As if to praise them all the states stood by.

O famous Leader of the Belgian fleet,
    Thy monument inscribed such praise shall wear
As Varro, timely flying, once did meet,
    Because he did not of his Rome despair.

Behold that navy which a while before
    Provoked the tardy English to the fight,
Now draw their beaten vessels close to shore,
    As larks die dared to shun the hobbies' flight.

Who ere would English monuments survey,
    In other records may our courage know:
But let them hide the story of this day,
    Whose fame was blemished by too base a foe.

Or if too busily they will enquire
    Into a victory which we disdain:
Then let them know, the Belgians did retire
    Before the Patron Saint of injured Spain.

Repenting England this revengeful day
    To Philip's manes did an off'ring bring:
England, which first, by leading them astray,
    Hatched up rebellion to destroy her King.

Our fathers bent their baneful industry
    To check a monarchy that slowly grew:
But did not France or Holland's fate foresee,
    Whose rising power to swift dominion flew.

In fortune's empire blindly thus we go,
  And wander after pathless destiny:
Whose dark resorts since prudence cannot know,
  In vain it would provide for what shall be.

But what ere English to the blessed shall go,
  And the fourth Harry or first Orange meet:
Find him disowning of a Bourbon foe,
  And him detesting a Batavian fleet.

Now on their coasts our conquering navy rides,
  Waylays their merchants, and their land besets:
Each day new wealth without their care provides,
  They lie asleep with prizes in their nets.

DANIEL DEFOE

1660–1731

30   from *The Spanish Descent**

The word's gone out, and now they spread the main
With swelling sails, and swelling hopes, for Spain:
To double vengeance pressed where'er they come,
Resolved to pay the haughty Spaniard home:
Resolved by future conduct to atone
For all our past mistakes, and all their own.
New life springs up in every English face,
And fits them all for glorious things apace:
The booty some excites, and some the cause;
But more the hope to gain their lost applause.
Eager their sullied honour to restore,
Some anger whets, some pride and vengeance more.
    The lazy minutes now pass on too slow,
Fancy flies faster than the winds can blow:

---

* In 1702, during the War of the Spanish Succession, an unsuccessful expedition to
Cadiz by the British and the Dutch was followed by a dramatic victory in the Bay of Vigo,
where, without losing a single ship themselves, they were able to capture an entire fleet,
including 12 Spanish galleons and 15 French men-of-war.

Impatient wishes lengthen out the day;
They chide the loitering winds for their delay.
But time is nature's faithful messenger,
And brings up all we wish, as well as all we fear.
      The mists clear up, and now the scout decries
The subject of their hopes and victories:
The wished for fleets embayed, in harbour lie,
Unfit to fight, and more unfit to fly.
Triumphant joy throughout the navy flies,
Echoed from shore with terror and surprise.
Strange power of noise! which at one simple sound
At once shall some encourage, some confound.
      In vain the lion tangled in the snare
With anguish roars, and rends the trembling air:
'Tis vain to struggle with Almighty Fate;
Vain and impossible the weak debate.
The mighty boom, the forts, resist in vain.
The guns with fruitless force in noise complain.
See how the troops intrepidly fall on!
Wish for more foes, and think they fly too soon.
With eager fury to their forts pursue,
And think the odds of four to one too few.
The land's first conquered and the prize attends;
Fate beckons in the fleet to back their friends:
Despair succeeds, they struggle now too late,
And soon submit to their prevailing fate:
Courage is madness when occasion's past,
Death's the securest refuge, and the last.
      And now the rolling flames come threat'ning on,
And mighty streams of melted gold run down.
The flaming ore down to its centre makes,
To form new mines beneath the oozy lakes.
      Here a galleon with spicy drugs inflamed,
In odoriferous folds of sulphur streamed.
The gods of old no such oblations knew,
Their spices weak, and their perfumes but few.
The frighted Spaniards from their treasure fly,
Loath to forsake their wealth, but loath to die.
      Here a vast carrack flies while none pursue,
Bulged on the shore by her distracted crew:
There like a mighty mountain she appears,
And groans beneath the golden weight she bears.
Conquest perverts the property of friend,

And makes men ruin what they can't defend:
Some blow their treasures up into the air
With all the wild excesses of despair.
Strange fate! that war such odd events should have;
Friends would destroy, and enemies would save:
Others their safety to their wealth prefer,
And mix some small discretion with their fear.
Life's the best gift that nature can bestow;
The first that we receive, the last which we forgo:
And he that's vainly prodigal of blood,
Forfeits his sense to do his cause no good.
All desperation's the effect of fear;
Courage is temper, valour can't despair.
  And now the victory's completely gained;
No ships to conquer now, no foes remained.
The mighty spoils exceed whate'er was known
That vanquished ever lost, or victor won:
So great, if Fame shall future times remind,
They'll think she lies, and libels all mankind.

JOSEPH ADDISON

1672–1719

31   from *The Campaign**

A Poem to His Grace the Duke of Marlborough

But, O my muse, what numbers wilt thou find
To sing the furious troops in battle joined!
Methinks I hear the drum's tumultuous sound
The victor's shouts and dying groans confound,
The dreadful burst of cannon rend the skies,
And all the thunder of the battle rise.
'Twas then great Marlborough's mighty soul was proved
That, in the shock of charging hosts unmoved,
Amidst confusion, horror, and despair,
Examined all the dreadful scenes of war;

---

* At the Battle of Blenheim, on 13 August 1704, the Duke of Marlborough and Prince
Eugene of Savoy won one of the most important victories of the War of the Spanish
Succession, defeating the French and Bavarians and capturing the French Marshal
Tallard.

In peaceful thought the field of death surveyed,
To fainting squadrons sent the timely aid,
Inspired repulsed battalions to engage,
And taught the doubtful battle where to rage.
So when an angel by divine command
With rising tempests shakes a guilty land,
Such as of late o'er pale Britannia past,
Calm and serene he drives the furious blast;
And, pleased the Almighty's orders to perform,
Rides in the whirlwind, and directs the storm.

ROBERT SOUTHEY

1774–1843

32   *The Battle of Blenheim*

I

It was a summer evening,
   Old Kaspar's work was done,
And he before his cottage door
   Was sitting in the sun,
And by him sported on the green
His little grandchild Wilhelmine.

II

She saw her brother Peterkin
   Roll something large and round,
Which he beside the rivulet
   In playing there had found;
He came to ask what he had found,
That was so large, and smooth, and round.

III

Old Kaspar took it from the boy,
   Who stood expectant by;
And then the old man shook his head,
   And, with a natural sigh,
' 'Tis some poor fellow's skull,' said he,
'Who fell in the great victory.

IV

'I find them in the garden,
　For there's many here about;
And often when I go to plough,
　The ploughshare turns them out!
For many thousand men,' said he,
'Were slain in that great victory.'

V

'Now tell us what 'twas all about,'
　Young Peterkin, he cries;
And little Wilhelmine looks up
　With wonder-waiting eyes;
'Now tell us all about the war,
And what they fought each other for.'

VI

'It was the English,' Kaspar cried,
　'Who put the French to rout;
But what they fought each other for,
　I could not well make out;
But everybody said,' quoth he,
'That 'twas a famous victory.

VII

'My father lived at Blenheim then,
　Yon little stream hard by;
They burnt his dwelling to the ground,
　And he was forced to fly;
So with his wife and child he fled,
Nor had he where to rest his head.

VIII

'With fire and sword the country round
　Was wasted far and wide,
And many a childing mother then,
　And new-born baby died;
But things like that, you know, must be
At every famous victory.

IX

'They say it was a shocking sight
　　After the field was won;
For many thousand bodies here
　　Lay rotting in the sun;
But things like that, you know, must be
After a famous victory.

X

'Great praise the Duke of Marlbro' won,
　　And our good Prince Eugene.'
'Why 'twas a very wicked thing!'
　　Said little Wilhelmine.
'Nay ... nay ... my little girl,' quoth he,
'It was a famous victory.

XI

'And everybody praised the Duke
　　Who this great fight did win.'
'But what good came of it at last?'
　　Quoth little Peterkin.
'Why that I cannot tell,' said he
'But 'twas a famous victory.'

JAMES THOMSON

1700–1748

33　　　　　*Rule, Britannia!*

When Britain first, at Heaven's command,
　　Arose from out the azure main,
This was the charter of the land,
　　And guardian angels sung this strain.
　　　'Rule, Britannia, rule the waves;
　　　Britons never will be slaves.'

The nations, not so blest as thee,
　　Must, in their turns, to tyrants fall;
While thou shalt flourish great and free,
　　The dread and envy of them all.
　　　'Rule,' &c.

Still more majestic shalt thou rise,
  More dreadful from each foreign stroke;
As the loud blast that tears the skies
  Serves but to root thy native oak.
    'Rule,' &c.

Thee haughty tyrants ne'er shall tame;
  All their attempts to bend thee down
Will but arouse thy generous flame,
  But work their woe, and thy renown.
    'Rule,' &c.

To thee belongs the rural reign;
  Thy cities shall with commerce shine;
All thine shall be the subject main;
  And every shore it circles, thine.
    'Rule,' &c.

The Muses, still with freedom found,
  Shall to thy happy coast repair:
Blest isle! with matchless beauty crowned,
  And manly hearts to guard the fair:
    'Rule, Britannia, rule the waves,
    Britons never will be slaves.'

SAMUEL JOHNSON

1709–1784

34   from *The Vanity of Human Wishes**

On what foundation stands the warrior's pride,
How just his hopes, let Swedish Charles decide;
A frame of adamant, a soul of fire,
No dangers fright him, and no labours tire;
O'er love, o'er fear, extends his wide domain,
Unconquered lord of pleasure and of pain;

* King Charles XII of Sweden invaded Russia in 1708, where he was disastrously defeated at Pultowa in 1709. Unsuccessful in his efforts to forge a lasting alliance against Russia with Turkey, he invaded Norway; in 1816 he was killed in the attack on Fredrikshald.

No joys to him pacific sceptres yield,
War sounds the trump, he rushes to the field;
Behold surrounding kings their powers combine,
And one capitulate, and one resign;
Peace courts his hand, but spreads her charms in vain;
'Think nothing gained,' he cries, 'till naught remain,
On Moscow's walls till Gothic standards fly,
And all be mine beneath the polar sky.'
The march begins in military state,
And nations on his eye suspended wait;
Stern Famine guards the solitary coast,
And Winter barricades the realms of Frost;
He comes, nor want nor cold his course delay—
Hide, blushing Glory, hide Pultowa's day:
The vanquished hero leaves his broken bands,
And shows his miseries in distant lands;
Condemned a needy supplicant to wait,
While ladies interpose, and slaves debate.
But did not Chance at length her error mend?
Did no subverted empire mark his end?
Did rival monarchs give the fatal wound?
Or hostile millions press him to the ground?
His fall was destined to a barren strand,
A petty fortress, and a dubious hand;
He left the name at which the world grew pale,
To point a moral, or adorn a tale.

JOHN SCOTT OF AMWELL

1730–1783

35 *The Drum*

I hate that drum's discordant sound,
Parading round, and round, and round:
To thoughtless youth it pleasure yields,
And lures from cities and from fields,
To sell their liberty for charms
Of tawdry lace, and glittering arms;
And when Ambition's voice commands,
To march, and fight, and fall, in foreign lands.

I hate that drum's discordant sound,
Parading round, and round, and round:
To me it talks of ravaged plains,
And burning towns, and ruined swains,
And mangled limbs, and dying groans,
And widows' tears, and orphans' moans;
And all that Misery's hand bestows,
To fill the catalogue of human woes.

THOMAS CAMPBELL

1777–1844

36   *Ye Mariners of England*

Ye Mariners of England
    That guard our native seas!
Whose flag has braved a thousand years
    The battle and the breeze!
Your glorious standard launch again
    To match another foe;
And sweep through the deep,
    While the stormy winds do blow!
While the battle rages loud and long
    And the stormy winds do blow.

The spirits of your fathers
    Shall start from every wave—
For the deck it was their field of fame,
    And Ocean was their grave:
Where Blake and mighty Nelson fell
    Your manly hearts shall glow,
As ye sweep through the deep,
    While the stormy winds do blow!
While the battle rages loud and long
    And the stormy winds do blow.

Britannia needs no bulwarks,
    No towers along the steep;
Her march is o'er the mountain-waves,
    Her home is on the deep.

With thunders from her native oak
　　She quells the floods below,
As they roar on the shore,
　　When the stormy winds do blow!
When the battle rages loud and long,
　　And the stormy winds do blow.

The meteor flag of England
　　Shall yet terrific burn;
Till danger's troubled night depart
　　And the star of peace return.
Then, then, ye ocean-warriors!
　　Our song and feast shall flow
To the fame of your name,
　　When the storm has ceased to blow!
When the fiery fight is heard no more,
　　And the storm has ceased to blow.

37　　　　　　　　　*Hohenlinden*＊

On Linden, when the sun was low,
All bloodless lay the untrodden snow,
And dark as winter was the flow
　　Of Iser, rolling rapidly.

But Linden saw another sight,
When the drum beat, at dead of night,
Commanding fires of death to light
　　The darkness of her scenery.

By torch and trumpet fast arrayed,
Each horseman drew his battle blade,
And furious every charger neighed
　　To join the dreadful revelry.

Then shook the hills, with thunder riven;
Then rushed the steed, to battle driven;
And, louder than the bolts of heaven,
　　Far flashed the red artillery.

＊ On 3 December 1800, the French General Jean Victor Moreau crossed the Rhine
with his troops, decisively defeating the Austrian and allied forces in the Bavarian village of
Hohenlinden. The battle marked a turning point in the French Revolutionary Wars.

But redder yet that light shall glow,
On Linden's hills of stainèd snow;
And bloodier yet, the torrent flow
    Of Iser, rolling rapidly.

'Tis morn; but scarce yon level sun
Can pierce the war-clouds, rolling dun,
Where furious Frank, and fiery Hun,
    Shout in their sulphurous canopy.

The combat deepens. On, ye brave,
Who rush to glory, or the grave!
Wave, Munich, all thy banners wave,
    And charge with all thy chivalry!

Few, few shall part, where many meet!
The snow shall be their winding sheet,
And every turf, beneath their feet,
    Shall be a soldier's sepulchre.

SAMUEL TAYLOR COLERIDGE

1772–1834

38   *Fears in Solitude*

Written in April 1798, during the alarm
of an invasion

A green and silent spot, amid the hills,
A small and silent dell! O'er stiller place
No singing sky-lark ever poised himself.
The hills are heathy, save that swelling slope,
Which hath a gay and gorgeous covering on,
All golden with the never-bloomless furze,
Which now blooms most profusely: but the dell,
Bathed by the mist, is fresh and delicate
As vernal corn-field, or the unripe flax,
When, through its half-transparent stalks, at eve,
The level sunshine glimmers with green light.
Oh! 'tis a quiet spirit-healing nook!

Which all, methinks, would love; but chiefly he,
The humble man, who, in his youthful years,
Knew just so much of folly, as had made
His early manhood more securely wise!
Here he might lie on fern or withered heath,
While from the singing lark (that sings unseen
The minstrelsy that solitude loves best),
And from the sun, and from the breezy air,
Sweet influences trembled o'er his frame;
And he, with many feelings, many thoughts,
Made up a meditative joy, and found
Religious meanings in the forms of Nature!
And so, his senses gradually wrapt
In a half sleep, he dreams of better worlds,
And dreaming hears thee still, O singing lark,
That singest like an angel in the clouds!

My God! it is a melancholy thing
For such a man, who would full fain preserve
His soul in calmness, yet perforce must feel
For all his human brethren—O my God!
It weighs upon the heart, that he must think
What uproar and what strife may now be stirring
This way or that way o'er these silent hills—
Invasion, and the thunder and the shout,
And all the crash of onset; fear and rage,
And undetermined conflict—even now,
Even now, perchance, and in his native isle:
Carnage and groans beneath this blessed sun!
We have offended, Oh! my countrymen!
We have offended very grievously,
And been most tyrannous. From east to west
A groan of accusation pierces Heaven!
The wretched plead against us; multitudes
Countless and vehement, the sons of God,
Our brethren! Like a cloud that travels on,
Steamed up from Cairo's swamps of pestilence,
Even so, my countrymen! have we gone forth
And borne to distant tribes slavery and pangs,
And, deadlier far, our vices, whose deep taint
With slow perdition murders the whole man,
His body and his soul! Meanwhile, at home,
All individual dignity and power

Engulfed in Courts, Committees, Institutions,
Associations and Societies,
A vain, speech-mouthing, speech-reporting Guild,
One Benefit-Club for mutual flattery,
We have drunk up, demure as at a grace,
Pollutions from the brimming cup of wealth;
Contemptuous of all honourable rule,
Yet bartering freedom and the poor man's life
For gold, as at a market! The sweet words
Of Christian promise, words that even yet
Might stem destruction, were they wisely preached,
Are muttered o'er by men, whose tones proclaim
How flat and wearisome they feel their trade:
Rank scoffers some, but most too indolent
To deem them falsehoods or to know their truth.
Oh! blasphemous! the Book of Life is made
A superstitious instrument, on which
We gabble o'er the oaths we mean to break;
For all must swear—all and in every place,
College and wharf, council and justice-court;
All, all must swear, the briber and the bribed,
Merchant and lawyer, senator and priest,
The rich, the poor, the old man and the young;
All, all make up one scheme of perjury,
That faith doth reel; the very name of God
Sounds like a juggler's charm; and, bold with joy,
Forth from his dark and lonely hiding-place,
(Portentous sight!) the owlet Atheism,
Sailing on obscene wings athwart the noon,
Drops his blue-fringèd lids, and holds them close,
And hooting at the glorious sun in Heaven,
Cries out, 'Where is it?'
                    Thankless too for peace,
(Peace long preserved by fleets and perilous seas)
Secure from actual warfare, we have loved
To swell the war-whoop, passionate for war!
Alas! for ages ignorant of all
Its ghastlier workings, (famine or blue plague,
Battle, or siege, or flight through wintry snows,)
We, this whole people, have been clamorous
For war and bloodshed; animating sports,
The which we pay for as a thing to talk of,
Spectators and not combatants! No guess

Anticipative of a wrong unfelt,
No speculation on contingency,
However dim and vague, too vague and dim
To yield a justifying cause; and forth,
(Stuffed out with big preamble, holy names,
And adjurations of the God in Heaven,)
We send our mandates for the certain death
Of thousands and ten thousands! Boys and girls,
And women, that would groan to see a child
Pull off an insect's leg, all read of war,
The best amusement for our morning meal!
The poor wretch, who has learnt his only prayers
From curses, who knows scarcely words enough
To ask a blessing from his Heavenly Father,
Becomes a fluent phraseman, absolute
And technical in victories and defeats,
And all our dainty terms for fratricide;
Terms which we trundle smoothly o'er our tongues
Like mere abstractions, empty sounds to which
We join no feeling and attach no form!
As if the soldier died without a wound;
As if the fibres of this godlike frame
Were gored without a pang; as if the wretch,
Who fell in battle, doing bloody deeds,
Passed off to Heaven, translated and not killed;
As though he had no wife to pine for him,
No God to judge him! Therefore, evil days
Are coming on us, O my countrymen!
And what if all-avenging Providence,
Strong and retributive, should make us know
The meaning of our words, force us to feel
The desolation and the agony
Of our fierce doings?
                              Spare us yet awhile,
Father and God! O! spare us yet awhile!
Oh! let not English women drag their flight
Fainting beneath the burthen of their babes,
Of the sweet infants, that but yesterday
Laughed at the breast! Sons, brothers, husbands, all
Who ever gazed with fondness on the forms
Which grew up with you round the same fire-side,
And all who ever heard the sabbath-bells
Without the infidel's scorn, make yourselves pure!

Stand forth! be men! repel an impious foe,
Impious and false, a light yet cruel race,
Who laugh away all virtue, mingling mirth
With deeds of murder; and still promising
Freedom, themselves too sensual to be free,
Poison life's amities, and cheat the heart
Of faith and quiet hope, and all that soothes,
And all that lifts the spirit! Stand we forth;
Render them back upon the insulted ocean,
And let them toss as idly on its waves
As the vile seaweed, which some mountain-blast
Swept from our shores! And oh! may we return
Not with a drunken triumph, but with fear,
Repenting of the wrongs with which we stung
So fierce a foe to frenzy!
                              I have told,
O Britons! O my brethren! I have told
Most bitter truth, but without bitterness.
Nor deem my zeal or factious or mistimed;
For never can true courage dwell with them,
Who, playing tricks with conscience, dare not look
At their own vices. We have been too long
Dupes of a deep delusion! Some, belike,
Groaning with restless enmity, expect
All change from change of constituted power;
As if a Government had been a robe,
On which our vice and wretchedness were tagged
Like fancy-points and fringes, with the robe
Pulled off at pleasure. Fondly these attach
A radical causation to a few
Poor drudges of chastising Providence,
Who borrow all their hues and qualities
From our own folly and rank wickedness,
Which gave them birth and nursed them. Others, meanwhile,
Dote with a mad idolatry; and all
Who will not fall before their images,
And yield them worship, they are enemies
Even of their country!
                              Such have I been deemed.—
But, O dear Britain! O my Mother Isle!
Needs must thou prove a name most dear and holy
To me, a son, a brother, and a friend,
A husband, and a father! who revere

All bonds of natural love, and find them all
Within the limits of thy rocky shores.
O native Britain! O my Mother Isle!
How shouldst thou prove aught else but dear and holy
To me, who from thy lakes and mountain-hills,
Thy clouds, thy quiet dales, thy rocks and seas,
Have drunk in all my intellectual life,
All sweet sensations, all ennobling thoughts,
All adoration of the God in nature,
All lovely and all honourable things,
Whatever makes this mortal spirit feel
The joy and greatness of its future being?
There lives nor form nor feeling in my soul
Unborrowed from my country! O divine
And beauteous island! thou hast been my sole
And most magnificent temple, in the which
I walk with awe, and sing my stately songs,
Loving the God that made me!—
                                        May my fears,
My filial fears, be vain! and may the vaunts
And menace of the vengeful enemy
Pass like the gust, that roared and died away
In the distant tree: which heard, and only heard
In this low dell, bowed not the delicate grass.

But now the gentle dew-fall sends abroad
The fruit-like perfume of the golden furze:
The light has left the summit of the hill,
Though still a sunny gleam lies beautiful,
Aslant the ivied beacon. Now farewell,
Farewell, awhile, O soft and silent spot!
On the green sheep-track, up the heathy hill,
Homeward I wind my way; and lo! recalled
From bodings that have well-nigh wearied me,
I find myself upon the brow, and pause
Startled! And after lonely sojourning
In such a quiet and surrounded nook,
This burst of prospect, here the shadowy main,
Dim-tinted, there the mighty majesty
Of that huge amphitheatre of rich
And elmy fields, seems like society—
Conversing with the mind, and giving it
A livelier impulse and a dance of thought!

And now, belovèd Stowey! I behold
Thy church-tower, and, methinks, the four huge elms
Clustering, which mark the mansion of my friend;
And close behind them, hidden from my view,
Is my own lowly cottage, where my babe
And my babe's mother dwell in peace! With light
And quickened footsteps thitherward I tend,
Remembering thee, O green and silent dell!
And grateful, that by nature's quietness
And solitary musings, all my heart
Is softened, and made worthy to indulge
Love, and the thoughts that yearn for human kind.

Nether Stowey, 20 April 1798

WILLIAM WORDSWORTH
1770–1850

39   *Old Man Travelling*

                    The little hedgerow birds,
That peck along the road, regard him not.
He travels on, and in his face, his step,
His gait, is one expression; every limb,
His look and bending figure, all bespeak
A man who does not move with pain, but moves
With thought—He is insensibly subdued
To settled quiet; he is one by whom
All effort seems forgotten, one to whom
Long patience has such mild composure given,
That patience now doth seem a thing, of which
He hath no need. He is by nature led
To peace so perfect, that the young behold
With envy, what the old man hardly feels.
—I asked him whither he was bound, and what
The object of his journey; he replied
'Sir! I am going many miles to take
A last leave of my son, a mariner,
Who from a sea-fight has been brought to Falmouth,
And there is dying in an hospital.'

1797

40 It is not to be thought of that the flood
Of British freedom, which to the open sea
Of the world's praise from dark antiquity
Hath flowed, 'with pomp of waters, unwithstood,'
Road by which all might come and go that would,
And bear out freights of worth to foreign lands;
That this most famous stream in bogs and sands
Should perish: and to evil and to good
Be lost for ever. In our halls is hung
Armoury of the invincible knights of old:
We must be free or die, who speak the tongue
That Shakespeare spake; the faith and morals hold
Which Milton held. In everything we are sprung
Of earth's first blood, have titles manifold.

41 *To the Men of Kent*

October, 1803

Vanguard of liberty, ye Men of Kent,
Ye children of a soil that doth advance
Its haughty brow against the coast of France,
Now is the time to prove your hardiment!
To France be words of invitation sent!
They from their fields can see the countenance
Of your fierce war, may ken the glittering lance,
And hear you shouting forth your brave intent.
Left single, in bold parley, ye, of yore,
Did from the Norman win a gallant wreath;
Confirmed the charters that were yours before;
No parleying now! In Britain is one breath;
We all are with you now from shore to shore;
Ye Men of Kent, 'tis victory or death!

42 *November, 1806**

Another year!—another deadly blow!
Another mighty empire overthrown!
And we are left, or shall be left alone;
The last that dare to struggle with the foe.

* The Battle of Jena, on 14 October 1806, resulted in the complete overthrow of Prussia by the French under Napoleon.

'Tis well! from this day forward we shall know
That in ourselves our safety must be sought;
That by our own right hands it must be wrought;
That we must stand unpropped, or be laid low.
O dastard whom such foretaste doth not cheer!
We shall exult, if they who rule the land
Be men who hold its many blessings dear,
Wise, upright, valiant; not a servile band,
Who are to judge of danger which they fear,
And honour which they do not understand.

PERCY BYSSHE SHELLEY

1792–1822

43   from *The Revolt of Islam*

Over the utmost hill at length I sped,
    A snowy-steep:—the moon was hanging low
Over the Asian mountains, and outspread
    The plain, the city, and the camp below,
    Skirted the midnight ocean's glimmering flow;
The city's moonlit spires and myriad lamps,
    Like stars in a sublunar sky did glow,
And fires blazed far amid the scattered camps,
Like springs of flame, which burst where'er swift earthquake
    stamps.

All slept but those in watchful arms who stood,
    And those who sate tending the beacon's light,
And the few sounds from that vast multitude
    Made silence more profound.—Oh, what a might
    Of human thought was cradled in that night!
How many hearts impenetrably veiled
    Beat underneath its shade, what secret fight
Evil and good, in woven passions mailed,
Waged through that silent throng; a war that never failed!

And now the Power of Good held victory,
  So, through the labyrinth of many a tent,
Among the silent millions who did lie
  In innocent sleep, exultingly I went;
  The moon had left Heaven desert now, but lent
From eastern morn the first faint lustre showed
  An armèd youth—over his spear he bent
His downward face.—'A friend!' I cried aloud,
And quickly common hopes made freemen understood.

I sate beside him while the morning beam
  Crept slowly over Heaven, and talked with him
Of those immortal hopes, a glorious theme!
  Which led us forth, until the stars grew dim:
  And all the while, methought, his voice did swim
As if it drownèd in remembrance were
  Of thoughts which make the moist eyes overbrim:
At last, when daylight 'gan to fill the air,
He looked on me, and cried in wonder—'Thou art here!'

Then, suddenly, I knew it was the youth
  In whom its earliest hopes my spirit found;
But envious tongues had stained his spotless truth,
  And thoughtless pride his love in silence bound,
  And shame and sorrow mine in toils had wound,
Whilst he was innocent, and I deluded;
  The truth now came upon me, on the ground
Tears of repenting joy, which fast intruded,
Fell fast, and o'er its peace our mingling spirits brooded.

Thus, while with rapid lips and earnest eyes
  We talked, a sound of sweeping conflict spread
As from the earth did suddenly arise;
  From every tent roused by that clamour dread,
  Our bands outsprung and seized their arms—we sped
Towards the sound: our tribes were gathering far.
  Those sanguine slaves amid ten thousand dead
Stabbed in their sleep, trampled in treacherous war
The gentle hearts whose power their lives had sought to spare.

Like rabid snakes, that sting some gentle child
  Who brings them food, when winter false and fair
Allures them forth with its cold smiles, so wild
  They rage among the camp;—they overbear
  The patriot hosts—confusion, then despair
Descends like night—when 'Laon!' one did cry:
  Like a bright ghost from Heaven that shout did scare
The slaves, and widening through the vaulted sky,
Seemed sent from Earth to Heaven in sign of victory.

In sudden panic those false murderers fled,
  Like insect tribes before the northern gale:
But swifter still, our hosts encompassèd
  Their shattered ranks, and in a craggy vale,
  Where even their fierce despair might nought avail,
Hemmed them around!—and then revenge and fear
  Made the high virtue of the patriots fail:
One pointed on his foe the mortal spear—
I rushed before its point, and cried, 'Forbear, forbear!'

The spear transfixed my arm that was uplifted
  In swift expostulation, and the blood
Gushed round its point: I smiled, and—'Oh! thou gifted
  With eloquence which shall not be withstood,
  Flow thus!'—I cried in joy, 'thou vital flood,
Until my heart be dry, ere thus the cause
  For which thou wert aught worthy be subdued—
Ah, ye are pale,—ye weep,—your passions pause,—
'Tis well! ye feel the truth of love's benignant laws.

'Soldiers, our brethren and our friends are slain.
  Ye murdered them, I think, as they did sleep!
Alas, what have ye done? the slightest pain
  Which ye might suffer, there were eyes to weep,
  But ye have quenched them—there were smiles to steep
Your hearts in balm, but they are lost in woe;
  And those whom love did set his watch to keep
Around your tents, truth's freedom to bestow,
Ye stabbed as they did sleep—but they forgive ye now.

'Oh wherefore should ill ever flow from ill,
   And pain still keener pain for ever breed?
We all are brethren—even the slaves who kill
   For hire, are men; and to avenge misdeed
   On the misdoer, doth but Misery feed
With her own broken heart! O Earth, O Heaven!
   And thou, dread Nature, which to every deed
And all that lives or is, to be hath given,
Even as to thee have these done ill, and are forgiven!

'Join then your hands and hearts, and let the past
   Be as a grave which gives not up its dead
To evil thoughts.'—A film then overcast
   My sense with dimness, for the wound, which bled
   Freshly, swift shadows o'er mine eyes had shed.
When I awoke, I lay mid friends and foes,
   And earnest countenances on me shed
The light of questioning looks, whilst one did close
My wound with balmiest herbs, and soothed me to repose;

And one whose spear had pierced me, leaned beside,
   With quivering lips and humid eyes;—and all
Seemed like some brothers on a journey wide
   Gone forth, whom now strange meeting did befall
   In a strange land, round one whom they might call
Their friend, their chief, their father, for assay
   Of peril, which had saved them from the thrall
Of death, now suffering. Thus the vast array
Of those fraternal bands were reconciled that day.

CHARLES WOLFE

1791–1823

44   *The Burial of Sir John Moore after Corunna**

Not a drum was heard, not a funeral note,
    As his corse to the rampart we hurried;
Not a soldier discharged his farewell shot
    O'er the grave where our hero we buried.

We buried him darkly at dead of night,
    The sods with our bayonets turning,
By the struggling moonbeam's misty light
    And the lanthorn dimly burning.

No useless coffin enclosed his breast,
    Not in sheet or in shroud we wound him;
But he lay like a warrior taking his rest
    With his martial cloak around him.

Few and short were the prayers we said,
    And we spoke not a word of sorrow;
But we steadfastly gazed on the face that was dead,
    And we bitterly thought of the morrow.

We thought, as we hollowed his narrow bed
    And smoothed down his lonely pillow,
That the foe and the stranger would tread o'er his head,
    And we far away on the billow!

Lightly they'll talk of the spirit that's gone,
    And o'er his cold ashes upbraid him—
But little he'll reck, if they let him sleep on
    In the grave where a Briton has laid him.

---

* Sir John Moore commanded British troops supporting the Spanish Army against Napoleon in the Peninsular War (1808–14). Forced into a 250-mile retreat by a French defeat of the Spanish, he fought valiantly at Corunna, Spain, where he won the battle against the French, but lost his own life (1809).

But half of our heavy task was done
    When the clock struck the hour for retiring;
And we heard the distant and random gun
    That the foe was sullenly firing.

Slowly and sadly we laid him down,
    From the field of his fame fresh and gory;
We carved not a line, and we raised not a stone,
    But we left him alone with his glory.

JOEL BARLOW

1754–1812

45   *Advice to a Raven in Russia*

December, 1812

Black fool, why winter here? These frozen skies,
Worn by your wings and deafened by your cries,
Should warn you hence, where milder suns invite,
And day alternates with his mother night.
    You fear perhaps your food will fail you there,
Your human carnage, that delicious fare
That lured you hither, following still your friend
The great Napoleon to the world's bleak end.
You fear, because the southern climes poured forth
Their clustering nations to infest the north,
Bavarians, Austrians, those who drink the Po
And those who skirt the Tuscan seas below,
With all Germania, Neustria, Belgia, Gaul,
Doomed here to wade through slaughter to their fall,
You fear he left behind no wars, to feed
His feathered cannibals and nurse the breed.
    Fear not, my screamer, call your greedy train,
Sweep over Europe, hurry back to Spain,
You'll find his legions there; the valiant crew
Please best their master when they toil for you.
Abundant there they spread the country o'er
And taint the breeze with every nation's gore,
Iberian, Lusian, British widely strown,
But still more wide and copious flows their own.

Go where you will; Calabria, Malta, Greece,
Egypt and Syria still his fame increase,
Domingo's fattened isle and India's plains
Glow deep with purple drawn from Gallic veins.
No raven's wing can stretch the flight so far
As the torn bandrols of Napoleon's war.
Choose then your climate, fix your best abode,
He'll make you deserts and he'll bring you blood.

How could you fear a dearth? have not mankind,
Though slain by millions, millions left behind?
Has not Conscription still the power to wield
Her annual faulchion o'er the human field?
A faithful harvester! or if a man
Escape that gleaner, shall he scape the Ban?
The triple Ban, that like the hound of hell
Gripes with three jowls, to hold his victim well.

Fear nothing then, hatch fast your ravenous brood,
Teach them to cry to Bonaparte for food;
They'll be like you, of all his suppliant train,
The only class that never cries in vain.
For see what mutual benefits you lend!
(The surest way to fix the mutual friend)
While on his slaughtered troops your tribe are fed,
You cleanse his camp and carry off his dead.
Imperial scavenger! but now you know
Your work is vain amid these hills of snow.
His tentless troops are marbled through with frost
And change to crystal when the breath is lost.
Mere trunks of ice, though limbed like human frames
And lately warmed with life's endearing flames,
They cannot taint the air, the world impest,
Nor can you tear one fibre from their breast.
No! from their visual sockets, as they lie,
With beak and claws you cannot pluck an eye.
The frozen orb, preserving still its form,
Defies your talons as it braves the storm,
But stands and stares to God, as if to know
In what cursed hands he leaves his world below.

Fly then, or starve; though all the dreadful road
From Minsk to Moscow with their bodies strowed
May count some myriads, yet they can't suffice
To feed you more beneath these dreary skies.
Go back, and winter in the wilds of Spain;

Feast there awhile, and in the next campaign
Rejoin your master; for you'll find him then,
With his new million of the race of men,
Clothed in his thunders, all his flags unfurled,
Raging and storming o'er the prostrate world.
  War after war his hungry soul requires,
State after state shall sink beneath his fires,
Yet other Spains in victim smoke shall rise
And other Moscows suffocate the skies,
Each land lie reeking with its people's slain
And not a stream run bloodless to the main.
Till men resume their souls, and dare to shed
Earth's total vengeance on the monster's head,
Hurl from his blood-built throne this king of woes,
Dash him to dust, and let the world repose.

ADAM MICKIEWICZ
1798–1855

46

The Year 1812

Year well remembered! Happy who beheld thee!
The commons knew thee as the year of yield,
But as the year of war, the soldiery.

Rumours and skyward prodigies revealed
The poet's dream, the tale on old men's lips,
The spring when kine preferred the barren field.

Short of the acres green with growing tips
They halted lowing, chewed the winter's cud;
The men awaited an apocalypse.

Languid the farmer sought his livelihood
And checked his team and gazed, as if enquiring
What marvels gathered westward while he stood.

He asked the stork, whose white returning wing
Already spread above its native pine
Had raised the early standard of the Spring.

From swallows gathering frozen mud to line
Their tiny homes, or in loud regiments
Ranged over water, he implored a sign.

The thickets hear each night as dusk descends
The woodcock's call. The forests hear the geese
Honk, and go down. The crane's voice never ends.

What storms have whirled them from what shaken seas,
The watchers ask, that they should come so soon?
Or in the feathered world, what mutinies?

For now fresh migrants of a brighter plume
Than finch or plover gleam above the hills,
Impend, descend, and on our meadows loom.

Cavalry! Troop after troop it spills
With strange insignia, strangely armed,
As snow in a spring thaw fills

The valley roads. From the forests long
Bright bayonets issue, as brigades of foot
Debouch like ants, form up, and densely throng;

All heading north as if the bird, the scout,
Had led men here from halcyon lands, impelled
By instincts too imperative to doubt.

War! the war!—a meaning that transpires
To the remotest corner. In the wood
Beyond whose bounds no rustic mind enquires,

Where in the sky the peasant understood
Only the wind's cry, and on earth the brute's
(And all his visitors the neighbourhood),

A sudden glare! A crash! A ball that shoots
Far from the field, makes its impeded way,
Rips through the branches and lays bare the roots.

The bearded bison trembles, and at bay
Heaves to his forelegs, ruffs his mane, and glares
At sudden sparks that glitter on the spray.

The stray bomb spins and hisses; as he stares,
Bursts. And the beast that never knew alarm
Blunders in panic to profounder lairs.

'Whither the battle?'—and the young men arm.
The women pray, 'God is Napoleon's shield,
Napoleon ours', as to the outcome calm.

Spring well remembered! Happy who saw thee then,
Spring of the war, Spring of the mighty yield,
That promised corn but ripened into men.

Translated from the Polish by Donald Davie via the prose version of George Rapall Noyes

VICTOR HUGO

1802–1885

47   *Russia 1812*

The snow fell, and its power was multiplied.
For the first time the Eagle bowed its head—
dark days! Slowly the Emperor returned—
behind him Moscow! Its onion domes still burned.
The snow rained down in blizzards—rained and froze.
Past each white waste a further white waste rose.
None recognized the captains or the flags.
Yesterday the Grand Army, today its dregs!
No one could tell the vanguard from the flanks.
The snow! The hurt men struggled from the ranks,
hid in the bellies of dead horse, in stacks
of shattered caissons. By the bivouacs,
one saw the picket dying at his post,
still standing in his saddle, white with frost,
the stone lips frozen to the bugle's mouth!
Bullets and grapeshot mingled with the snow,
that hailed ... The Guard, surprised at shivering, march
in a dream now; ice rimes the grey moustache.
The snow falls, always snow! The driving mire
submerges; men, trapped in that white empire,
have no more bread and march on barefoot—gaps!

They were no longer living men and troops,
but a dream drifting in a fog, a mystery,
mourners parading under the black sky.
The solitude, vast, terrible to the eye,
was like a mute avenger everywhere,
as snowfall, floating through the quiet air,
buried the huge army in a huge shroud.
Could anyone leave this kingdom? A crowd—
each man, obsessed with dying, was alone.
Men slept—and died! The beaten mob sludged on,
ditching the guns to burn their carriages.
Two foes. The North, the Czar. The North was worse.
In hollows where the snow was piling up,
one saw whole regiments fallen asleep.
Attila's dawn, Cannaes of Hannibal!
The army marching to its funeral!
Litters, wounded, the dead, deserters—swarm,
crushing the bridges down to cross a stream.
They went to sleep ten thousand, woke up four.
Ney, bringing up the former army's rear,
hacked his horse loose from three disputing Cossacks . . .
All night, the *qui vive?* The alert! Attacks;
retreats! White ghosts would wrench away our guns,
or we would see dim, terrible squadrons,
circles of steel, whirlpools of savages,
rush sabring through the camp like dervishes.
And in this way, whole armies died at night.

The Emperor was there, standing—he saw.
This oak already trembling from the axe,
watched his glories drop from him branch by branch:
chiefs, soldiers. Each one had his turn and chance—
they died! Some lived. These still believed his star,
and kept their watch. They loved the man of war,
this small man with his hands behind his back,
whose shadow, moving to and fro, was black
behind the lighted tent. Still believing, they
accused their destiny of *lèse-majesté*.
His misfortune had mounted on their back.
The man of glory shook. Cold stupefied
him, then suddenly he felt terrified.
Being without belief, he turned to God:
'God of armies, is this the end?' he cried.

89

And then at last the expiation came,
as he heard someone call him by his name,
someone half-lost in shadow, who said, 'No,
Napoleon.' Napoleon understood,
restless, bareheaded, leaden, as he stood
before his butchered legions in the snow.

Translated from the French by Robert Lowell

FYODOR TYUTCHEV

1803–1873

48   *At Vshchizh*

After the tumult and the blood
Had died, had dried,
Silence unmade its history:
A group of mounds; on them
A group of oaks. They spread
Their broad unmindful glories
Over the unheard rumour of those dead
And rustle there, rooted on ruin.
All nature's knowledge
Is to stay unknowing—
Ours, to confess confusion:
Dreamt-out by her,
Our years are apparitions in their coming-going.
Her random seed
Spread to their fruitless feat, she then
Regathers them
Into that peace all history must feed.

Translated from the Russian by Charles Tomlinson

ROBERT BROWNING
1812–1889

49   *Incident of the French Camp*

I

You know, we French stormed Ratisbon:
 A mile or so away,
On a little mound, Napoleon
 Stood on our storming-day;
With neck out-thrust, you fancy how,
 Legs wide, arms locked behind,
As if to balance the prone brow
 Oppressive with its mind.

II

Just as perhaps he mused 'My plans
 That soar, to earth may fall,
Let once my army-leader Lannes
 Waver at yonder wall,'—
Out 'twixt the battery-smokes there flew
 A rider, bound on bound
Full-galloping; nor bridle drew
 Until he reached the mound.

III

Then off there flung in smiling joy,
 And held himself erect
By just his horse's mane, a boy:
 You hardly could suspect—
(So tight he kept his lips compressed,
 Scarce any blood came through)
You looked twice ere you saw his breast
 Was all but shot in two.

IV

'Well,' cried he, 'Emperor, by God's grace
 We've got you Ratisbon!
The Marshal's in the market-place,
 And you'll be there anon

To see your flag-bird flap his vans
  Where I, to heart's desire,
Perched him!' The chief's eye flashed; his plans
  Soared up again like fire.

V

The chief's eye flashed; but presently
  Softened itself, as sheathes
A film the mother-eagle's eye
  When her bruised eaglet breathes;
'You're wounded!' 'Nay,' the soldier's pride
  Touched to the quick, he said:
'I'm killed, Sire!' And his chief beside,
  Smiling the boy fell dead.

THOMAS HARDY

1840–1928

50   from *The Dynasts*

*[The Eve of Waterloo]**

(Chorus of Phantoms)

The eyelids of eve fall together at last,
And the forms so foreign to field and tree
Lie down as though native, and slumber fast!

Sore are the thrills of misgiving we see
In the artless champaign at this harlequinade,
Distracting a vigil where calm should be!

The green seems opprest, and the Plain afraid
Of a Something to come, whereof these are the proofs,—
Neither earthquake, nor storm, nor eclipse's shade!

* The French defeat at the Battle of Waterloo, on 18 June 1815, concluded the Napoleonic Wars. British and Prussian forces under the Duke of Wellington and Field Marshal Blücher routed Napoleon's army; on 22 June Napoleon left the field and signed his abdication. French casualties totalled over 32,000, British and Prussian 23,000.

Yea, the coneys are scared by the thud of hoofs,
And their white scuts flash at their vanishing heels,
And swallows abandon the hamlet-roofs.

The mole's tunnelled chambers are crushed by wheels,
The lark's eggs scattered, their owners fled;
And the hedgehog's household the sapper unseals.

The snail draws in at the terrible tread,
But in vain; he is crushed by the felloe-rim;
The worm asks what can be overhead,

And wriggles deep from a scene so grim,
And guesses him safe; for he does not know
What a foul red flood will be soaking him!

Beaten about by the heel and toe
Are butterflies, sick of the day's long rheum,
To die of a worse than the weather-foe.

Trodden and bruised to a miry tomb
Are ears that have greened but will never be gold,
And flowers in the bud that will never bloom.

So the season's intent, ere its fruit unfold,
Is frustrate, and mangled, and made succumb,
Like a youth of promise struck stark and cold! . . .

And what of these who tonight have come?
—The young sleep sound; but the weather awakes
In the veterans, pains from the past that numb;

Old stabs of Ind, old Peninsular aches,
Old Friedland chills, haunt their moist mud bed,
Cramps from Austerlitz; till their slumber breaks.

And each soul shivers as sinks his head
On the loam he's to lease with the other dead
From tomorrow's mist-fall till Time be sped!

GEORGE GORDON NOEL, LORD BYRON
1788–1824

51   *The Destruction of Sennacherib**

I

The Assyrian came down like the wolf on the fold,
And his cohorts were gleaming in purple and gold;
And the sheen of their spears was like stars on the sea,
When the blue wave rolls nightly on deep Galilee.

II

Like the leaves of the forest when Summer is green,
That host with their banners at sunset were seen:
Like the leaves of the forest when Autumn hath blown,
That host on the morrow lay withered and strown.

III

For the Angel of Death spread his wings on the blast,
And breathed in the face of the foe as he passed;
And the eyes of the sleepers waxed deadly and chill,
And their hearts but once heaved, and for ever grew still!

IV

And there lay the steed with his nostril all wide,
But through it there rolled not the breath of his pride:
And the foam of his gasping lay white on the turf,
And cold as the spray of the rock-beating surf.

V

And there lay the rider distorted and pale,
With the dew on his brow, and the rust on his mail;
And the tents were all silent, the banners alone,
The lances unlifted, the trumpet unblown.

---

* Sennacherib, King of Assyria from 709 BC to his death in 681 BC, demolished a series
of Judaean cities and besieged Jerusalem. In the account in 2 Chronicles 32, upon which
Byron based his poem, the Assyrian army was destroyed by an angel, and Sennacherib
retreated in defeat.

VI

And the widows of Ashur are loud in their wail,
And the idols are broke in the temple of Baal;
And the might of the Gentile, unsmote by the sword,
Hath melted like snow in the glance of the Lord!

52   from *Childe Harold's Pilgrimage**

There was a sound of revelry by night,
   And Belgium's Capital had gathered then
   Her Beauty and her Chivalry, and bright
   The lamps shone o'er fair women and brave men;
   A thousand hearts beat happily; and when
   Music arose with its voluptuous swell,
   Soft eyes looked love to eyes which spake again,
   And all went merry as a marriage bell;
But hush! hark! a deep sound strikes like a rising knell!

Did ye not hear it?—No; 'twas but the wind,
   Or the car rattling o'er the stony street;
   On with the dance! let joy be unconfined;
   No sleep till morn, when Youth and Pleasure meet
   To chase the glowing Hours with flying feet—
   But hark!—that heavy sound breaks in once more,
   As if the clouds its echo would repeat;
   And nearer, clearer, deadlier than before!
Arm! Arm! it is—it is—the cannon's opening roar!

Within a windowed niche of that high hall
   Sate Brunswick's fated chieftain; he did hear
   That sound the first amidst the festival,
   And caught its tone with Death's prophetic ear;
   And when they smiled because he deemed it near,
   His heart more truly knew that peal too well
   Which stretched his father on a bloody bier,
   And roused the vengeance blood alone could quell;
He rushed into the field, and, foremost fighting, fell.

* The Duchess of Richmond gave a famous ball in Brussels, Wellington's head-quarters, on the evening before the Battle of Waterloo. The Duke of Wellington and most of his officers were present.

Ah! then and there was hurrying to and fro,
   And gathering tears, and tremblings of distress,
   And cheeks all pale, which but an hour ago
   Blushed at the praise of their own loveliness;
   And there were sudden partings, such as press
   The life from out young hearts, and choking sighs
   Which ne'er might be repeated; who could guess
   If ever more should meet those mutual eyes,
Since upon night so sweet such awful morn could rise!

And there was mounting in hot haste: the steed,
   The mustering squadron, and the clattering car,
   Went pouring forward with impetuous speed,
   And swiftly forming in the ranks of war;
   And the deep thunder peal on peal afar;
   And near, the beat of the alarming drum
   Roused up the soldier ere the morning star;
   While thronged the citizens with terror dumb,
Or whispering, with white lips—'The foe! They come! they come!'

And wild and high the 'Cameron's Gathering' rose!
   The war-note of Lochiel, which Albyn's hills
   Have heard, and heard, too, have her Saxon foes:—
   How in the noon of night that pibroch thrills,
   Savage and shrill! But with the breath which fills
   Their mountain-pipe, so fill the mountaineers
   With the fierce native daring which instils
   The stirring memory of a thousand years,
And Evan's, Donald's fame rings in each clansman's ears!

And Ardennes waves above them her green leaves,
   Dewy with nature's tear-drops, as they pass,
   Grieving, if aught inanimate e'er grieves,
   Over the unreturning brave,—alas!
   Ere evening to be trodden like the grass
   Which now beneath them, but above shall grow
   In its next verdure, when this fiery mass
   Of living valour, rolling on the foe
And burning with high hope, shall moulder cold and low.

Last noon beheld them full of lusty life,
    Last eve in Beauty's circle proudly gay,
The midnight brought the signal-sound of strife,
The morn the marshalling in arms,—the day
Battle's magnificently-stern array!
The thunder-clouds close o'er it, which when rent
The earth is covered thick with other clay
Which her own clay shall cover, heaped and pent,
Rider and horse,—friend, foe,—in one red burial blent!

53   from *Don Juan*

'Let there be light!' said God, and there was light!
    'Let there be blood!' says man, and there's a sea!
The fiat of this spoiled child of the Night
    (For Day ne'er saw his merits) could decree
More evil in an hour, than thirty bright
    Summers could renovate, though they should be
Lovely as those which ripened Eden's fruit;
For war cuts up not only branch, but root.

     .   .   .   .

Oh, thou eternal Homer! who couldst charm
    All ears, though long; all ages, though so short,
By merely wielding with poetic arm
    Arms to which men will never more resort,
Unless gunpowder should be found to harm
    Much less than is the hope of every court,
Which now is leagued young Freedom to annoy;
But they will not find Liberty a Troy:—

Oh, thou eternal Homer! I have now
    To paint a siege, wherein more men were slain,
With deadlier engines and a speedier blow,
    Than in thy Greek gazette of that campaign;
And yet, like all men else, I must allow,
    To vie with thee would be about as vain
As for a brook to cope with ocean's flood;
But still we moderns equal you in blood;

If not in poetry, at least in fact;
   And fact is truth, the grand desideratum!
Of which, howe'er the Muse describes each act,
   There should be ne'ertheless a slight substratum.
But now the town is going to be attacked;
   Great deeds are doing—how shall I relate 'em?
Souls of immortal generals! Phœbus watches
To colour up his rays from your despatches.

Oh, ye great bulletins of Bonaparte!
   Oh, ye less grand long lists of killed and wounded!
Shade of Leonidas, who fought so hearty,
   When my poor Greece was once, as now, surrounded!
Oh, Cæsar's Commentaries! now impart, ye
   Shadows of glory! (lest I be confounded)
A portion of your fading twilight hues,
So beautiful, so fleeting, to the Muse.

When I call 'fading' martial immortality,
   I mean, that every age and every year,
And almost every day, in sad reality,
   Some sucking hero is compelled to rear,
Who, when we come to sum up the totality
   Of deeds to human happiness most dear,
Turns out to be a butcher in great business,
Afflicting young folks with a sort of dizziness.

Medals, rank, ribands, lace, embroidery, scarlet,
   Are things immortal to immortal man,
As purple to the Babylonian harlot:
   An uniform to boys is like a fan
To women; there is scarce a crimson varlet
   But deems himself the first in Glory's van.
But Glory's glory; and if you would find
What that is—ask the pig who sees the wind!

At least *he feels it*, and some say he *sees*,
   Because he runs before it like a pig;
Or, if that simple sentence should displease,
   Say, that he scuds before it like a brig,
A schooner, or—but it is time to ease
   This Canto, ere my Muse perceives fatigue.
The next shall ring a peal to shake all people,
Like a bob-major from a village steeple.

Hark! through the silence of the cold, dull night,
    The hum of armies gathering rank on rank!
Lo! dusky masses steal in dubious sight
    Along the leaguered wall and bristling bank
Of the armed river, while with straggling light
    The stars peep through the vapours dim and dank,
Which curl in curious wreaths:—how soon the smoke
Of Hell shall pall them in a deeper cloak!

Here pause we for the present—as even then
    That awful pause, dividing life from death,
Struck for an instant on the hearts of men,
    Thousands of whom were drawing their last breath!
A moment—and all will be life again!
    The march! the charge! the shouts of either faith!
Hurra! and Allah! and—one moment more,
The death-cry drowning in the battle's roar.

54   *On This Day I Complete My Thirty-Sixth Year*

I

'Tis time this heart should be unmoved,
        Since others it hath ceased to move:
Yet, though I cannot be beloved,
        Still let me love!

II

My days are in the yellow leaf;
        The flowers and fruits of Love are gone;
The worm, the canker, and the grief
        Are mine alone!

III

The fire that on my bosom preys
        Is lone as some volcanic isle;
No torch is kindled at its blaze—
        A funeral pile.

IV

The hope, the fear, the jealous care,
    The exalted portion of the pain
And power of love, I cannot share,
        But wear the chain.

V

But 'tis not *thus*—and 'tis not *here*—
    Such thoughts should shake my soul, nor *now*
Where Glory decks the hero's bier,
        Or binds his brow.

VI

The Sword, the Banner, and the Field,
    Glory and Greece, around me see!
The Spartan, borne upon his shield,
        Was not more free.

VII

Awake! (not Greece—she *is* awake!)
    Awake, my spirit! Think through *whom*
Thy life-blood tracks its parent lake,
        And then strike home!

VIII

Tread those reviving passions down,
    Unworthy manhood!—unto thee
Indifferent should the smile or frown
        Of Beauty be.

IX

If thou regret'st thy youth, *why live?*
    The land of honourable death
Is here:—up to the Field, and give
        Away thy breath!

X

Seek out—less often sought than found—
    A soldier's grave, for thee the best;
Then look around, and choose thy ground,
        And take thy Rest.

THOMAS BABINGTON MACAULAY,
LORD MACAULAY
1800–1859

55   from *Horatius*

A Lay Made about the Year of the City CCCLX

But hark! the cry is Astur:
  And lo! the ranks divide;
And the great Lord of Luna
  Comes with his stately stride.
Upon his ample shoulders
  Clangs loud the four-fold shield,
And in his hand he shakes the brand
  Which none but he can wield.

He smiled on those bold Romans
  A smile serene and high;
He eyed the flinching Tuscans,
  And scorn was in his eye.
Quoth he, 'The she-wolf's litter
  Stand savagely at bay:
But will ye dare to follow,
  If Astur clears the way?'

Then, whirling up his broadsword
  With both hands to the height,
He rushed against Horatius,
  And smote with all his might.
With shield and blade Horatius
  Right deftly turned the blow.
The blow, though turned, came yet too nigh;
It missed his helm, but gashed his thigh:
The Tuscans raised a joyful cry
  To see the red blood flow.

He reeled, and on Herminius
  He leaned one breathing-space;
Then, like a wild cat mad with wounds,
  Sprang right at Astur's face.

Through teeth, and skull, and helmet
  So fierce a thrust he sped,
The good sword stood a hand-breadth out
  Behind the Tuscan's head.

And the great Lord of Luna
  Fell at that deadly stroke,
As falls on Mount Alvernus
  A thunder-smitten oak.
Far o'er the crashing forest
  The giant arms lie spread;
And the pale augurs, muttering low,
  Gaze on the blasted head.

On Astur's throat Horatius
  Right firmly pressed his heel,
And thrice and four times tugged amain,
  Ere he wrenched out the steel.
'And see,' he cried, 'the welcome,
  Fair guests, that waits you here!
What noble Lucumo comes next
  To taste our Roman cheer?'

But at his haughty challenge
  A sullen murmur ran,
Mingled of wrath, and shame, and dread,
  Along that glittering van.
There lacked not men of prowess,
  Nor men of lordly race;
For all Etruria's noblest
  Were round the fatal place.

But all Etruria's noblest
  Felt their hearts sink to see
On the earth the bloody corpses,
  In the path the dauntless Three:
And, from the ghastly entrance
  Where those bold Romans stood,
All shrank, like boys who unaware,
Ranging the woods to start a hare,
Come to the mouth of the dark lair
Where, growling low, a fierce old bear
  Lies amidst bones and blood.

Was none who would be foremost
　To lead such dire attack:
But those behind cried 'Forward!'
　And those before cried 'Back!'
And backward now and forward
　Wavers the deep array;
And on the tossing sea of steel,
To and fro the standards reel;
And the victorious trumpet-peal
　Dies fitfully away.

Yet one man for one moment
　Strode out before the crowd;
Well known was he to all the Three,
　And they gave him greeting loud.
'Now welcome, welcome, Sextus!
　Now welcome to thy home!
Why dost thou stay, and turn away?
　Here lies the road to Rome.'

Thrice looked he at the city;
　Thrice looked he at the dead;
And thrice came on in fury,
　And thrice turned back in dread:
And, white with fear and hatred,
　Scowled at the narrow way
Where, wallowing in a pool of blood,
　The bravest Tuscans lay.

But meanwhile axe and lever
　Have manfully been plied;
And now the bridge hangs tottering
　Above the boiling tide.
'Come back, come back, Horatius!'
　Loud cried the Fathers all.
'Back, Lartius! back, Herminius!
　Back, ere the ruin fall!'

Back darted Spurius Lartius;
　Herminius darted back:
And, as they passed, beneath their feet
　They felt the timbers crack.

But when they turned their faces,
    And on the farther shore
Saw brave Horatius stand alone,
    They would have crossed once more.

But with a crash like thunder
    Fell every loosened beam,
And, like a dam, the mighty wreck
    Lay right athwart the stream:
And a long shout of triumph
    Rose from the walls of Rome,
As to the highest turret-tops
    Was splashed the yellow foam.

And, like a horse unbroken
    When first he feels the rein,
The furious river struggled hard,
    And tossed his tawny mane,
And burst the curb and bounded,
    Rejoicing to be free,
And whirling down, in fierce career,
Battlement, and plank, and pier,
    Rushed headlong to the sea.

Alone stood brave Horatius,
    But constant still in mind;
Thrice thirty thousand foes before,
    And the broad flood behind.
'Down with him!' cried false Sextus.
    With a smile on his pale face.
'Now yield thee,' cried Lars Porsena,
    'Now yield thee to our grace.'

Round turned he, as not deigning
    Those craven ranks to see;
Nought spake he to Lars Porsena,
    To Sextus nought spake he;
But he saw on Palatinus
    The white porch of his home;
And he spake to the noble river
    That rolls by the towers of Rome.

'Oh, Tiber! father Tiber!
To whom the Romans pray,
A Roman's life, a Roman's arms,
Take thou in charge this day!'
So he spake, and speaking sheathed
The good sword by his side,
And with his harness on his back,
Plunged headlong in the tide.

No sound of joy or sorrow
Was heard from either bank;
But friends and foes in dumb surprise,
With parted lips and straining eyes,
Stood gazing where he sank;
And when above the surges
They saw his crest appear,
All Rome sent forth a rapturous cry,
And even the ranks of Tuscany
Could scarce forbear to cheer.

But fiercely ran the current,
Swollen high by months of rain:
And fast his blood was flowing,
And he was sore in pain,
And heavy with his armour,
And spent with changing blows:
And oft they thought him sinking,
But still again he rose.

Never, I ween, did swimmer,
In such an evil case,
Struggle through such a raging flood
Safe to the landing place:
But his limbs were borne up bravely
By the brave heart within,
And our good father Tiber
Bare bravely up his chin.

'Curse on him!' quoth false Sextus;
'Will not the villain drown?
But for this stay, ere close of day
We should have sacked the town!'

'Heaven help him!' quoth Lars Porsena,
　'And bring him safe to shore;
For such a gallant feat of arms
　Was never seen before.'

And now he feels the bottom;
　Now on dry earth he stands;
Now round him throng the Fathers;
　To press his gory hands;
And now, with shouts and clapping,
　And noise of weeping loud,
He enters through the River-Gate,
　Borne by the joyous crowd.

WILLIAM EDMONSTOUNE AYTOUN
1813–1865

56　　　　from *Edinburgh after Flodden**

Then the Provost he uprose,
　And his lip was ashen white;
But a flush was on his brow,
　And his eye was full of light.
'Thou hast spoken, Randolph Murray,
　Like a soldier stout and true;
Thou hast done a deed of daring
　Had been perilled but by few.
For thou hast not shamed to face us,
　Nor to speak thy ghastly tale,
Standing—thou a knight and captain—
　Here, alive within thy mail!
Now, as my God shall judge me,
　I hold it braver done,
Than hadst thou tarried in thy place,
　And died above my son!

---

* In an unsuccessful invasion of England in 1513, King James IV of Scotland was killed in battle at Flodden Field, Northumberland, just over the Scottish border.

Thou needst not tell it: he is dead.
    God help us all this day!
But speak—how fought the citizens
    Within the furious fray?
For by the might of Mary!
    'Twere something still to tell
That no Scottish foot went backward
    When the Royal Lion fell!'

'No one failed him! He is keeping
    Royal state and semblance still;
Knight and noble lie around him,
    Cold on Flodden's fatal hill.
Of the brave and gallant-hearted,
    Whom ye sent with prayers away,
Not a single man departed
    From his Monarch yesterday.
Had you seen them, O my masters!
    When the night began to fall,
And the English spearmen gathered
    Round a grim and ghastly wall!
As the wolves in winter circle
    Round the leaguer on the heath,
So the greedy foe glared upward,
    Panting still for blood and death.
But a rampart rose before them,
    Which the boldest dared not scale;
Every stone a Scottish body,
    Every step a corpse in mail!
And behind it lay our Monarch,
    Clenching still his shivered sword;
By his side Montrose and Athole,
    At his feet a Southron lord.
All so thick they lay together,
    When the stars lit up the sky,
That I knew not who were stricken,
    Or who yet remained to die.
Few there were when Surrey halted,
    And his wearied host withdrew;
None but dying men around me,
    When the English trumpet blew.
Then I stooped, and took the banner,
    As you see it, from his breast,

And I closed our hero's eyelids,
   And I left him to his rest.
In the mountains growled the thunder,
   As I leaped the woeful wall,
And the heavy clouds were settling
   Over Flodden, like a pall.'

MATTHEW ARNOLD
1822–1888

57   from *Sohrab and Rustum*

Then Sohrab with his sword smote Rustum's helm,
Nor clove its steel quite through; but all the crest
He shore away, and that proud horsehair plume,
Never till now defiled, sank to the dust;
And Rustum bowed his head; but then the gloom
Grew blacker, thunder rumbled in the air,
And lightnings rent the cloud; and Ruksh, the horse,
Who stood at hand, uttered a dreadful cry;
No horse's cry was that, most like the roar
Of some pained desert-lion, who all day
Hath trailed the hunter's javelin in his side,
And comes at night to die upon the sand.
The two hosts heard that cry, and quaked for fear,
And Oxus curdled as it crossed his stream.
But Sohrab heard, and quailed not, but rushed on,
And struck again; and again Rustum bowed
His head; but this time all the blade, like glass,
Sprang in a thousand shivers on the helm,
And in the hand the hilt remained alone.
Then Rustum raised his head; his dreadful eyes
Glared, and he shook on high his menacing spear,
And shouted: *Rustum!*—Sohrab heard that shout,
And shrank amazed; back he recoiled one step,
And scanned with blinking eyes the advancing form;
And then he stood bewildered; and he dropped
His covering shield, and the spear pierced his side.
He reeled, and staggering back, sank to the ground;
And then the gloom dispersed, and the wind fell,

And the bright sun broke forth, and melted all
The cloud; and the two armies saw the pair—
Saw Rustum standing, safe upon his feet,
And Sohrab, wounded, on the bloody sand.
  Then, with a bitter smile, Rustum began:—
'Sohrab, thou thoughtest in thy mind to kill
A Persian lord this day, and strip his corpse,
And bear thy trophies to Afrasiab's tent.
Or else that the great Rustum would come down
Himself to fight, and that thy wiles would move
His heart to take a gift, and let thee go.
And then that all the Tartar host would praise
Thy courage or thy craft, and spread thy fame,
To glad thy father in his weak old age.
Fool, thou art slain, and by an unknown man!
Dearer to the red jackals shalt thou be
Than to thy friends, and to thy father old.'

　　·　　·　　·　　·　　·　　·　　·　　·

  Then, at the point of death, Sohrab replied:—
'A life of blood indeed, thou dreadful man!
But thou shalt yet have peace; only not now,
Not yet! but thou shalt have it on that day,
When thou shalt sail in a high-masted ship,
Thou and the other peers of Kai Khosroo,
Returning home over the salt blue sea,
From laying thy dear master in his grave.'
  And Rustum gazed in Sohrab's face, and said:—
'Soon be that day, my son, and deep that sea!
Till then, if fate so wills, let me endure.'
  He spoke; and Sohrab smiled on him, and took
The spear, and drew it from his side, and eased
His wound's imperious anguish; but the blood
Came welling from the open gash, and life
Flowed with the stream; all down his cold white side
The crimson torrent ran, dim now and soiled,
Like the soiled tissue of white violets
Left, freshly gathered, on their native bank,
By children whom their nurses call with haste
Indoors from the sun's eye; his head drooped low,
His limbs grew slack; motionless, white, he lay—
White, with eyes closed; only when heavy gasps,
Deep heavy gasps quivering through all his frame,

Convulsed him back to life, he opened them,
And fixed them feebly on his father's face;
Till now all strength was ebbed, and from his limbs
Unwillingly the spirit fled away,
Regretting the warm mansion which it left,
And youth, and bloom, and this delightful world.

So, on the bloody sand, Sohrab lay dead;
And the great Rustum drew his horseman's cloak
Down o'er his face, and sate by his dead son.
As those black granite pillars, once high-reared
By Jemshid in Persepolis, to bear
His house, now 'mid their broken flights of steps
Lie prone, enormous, down the mountain side—
So in the sand lay Rustum by his son.

And night came down over the solemn waste,
And the two gazing hosts, and that sole pair,
And darkened all; and a cold fog, with night,
Crept from the Oxus. Soon a hum arose,
As of a great assembly loosed, and fires
Began to twinkle through the fog; for now
Both armies moved to camp, and took their meal;
The Persians took it on the open sands
Southward, the Tartars by the river marge;
And Rustum and his son were left alone.

But the majestic river floated on,
Out of the mist and hum of that low land,
Into the frosty starlight, and there moved,
Rejoicing, through the hushed Chorasmian waste,
Under the solitary moon; he flowed
Right for the polar star, past Orgunjè,
Brimming, and bright, and large; then sands begin
To hem his watery march, and dam his streams,
And split his currents; that for many a league
The shorn and parcelled Oxus strains along
Through beds of sand and matted rushy isles—
Oxus, forgetting the bright speed he had
In his high mountain-cradle in Pamere,
A foiled circuitous wanderer—till at last
The longed-for dash of waves is heard, and wide
His luminous home of waters opens, bright
And tranquil, from whose floor the new-bathed stars
Emerge, and shine upon the Aral Sea.

ALFRED, LORD TENNYSON

1809–1892

58   *The Revenge*

A Ballad of the Fleet

I

At Flores in the Azores Sir Richard Grenville lay,
And a pinnace, like a fluttered bird, came flying from far away:
'Spanish ships of war at sea! we have sighted fifty-three!'
Then sware Lord Thomas Howard: ' 'Fore God I am no coward;
But I cannot meet them here, for my ships are out of gear,
And the half my men are sick. I must fly, but follow quick.
We are six ships of the line; can we fight with fifty-three?'

II

Then spake Sir Richard Grenville: 'I know you are no coward;
You fly them for a moment to fight with them again.
But I've ninety men and more that are lying sick ashore.
I should count myself the coward if I left them, my Lord Howard,
To these Inquisition dogs and the devildoms of Spain.'

III

So Lord Howard past away with five ships of war that day,
Till he melted like a cloud in the silent summer heaven;
But Sir Richard bore in hand all his sick men from the land
Very carefully and slow,
Men of Bideford in Devon,
And we laid them on the ballast down below;
For we brought them all aboard,
And they blest him in their pain, that they were not left to Spain,
To the thumbscrew and the stake, for the glory of the Lord.

IV

He had only a hundred seamen to work the ship and to fight,
And he sailed away from Flores till the Spaniard came in sight,
With his huge sea-castles heaving upon the weather bow.
'Shall we fight or shall we fly?

Good Sir Richard, tell us now,
For to fight is but to die!
There'll be little of us left by the time this sun be set.'
And Sir Richard said again: 'We be all good English men.
Let us bang these dogs of Seville, the children of the devil,
For I never turned my back upon Don or devil yet.'

V

Sir Richard spoke and he laughed, and we roared a hurrah, and so
The little *Revenge* ran on sheer into the heart of the foe,
With her hundred fighters on deck, and her ninety sick below;
For half of their fleet to the right and half to the left were seen,
And the little *Revenge* ran on through the long sea-lane between.

VI

Thousands of their soldiers looked down from their decks and laughed,
Thousands of their seamen made mock at the mad little craft
Running on and on, till delayed
By their mountain-like San Philip that, of fifteen hundred tons,
And up-shadowing high above us with her yawning tiers of guns,
Took the breath from our sails, and we stayed.

VII

And while now the great San Philip hung above us like a cloud
Whence the thunderbolt will fall
Long and loud,
Four galleons drew away
From the Spanish fleet that day,
And two upon the larboard and two upon the starboard lay,
And the battle-thunder broke from them all.

VIII

But anon the great San Philip, she bethought herself and went
Having that within her womb that had left her ill content;
And the rest they came aboard us, and they fought us hand to hand,
For a dozen times they came with their pikes and musqueteers,
And a dozen times we shook 'em off as a dog that shakes his ears
When he leaps from the water to the land.

IX

And the sun went down, and the stars came out far over the summer sea,
But never a moment ceased the fight of the one and the fifty-three.
Ship after ship, the whole night long, their high-built galleons came,
Ship after ship, the whole night long, with her battle-thunder and flame;
Ship after ship, the whole night long, drew back with her dead and her
shame.
For some were sunk and many were shattered, and so could fight us no
more—
God of battles, was ever a battle like this in the world before?

X

For he said 'Fight on! fight on!'
Though his vessel was all but a wreck;
And it chanced that, when half of the short summer night was gone,
With a grisly wound to be dressed he had left the deck,
But a bullet struck him that was dressing it suddenly dead,
And himself he was wounded again in the side and the head,
And he said 'Fight on! fight on!'

XI

And the night went down, and the sun smiled out far over the summer
sea,
And the Spanish fleet with broken sides lay round us all in a ring;
But they dared not touch us again, for they feared that we still could
sting,
So they watched what the end would be.
And we had not fought them in vain,
But in perilous plight were we,
Seeing forty of our poor hundred were slain,
And half of the rest of us maimed for life
In the crash of the cannonades and the desperate strife;
And the sick men down in the hold were most of them stark and cold,
And the pikes were all broken or bent, and the powder was all of it spent;
And the masts and the rigging were lying over the side;
But Sir Richard cried in his English pride,
'We have fought such a fight for a day and a night
As may never be fought again!
We have won great glory, my men!
And a day less or more

At sea or ashore,
We die—does it matter when?
Sink me the ship, Master Gunner—sink her, split her in twain!
Fall into the hands of God, not into the hands of Spain!'

XII

And the gunner said 'Ay, ay,' but the seamen made reply:
'We have children, we have wives,
And the Lord hath spared our lives.
We will make the Spaniard promise, if we yield, to let us go;
We shall live to fight again and to strike another blow.'
And the lion there lay dying, and they yielded to the foe.

XIII

And the stately Spanish men to their flagship bore him then,
Where they laid him by the mast, old Sir Richard caught at last,
And they praised him to his face with their courtly foreign grace;
But he rose upon their decks, and he cried:
'I have fought for Queen and Faith like a valiant man and true;
I have only done my duty as a man is bound to do:
With a joyful spirit I Sir Richard Grenville die!'
And he fell upon their decks, and he died.

XIV

And they stared at the dead that had been so valiant and true,
And had holden the power and glory of Spain so cheap
That he dared her with one little ship and his English few;
Was he devil or man? He was devil for aught they knew,
But they sank his body with honour down into the deep,
And they manned the *Revenge* with a swarthier alien crew,
And away she sailed with her loss and longed for her own;
When a wind from the lands they had ruined awoke from sleep,
And the water began to heave and the weather to moan,
And or ever that evening ended a great gale blew,
And a wave like the wave that is raised by an earthquake grew,
Till it smote on their hulls and their sails and their masts and their flags,
And the whole sea plunged and fell on the shot-shattered navy of Spain,
And the little *Revenge* herself went down by the island crags
To be lost evermore in the main.

59 *The Charge of the Light Brigade**

I

Half a league, half a league,
  Half a league onward,
All in the valley of Death
  Rode the six hundred.
'Forward, the Light Brigade!
Charge for the guns!' he said:
Into the valley of Death
  Rode the six hundred.

II

'Forward, the Light Brigade!'
Was there a man dismayed?
Not though the soldier knew
  Some one had blundered:
Their's not to make reply,
Their's not to reason why,
Their's but to do and die:
Into the valley of Death
  Rode the six hundred.

III

Cannon to right of them,
Cannon to left of them,
Cannon in front of them
  Volleyed and thundered;
Stormed at with shot and shell,
Boldly they rode and well,
Into the jaws of Death,
Into the mouth of Hell
  Rode the six hundred.

---

* In 1854, during the Crimean War, an English light-cavalry brigade of over 600 men was led into a hopeless charge against well-protected batteries of Russian artillery at Balaklava. The blunder resulted in the deaths of well over two-thirds of the British soldiers.

IV

Flashed all their sabres bare,
Flashed as they turned in air
Sabring the gunners there,
Charging an army, while
　All the world wondered:
Plunged in the battery-smoke
Right through the line they broke;
Cossack and Russian
Reeled from the sabre-stroke
　Shattered and sundered.
Then they rode back, but not
　Not the six hundred.

V

Cannon to right of them,
Cannon to left of them,
Cannon behind them
　Volleyed and thundered;
Stormed at with shot and shell,
While horse and hero fell,
They that had fought so well
Came through the jaws of Death,
Back from the mouth of Hell,
All that was left of them,
　Left of six hundred.

VI

When can their glory fade?
O the wild charge they made!
　All the world wondered.
Honour the charge they made!
Honour the Light Brigade,
　Noble six hundred!

60   from *Maud*

I

My life has crept so long on a broken wing
Through cells of madness, haunts of horror and fear,
That I come to be grateful at last for a little thing:
My mood is changed, for it fell at a time of year
When the face of night is fair on the dewy downs,
And the shining daffodil dies, and the Charioteer
And starry Gemini hang like glorious crowns
Over Orion's grave low down in the west,
That like a silent lightning under the stars
She seemed to divide in a dream from a band of the blest,
And spoke of a hope for the world in the coming wars—
'And in that hope, dear soul, let trouble have rest,
Knowing I tarry for thee,' and pointed to Mars
As he glowed like a ruddy shield on the Lion's breast.

II

And it was but a dream, yet it yielded a dear delight
To have looked, though but in a dream, upon eyes so fair,
That had been in a weary world my one thing bright;
And it was but a dream, yet it lightened my despair
When I thought that a war would arise in defence of the
      right,
That an iron tyranny now should bend or cease,
The glory of manhood stand on his ancient height,
Nor Britain's one sole God be the millionaire:
No more shall commerce be all in all, and Peace
Pipe on her pastoral hillock a languid note,
And watch her harvest ripen, her herd increase,
Nor the cannon-bullet rust on a slothful shore,
And the cobweb woven across the cannon's throat
Shall shake its threaded tears in the wind no more.

III

And as months ran on and rumour of battle grew,
'It is time, it is time, O passionate heart,' said I
(For I cleaved to a cause that I felt to be pure and true),
'It is time, O passionate heart and morbid eye,
That old hysterical mock-disease should die.'

And I stood on a giant deck and mixed my breath
With a loyal people shouting a battle cry,
Till I saw the dreary phantom arise and fly
Far into the North, and battle, and seas of death.

IV

Let it go or stay, so I wake to the higher aims
Of a land that has lost for a little her lust of gold,
And love of a peace that was full of wrongs and shames,
Horrible, hateful, monstrous, not to be told;
And hail once more to the banner of battle unrolled!
Though many a light shall darken, and many shall weep
For those that are crushed in the clash of jarring claims,
Yet God's just wrath shall be wreaked on a giant liar;
And many a darkness into the light shall leap,
And shine in the sudden making of splendid names,
And noble thought be freer under the sun,
And the heart of a people beat with one desire;
For the peace, that I deemed no peace, is over and done,
And now by the side of the Black and the Baltic deep,
And deathful-grinning mouths of the fortress, flames
The blood-red blossom of war with a heart of fire.

V

Let it flame or fade, and the war roll down like a wind,
We have proved we have hearts in a cause, we are noble still,
And myself have awaked, as it seems, to the better mind;
It is better to fight for the good than to rail at the ill;
I have felt with my native land, I am one with my kind,
I embrace the purpose of God, and the doom assigned.

WILLIAM MAKEPEACE THACKERAY
1811–1863

61 *The Due of the Dead**

I sit beside my peaceful hearth,
  With curtains drawn and lamp trimmed bright
I watch my children's noisy mirth;
  I drink in home, and its delight.

I sip my tea, and criticise
  The war, from flying rumours caught;
Trace on the map, to curious eyes,
  How here they marched, and there they fought.

In intervals of household chat,
  I lay down strategetic laws;
Why this manœuvre, and why that;
  Shape the event, or show the cause.

Or, in smooth dinner-table phrase,
  'Twixt soup and fish, discuss the fight;
Give to each chief his blame or praise;
  Say who was wrong and who was right.

Meanwhile o'er Alma's bloody plain
  The scathe of battle has rolled by—
The wounded writhe and groan—the slain
  Lie naked staring to the sky.

The out-worn surgeon plies his knife,
  Nor pauses with the closing day;
While those who have escaped with life
  Find food and fuel as they may.

And when their eyes in sleep they close,
  After scant rations duly shared,
Plague picks his victims out, from those
  Whom chance of battle may have spared.

* Allied British and French forces entered the Crimea in September 1854, engaging in
a year-long series of debilitating battles in the area of the Alma River before finally
capturing Sevastopol.

Still when the bugle sounds the march,
　　He tracks his prey through steppe and dell;
Hangs fruit to tempt the throats that parch,
　　And poisons every stream and well.

All this with gallant hearts is done;
　　All this with patient hearts is borne:
And they by whom the laurel's won
　　Are seldom they by whom 'tis worn.

No deed, no suffering of the war,
　　But wins us fame, or spares us ill;
Those noble swords, though drawn afar,
　　Are guarding English homesteads still.

Owe we a debt to these brave men,
　　Unpaid by aught that's said or sung;
By leaders from a ready pen,
　　Or phrases from a flippant tongue.

The living, England's hand may crown
　　With recognition, frank and free;
With titles, medals, and renown;
　　The wounded shall our pensioners be.

But they, who meet a soldier's doom—
　　Think you, it is enough, good friend,
To plant the laurel at their tomb,
　　And carve their names—and there an end?

No. They are gone: but there are left
　　Those they loved best while they were here—
Parents made childless, babes bereft,
　　Desolate widows, sisters dear.

All these let grateful England take;
　　And, with a large and liberal heart,
Cherish, for her slain soldiers' sake,
　　And of her fullness give them part.

Fold them within her sheltering breast;
　　Their parent, husband, brother, prove.
That so the dead may be at rest,
　　Knowing those cared for whom they love.

RALPH WALDO EMERSON
1803–1882

62   *Concord Hymn**

Sung at the completion of the Battle Monument,
19 April 1836

By the rude bridge that arched the flood,
   Their flag to April's breeze unfurled,
Here once the embattled farmers stood,
   And fired the shot heard round the world.

The foe long since in silence slept;
   Alike the conqueror silent sleeps;
And Time the ruined bridge has swept
   Down the dark stream which seaward creeps.

On this green bank, by this soft stream,
   We set today a votive stone;
That memory may their deed redeem,
   When, like our sires, our sons are gone.

Spirit, that made those heroes dare
   To die, and leave their children free,
Bid Time and Nature gently spare
   The shaft we raise to them and thee.

WALT WHITMAN
1819–1892

63   *Beat! Beat! Drums!*

Beat! beat! drums!—blow! bugles! blow!
Through the windows—through doors—burst like a ruthless force,
Into the solemn church, and scatter the congregation,
Into the school where the scholar is studying;

---

* On the night of 18–19 April 1775, Paul Revere and other riders gathered a band of
minute men from the Massachusetts countryside to confront advancing British troops.
Battles with the British in Lexington and Concord the following day marked the beginning
of the American War of Independence.

Leave not the bridegroom quiet—no happiness must he have now with
  his bride,
Nor the peaceful farmer any peace, ploughing his field or gathering his
  grain,
So fierce you whirr and pound you drums—so shrill you bugles blow.

Beat! beat! drums!—blow! bugles! blow!
Over the traffic of cities—over the rumble of wheels in the streets;
Are beds prepared for sleepers at night in the houses? no sleepers must
  sleep in those beds,
No bargainers' bargains by day—no brokers or speculators—would
  they continue?
Would the talkers be talking? would the singer attempt to sing?
Would the lawyer rise in the court to state his case before the judge?
Then rattle quicker, heavier drums—you bugles wilder blow.

Beat! beat! drums!—blow! bugles! blow!
Make no parley—stop for no expostulation,
Mind not the timid—mind not the weeper or prayer,
Mind not the old man beseeching the young man,
Let not the child's voice be heard, nor the mother's entreaties,
Make even the trestles to shake the dead where they lie awaiting the
  hearses,
So strong you thump O terrible drums—so loud you bugles blow.

64   *Come up from the Fields Father*

Come up from the fields father, here's a letter from our Pete,
And come to the front door mother, here's a letter from thy dear son.

Lo, 'tis autumn,
Lo, where the trees, deeper green, yellower and redder,
Cool and sweeten Ohio's villages with leaves fluttering in the moderate
  wind,
Where apples ripe in the orchards hang and grapes on the trellised
  vines,
(Smell you the smell of the grapes on the vines?
Smell you the buckwheat where the bees were lately buzzing?)
Above all, lo, the sky so calm, so transparent after the rain, and with
  wondrous clouds,
Below too, all calm, all vital and beautiful, and the farm prospers well.

Down in the fields all prospers well,
But now from the fields come father, come at the daughter's call,
And come to the entry mother, to the front door come right away.

Fast as she can she hurries, something ominous, her steps trembling,
She does not tarry to smooth her hair nor adjust her cap.

Open the envelope quickly,
O this is not our son's writing, yet his name is signed,
O a strange hand writes for our dear son, O stricken mother's soul!

All swims before her eyes, flashes with black, she catches the main
    words only,
Sentences broken, *gunshot wound in the breast, cavalry skirmish, taken to
    hospital,*
At present low, but will soon be better.

Ah now the single figure to me,
Amid all teeming and wealthy Ohio with all its cities and farms,
Sickly white in the face and dull in the head, very faint,
By the jamb of a door leans.

Grieve not so, dear mother, (the just-grown daughter speaks through her
    sobs,
The little sisters huddle around speechless and dismayed,)
See, dearest mother, the letter says Pete will soon be better.

Alas poor boy, he will never be better, (nor may-be needs to be better,
    that brave and simple soul,)
While they stand at home at the door he is dead already,
The only son is dead.

But the mother needs to be better,
She with thin form presently dressed in black,
By day her meals untouched, then at night fitfully sleeping, often
    waking,
In the midnight waking, weeping, longing with one deep longing,
O that she might withdraw unnoticed, silent from life escape and
    withdraw,
To follow, to seek, to be with her dear dead son.

65   *Vigil Strange I Kept on the Field one Night*

Vigil strange I kept on the field one night;
When you my son and my comrade dropped at my side that day,
One look I but gave which your dear eyes returned with a look I shall
    never forget,
One touch of your hand to mine O boy, reached up as you lay on the
    ground,
Then onward I sped in the battle, the even-contested battle,
Till late in the night relieved to the place at last again I made my way,
Found you in death so cold dear comrade, found your body son of
    responding kisses, (never again on earth responding,)
Bared your face in the starlight, curious the scene, cool blew the
    moderate night-wind,
Long there and then in vigil I stood, dimly around me the battlefield
    spreading,
Vigil wondrous and vigil sweet there in the fragrant silent night,
But not a tear fell, not even a long-drawn sigh, long, long I gazed,
Then on the earth partially reclining sat by your side leaning my chin in
    my hands,
Passing sweet hours, immortal and mystic hours with you dearest
    comrade—not a tear, not a word,
Vigil of silence, love and death, vigil for you my son and my soldier,
As onward silently stars aloft, eastward new ones upward stole,
Vigil final for you brave boy, (I could not save you, swift was your death,
I faithfully loved you and cared for you living, I think we shall surely
    meet again,)
Till at latest lingering of the night, indeed just as the dawn appeared,
My comrade I wrapped in his blanket, enveloped well his form,
Folded the blanket well, tucking it carefully over head and carefully
    under feet,
And there and then and bathed by the rising sun, my son in his grave, in
    his rude-dug grave I deposited,
Ending my vigil strange with that, vigil of night and battlefield dim,
Vigil for boy of responding kisses, (never again on earth responding,)
Vigil for comrade swiftly slain, vigil I never forget, how as day
    brightened,
I rose from the chill ground and folded my soldier well in his blanket,
And buried him where he fell.

66 *The Wound-Dresser*

An old man bending I come among new faces,
Years looking backward resuming in answer to children,
Come tell us old man, as from young men and maidens that love me,
(Aroused and angry, I'd thought to beat the alarum, and urge relentless war,
But soon my fingers failed me, my face drooped and I resigned myself,
To sit by the wounded and soothe them, or silently watch the dead;)
Years hence of these scenes, of these furious passions, these chances,
Of unsurpassed heroes, (was one side so brave? the other was equally brave;)
Now be witness again, paint the mightiest armies of earth,
Of those armies so rapid so wondrous what saw you to tell us?
What stays with you latest and deepest? of curious panics,
Of hard-fought engagements or sieges tremendous what deepest remains?

*

O maidens and young men I love and that love me,
What you ask of my days those the strangest and sudden your talking recalls,
Soldier alert I arrive after a long march covered with sweat and dust,
In the nick of time I come, plunge in the fight, loudly shout in the rush of successful charge,
Enter the captured works—yet lo, like a swift-running river they fade,
Pass and are gone they fade—I dwell not on soldiers' perils or soldiers' joys,
(Both I remember well—many the hardships, few the joys, yet I was content.)

But in silence, in dreams' projections,
While the world of gain and appearance and mirth goes on,
So soon what is over forgotten, and waves wash the imprints off the sand,
With hinged knees returning I enter the doors, (while for you up there,
Whoever you are, follow without noise and be of strong heart.)

Bearing the bandages, water and sponge,
Straight and swift to my wounded I go,
Where they lie on the ground after the battle brought in,
Where their priceless blood reddens the grass the ground,

Or to the rows of the hospital tent, or under the roofed hospital,
To the long rows of cots up and down each side I return,
To each and all one after another I draw near, not one do I miss,
An attendant follows holding a tray, he carries a refuse pail,
Soon to be filled with clotted rags and blood, emptied, and filled again.

I onward go, I stop,
With hinged knees and steady hand to dress wounds,
I am firm with each, the pangs are sharp yet unavoidable,
One turns to me his appealing eyes—poor boy! I never knew you,
Yet I think I could not refuse this moment to die for you, if that would
    save you.

*

On, on I go, (open doors of time! open hospital doors!)
The crushed head I dress, (poor crazed hand tear not the bandage
    away,)
The neck of the cavalry-man with the bullet through and through I
    examine,
Hard the breathing rattles, quite glazed already the eye, yet life struggles
    hard,
(Come sweet death! be persuaded O beautiful death!
In mercy come quickly.)

From the stump of the arm, the amputated hand,
I undo the clotted lint, remove the slough, wash off the matter and
    blood,
Back on his pillow the soldier bends with curved neck and side-falling
    head,
His eyes are closed, his face is pale, he dares not look on the bloody
    stump,
And has not yet looked on it.

I dress a wound in the side, deep, deep,
But a day or two more, for see the frame all wasted and sinking,
And the yellow-blue countenance see.

I dress the perforated shoulder, the foot with the bullet-wound,
Cleanse the one with a gnawing and putrid gangrene, so sickening, so
    offensive,
While the attendant stands behind aside me holding the tray and pail.

I am faithful, I do not give out,

The fractured thigh, the knee, the wound in the abdomen,
These and more I dress with impassive hand, (yet deep in my breast a
  fire, a burning flame.)

*

Thus in silence in dreams' projections,
Returning, resuming, I thread my way through the hospitals,
The hurt and wounded I pacify with soothing hand,
I sit by the restless all the dark night, some are so young,
Some suffer so much, I recall the experience sweet and sad,
(Many a soldier's loving arms about this neck have crossed and rested,
Many a soldier's kiss dwells on these bearded lips.)

67   *Reconciliation*

Word over all, beautiful as the sky,
Beautiful that war and all its deeds of carnage must in time be utterly
  lost,
That the hands of the sisters Death and Night incessantly softly wash
  again, and ever again, this soiled world;
For my enemy is dead, a man divine as myself is dead,
I look where he lies white-faced and still in the coffin—I draw near,
Bend down, and touch lightly with my lips the white face in the coffin.

HERMAN MELVILLE

1819–1891

68   *The Portent**

(1859)

Hanging from the beam,
    Slowly swaying (such the law),
Gaunt the shadow on your green,
    Shenandoah!

---

* On 16 October 1859, the abolitionist John Brown and a troop of eighteen men raided
the United States Arsenal at Harper's Ferry, Virginia, near the Shenandoah Valley. He
was captured two days later, tried on a charge of treason and inciting a slave uprising,
convicted, and in December 1859, hanged.

The cut is on the crown
(Lo, John Brown),
And the stabs shall heal no more.

Hidden in the cap
　　Is the anguish none can draw;
So your future veils its face,
　　Shenandoah!
But the streaming beard is shown
(Weird John Brown),
The meteor of the war.

69 　　　　　　　*Ball's Bluff* *

A Reverie

(October 1861)

One noonday, at my window in the town,
　　I saw a sight—saddest that eyes can see—
　　Young soldiers marching lustily
　　　　Unto the wars,
With fifes, and flags in mottoed pageantry;
　　　　While all the porches, walks, and doors
Were rich with ladies cheering royally.

They moved like Juny morning on the wave,
　　Their hearts were fresh as clover in its prime
　　(It was the breezy summer time),
　　　　Life throbbed so strong,
How should they dream that Death in a rosy clime
　　　　Would come to thin their shining throng?
Youth feels immortal, like the gods sublime.

Weeks passed; and at my window, leaving bed,
　　By night I mused, of easeful sleep bereft,
　　On those brave boys (Ah War! thy theft);
　　　　Some marching feet
Found pause at last by cliffs Potomac cleft;
　　　　Wakeful I mused, while in the street
Far footfalls died away till none were left.

---

* On 21 October 1861, four regiments of Union troops packed into boats on the Potomac River faced Confederate attack at Ball's Bluff, where they were pinned against a hundred-foot cliff. More than 1,000 Union soldiers were killed in the massacre that ensued.

70 *Shiloh**

A Requiem

(April 1862)

Skimming lightly, wheeling still,
The swallows fly low
Over the field in clouded days,
The forest-field of Shiloh—
Over the field where April rain
Solaced the parched ones stretched in pain
Through the pause of night
That followed the Sunday fight
Around the church of Shiloh—
The church so lone, the log-built one,
That echoed to many a parting groan
And natural prayer
Of dying foemen mingled there—
Foemen at morn, but friends at eve—
Fame or country least their care:
(What like a bullet can undeceive!)
But now they lie low,
While over them the swallows skim,
And all is hushed at Shiloh.

71 *The College Colonel*

He rides at their head;
A crutch by his saddle just slants in view,
One slung arm is in splints, you see,
Yet he guides his strong steed—how coldly
too.

He brings his regiment home—
Not as they filed two years before,
But a remnant half-tattered, and battered, and
worn,

* One of the bloodiest battles of the American Civil War was fought around the Shiloh Baptist Church in Tennessee on 6 and 7 April 1862. Union losses totalled more than 13,000 men, Confederate losses more then 10,000.

Like castaway sailors, who—stunned
   By the surf's loud roar,
  Their mates dragged back and seen no more—
Again and again breast the surge,
   And at last crawl, spent, to shore.

A still rigidity and pale—
   An Indian aloofness lones his brow;
He has lived a thousand years
Compressed in battle's pains and prayers,
   Marches and watches slow.

There are welcoming shouts, and flags;
   Old men off hat to the Boy,
Wreaths from gay balconies fall at his feet,
   But to *him*—there comes alloy.

It is not that a leg is lost,
   It is not that an arm is maimed,
It is not that the fever has racked—
   Self he has long disclaimed.

But all through the Seven Days' Fight,
   And deep in the Wilderness grim,
And in the field-hospital tent,
   And Petersburg crater, and dim
Lean brooding in Libby, there came—
   Ah heaven!—what *truth* to him.

EMILY DICKINSON
1830–1886

72   My Portion is Defeat—today—
       A paler luck than Victory—
       Less Paeans—fewer Bells—
       The Drums don't follow Me—with tunes—
       Defeat—a somewhat slower—means—
       More Arduous than Balls—

'Tis populous with Bone and stain—
And Men too straight to stoop again,
And Piles of solid Moan—
And Chips of Blank—in Boyish Eyes—
And scraps of Prayer—
And Death's surprise,
Stamped visible—in Stone—

There's somewhat prouder, over there—
The Trumpets tell it to the Air—
How different Victory
To Him who has it—and the One
Who to have had it, would have been
Contenteder—to die—

73
My Triumph lasted till the Drums
Had left the Dead alone
And then I dropped my Victory
And chastened stole along
To where the finished Faces
Conclusion turned on me
And then I hated Glory
And wished myself were They.

What is to be is best descried
When it has also been—
Could Prospect taste of Retrospect
The tyrannies of Men
Were Tenderer—diviner
The Transitive toward.
A Bayonet's contrition
Is nothing to the Dead.

STEPHEN CRANE

1871–1900

74
Do not weep, maiden, for war is kind.
Because your lover threw wild hands toward the sky
And the affrighted steed ran on alone,
Do not weep.
War is kind.

Hoarse, booming drums of the regiment,
Little souls who thirst for fight,
These men were born to drill and die.
The unexplained glory flies above them,
Great is the Battle-God, great, and his Kingdom—
A field where a thousand corpses lie.

Do not weep, babe, for war is kind.
Because your father tumbled in the yellow trenches,
Raged at his breast, gulped and died,
Do not weep.
War is kind.

Swift blazing flag of the regiment,
Eagle with crest of red and gold,
These men were born to drill and die.
Point for them the virtue of slaughter,
Make plain to them the excellence of killing
And a field where a thousand corpses lie.

Mother whose heart hung humble as a button
On the bright splendid shroud of your son,
Do not weep.
War is kind.

JAMES RUSSELL LOWELL

1819–1891

75   from *Ode Recited at the Harvard Commemoration*

21 July 1865

Weak-winged is song,
Nor aims at that clear-ethered height
Whither the brave deed climbs for light:
    We seem to do them wrong,
Bringing our robin's-leaf to deck their hearse
Who in warm life-blood wrote their nobler verse,
Our trivial song to honor those who come
With ears attuned to strenuous trump and drum,

And shaped in squadron-strophes their desire,
Live battle-odes whose lines were steel and fire:
    Yet sometimes feathered words are strong,
A gracious memory to buoy up and save
From Lethe's dreamless ooze, the common grave
    Of the unventurous throng.

.   .   .   .

    Who now shall sneer?
    Who dare again to say we trace
    Our lines to a plebeian race?
    Roundhead and Cavalier!
Dumb are those names erewhile in battle loud;
Dream-footed as the shadow of a cloud,
    They flit across the ear:
That is best blood that hath most iron in't.
To edge resolve with, pouring without stint
    For what makes manhood dear.
    Tell us not of Plantagenets,
Hapsburgs, and Guelfs, whose thin bloods crawl
Down from some victor in a border-brawl!
    How poor their outworn coronets,
Matched with one leaf of that plain civic wreath
Our brave for honor's blazon shall bequeath,
    Through whose desert a rescued Nation sets
Her heel on treason, and the trumpet hears
Shout victory, tingling Europe's sullen ears
    With vain resentments and more vain regrets!

    Not in anger, not in pride,
    Pure from passion's mixture rude
    Ever to base earth allied,
    But with far-heard gratitude,
    Still with heart and voice renewed,
To heroes living and dear martyrs dead,
The strain should close that consecrates our brave.
    Lift the heart and lift the head!
    Lofty be its mood and grave,
    Not without a martial ring,
    Not without a prouder tread
    And a peal of exultation:
    Little right has he to sing
    Through whose heart in such an hour

Beats no march of conscious power,
Sweeps no tumult of elation!
'Tis no Man we celebrate,
By his country's victories great,
A hero half, and half the whim of Fate,
But the pith and marrow of a Nation
Drawing force from all her men,
Highest, humblest, weakest, all,
For her time of need, and then
Pulsing it again through them,
Till the basest can no longer cower,
Feeling his soul spring up divinely tall,
Touched but in passing by her mantle-hem.
Come back, then, noble pride, for 'tis her dower!
How could poet ever tower,
If his passions, hopes, and fears,
If his triumphs and his tears,
Kept not measure with his people?
Boom, cannon, boom to all the winds and waves!
Clash out, glad bells, from every rocking steeple!
Banners, adance with triumph, bend your staves!
And from every mountain-peak
Let beacon-fire to answering beacon speak,
Katahdin tell Monadnock, Whiteface he,
And so leap on in light from sea to sea,
Till the glad news be sent
Across a kindling continent,
Making earth feel more firm and air breathe braver:
'Be proud! for she is saved, and all have helped to save her!
She that lifts up the manhood of the poor,
She of the open soul and open door,
With room about her hearth for all mankind!
The fire is dreadful in her eyes no more;
From her bold front the helm she doth unbind,
Sends all her handmaid armies back to spin,
And bids her navies, that so lately hurled
Their crashing battle, hold their thunders in,
Swimming like birds of calm along the unharmful shore.
No challenge sends she to the elder world,
That looked askance and hated; a light scorn
Plays o'er her mouth, as round her mighty knees
She calls her children back, and waits the morn
Of nobler day, enthroned between her subject seas.'

JULIA WARD HOWE

1819–1910

76   *The Battle Hymn of the Republic*

Mine eyes have seen the glory of the coming of the Lord:
He is trampling out the vintage where the grapes of wrath are stored;
He hath loosed the fatal lightning of His terrible swift sword:
     His truth is marching on.

I have seen Him in the watch-fires of a hundred circling camps,
They have builded Him an altar in the evening dews and damps;
I can read His righteous sentence by the dim and flaring lamps:
     His day is marching on.

I have read a fiery gospel writ in burnished rows of steel:
'As ye deal with my contemners, so with you my grace shall deal;
Let the Hero, born of woman, crush the serpent with his heel,
     Since God is marching on.'

He has sounded forth the trumpet that shall never call retreat;
He is sifting out the hearts of men before his judgement seat:
Oh, be swift, my soul, to answer Him! Be jubilant, my feet!
     Our God is marching on.

In the beauty of the lilies Christ was born across the sea,
With a glory in his bosom that transfigures you and me:
As he died to make men holy, let us die to make men free,
     While God is marching on.

ALLEN TATE

1889–1979

77   *Ode to the Confederate Dead*

     Row after row with strict impunity
     The headstones yield their names to the element,
     The wind whirrs without recollection;
     In the riven troughs the splayed leaves

Pile up, of nature the casual sacrament
To the seasonal eternity of death;
Then driven by the fierce scrutiny
Of heaven to their election in the vast breath,
They sough the rumour of mortality.

Autumn is desolation in the plot
Of a thousand acres where these memories grow
From the inexhaustible bodies that are not
Dead, but feed the grass row after rich row.
Think of the autumns that have come and gone!—
Ambitious November with the humors of the year,
With a particular zeal for every slab,
Staining the uncomfortable angels that rot
On the slabs, a wing chipped here, an arm there:
The brute curiosity of an angel's stare
Turns you, like them, to stone,
Transforms the heaving air
Till plunged to a heavier world below
You shift your sea-space blindly
Heaving, turning like the blind crab.

    Dazed by the wind, only the wind
    The leaves flying, plunge

You know who have waited by the wall
The twilight certainty of an animal,
Those midnight restitutions of the blood
You know—the immitigable pines, the smoky frieze
Of the sky, the sudden call: you know the rage,
The cold pool left by the mounting flood,
Of muted Zeno and Parmenides.
You who have waited for the angry resolution
Of those desires that should be yours tomorrow,
You know the unimportant shrift of death
And praise the vision
And praise the arrogant circumstance
Of those who fall
Rank upon rank, hurried beyond decision—
Here by the sagging gate, stopped by the wall.

    Seeing, seeing only the leaves
    Flying, plunge and expire

Turn your eyes to the immoderate past,
Turn to the inscrutable infantry rising
Demons out of the earth—they will not last.
Stonewall, Stonewall, and the sunken fields of hemp,
Shiloh, Antietam, Malvern Hill, Bull Run.
Lost in that orient of the thick-and-fast
You will curse the setting sun.

   Cursing only the leaves crying
   Like an old man in a storm

You hear the shout, the crazy hemlock point
With troubled fingers to the silence which
Smothers you, a mummy, in time.

                        The hound bitch
Toothless and dying, in a musty cellar
Hears the wind only.

                    Now that the salt of their blood
Stiffens the saltier oblivion of the sea,
Seals the malignant purity of the flood,
What shall we who count our days and bow
Our heads with a commemorial woe
In the ribboned coats of grim felicity,
What shall we say of the bones, unclean,
Whose verdurous anonymity will grow?
The ragged arms, the ragged heads and eyes
Lost in these acres of the insane green?
The gray lean spiders come, they come and go;
In a tangle of willows without light
The singular screech-owl's tight
Invisible lyric seeds the mind
With the furious murmur of their chivalry.

   We shall say only the leaves
   Flying, plunge and expire

We shall say only the leaves whispering
In the improbable mist of nightfall
That flies on multiple wing;
Night is the beginning and the end
And in between the ends of distraction

Waits mute speculation, the patient curse
That stones the eyes, or like the jaguar leaps
For his own image in a jungle pool, his victim.
What shall we say who have knowledge
Carried to the heart? Shall we take the act
To the grave? Shall we, more hopeful set up the grave
In the house? The ravenous grave?

                              Leave now
The shut gate and the decomposing wall:
The gentle serpent, green in the mulberry bush,
Riots with his tongue through the hush—
Sentinel of the grave who counts us all!

RAINER MARIA RILKE

1875–1926

78   *Last Evening*

And night and distant travel; for the train
of the whole army swept along the park.
He looked up from the harpsichord again
and played and glanced at her without remark,

almost like looking in a mirror's round:
so filled with his young features was that face,
features that bore his sadness with a grace
suing more seductively at every sound.

Then all at once that seemed to disappear:
she stood, as though with a great effort, near
the window-seat, and clasped her beating breast.

His playing stopped. Outside a fresh wind blew.
And on the mirror-table, strange and new,
stood the black shako with the death's head crest.

Translated from the German by J. B. Leishman

ARTHUR RIMBAUD
1854–1891

from *Eighteen-Seventy**

I

A POSTER OF OUR DAZZLING VICTORY
AT SAARBRUCKEN

In the centre of the poster, Napoleon
rides in apotheosis, sallow, medalled, a ramrod
perched on a merrygoround horse. He sees life
through rosy glasses, terrible as God,

and sentimental as a bourgeois papa.
Four little conscripts take their nap below
on scarlet guns and drums. One, unbuckling, cheers
Napoleon—he's stunned by the big name!

Another lounges on the butt of his Chassepot,
another feels his hair rise on his neck.
A bearskin shako bounds like a black sun:

VIVE L'EMPEREUR! They're holding back their breath.
And last, some moron, struggling to his knees,
presents a blue and scarlet ass—to what?

II

NAPOLEON AFTER SEDAN

The man waxy—he jogs along the fields
in flower, black, a cigar between his teeth.
The wax man thinks about the Tuilleries
in flower. At times his mossy eye takes fire.

* After the outbreak of the Franco-Prussian War in July 1870, Emperor Napoleon III greatly exaggerated the significance of the French victory in the battle at Saarbrucken on 2 August. Two days later, the Germans crossed the French border into Alsace; a wave of French defeats followed, culminating in the German capture of Napoleon and 100,000 of his men in September at Sedan.

Twenty years of orgy have made him drunk:
he'd said: 'My hand will snuff out Liberty,
politely, gently, as I snuff my stogie.'
Liberty lives; the Emperor is out—

he's captured. Oh what name is shaking on
his lips? What plebiscites? Napoleon
cannot tell you. His shark's eye is dead.

An opera glass on the horses at Compere . . .
he watches his cigar fume off in smoke . . .
soirées at Saint Cloud . . . a bluish vapour.

III

TO THE FRENCH OF THE SECOND EMPIRE

You, dead in '92 and '93,
still pale from the great kiss of Liberty—
when tyrants trampled on humanity,
you broke them underneath your wooden shoes.

You were reborn and great by agony,
your hearts in rage still beat for our salvation—
Oh soldiers, sown by death, your noble lover,
in our old furrows you regenerate!

You, whose life-blood washed our soiled standards red,
the dead of Valmy, Italy, Fleurus,
thousands of Christs, red-bonneted . . . we

have let you die with our Republic, we
who lick the boots of our bored kings like dogs—
men of the Second Empire, I mean you!

.   .   .   .

VII

THE SLEEPER IN THE VALLEY

The swollen river sang through the green hole,
and madly hooked white tatters on the grass.
Light escaladed the hot hills. The whole
valley bubbled with sunbeams like a beer-glass.

The conscript was open-mouthed; his bare head
and neck swam in the bluish water cress.
He slept. The mid-day soothed his heaviness,
sunlight was raining into his green bed,

and baked the bruises from his body, rolled
as a sick child might hug itself asleep . . .
Oh Nature, rock him warmly, he is cold.

The flowers no longer make his hot eyes weep.
The river sucks his hair. His blue eye rolls.
He sleeps. In his right side are two red holes.

VIII

EVIL

All day the red spit of the chain-shot tore
whistling across the infinite blue sky,
while the great captain saw his infantry
flounder in massed battalions into fire.

The criminal injustice that deceives
and rules us, lays our corpses end on end,
then burns us like the summer grass or leaves;
La Patrie is avaricious to this end!

She is a god that laughs at Papal bulls,
the great gold chalice and the thuribles.
She dozes while our grand hosannas drown

the guns and drums, and wakes to hear the grief
of widows or a mother who lays down
her great sou knotted in a handkerchief.

Translated from the French by Robert Lowell

RUDYARD KIPLING
1865–1936

80

Arithmetic on the Frontier

A great and glorious thing it is
　　To learn, for seven years or so,
The Lord knows what of that and this,
　　Ere reckoned fit to face the foe—
The flying bullet down the Pass,
That whistles clear: 'All flesh is grass.'

Three hundred pounds per annum spent
　　On making brain and body meeter
For all the murderous intent
　　Comprised in 'villainous saltpeter'!
And after?—Ask the Yusufzaies
What comes of all our 'ologies.

A scrimmage in a Border Station—
　　A canter down some dark defile—
Two thousand pounds of education
　　Drops to a ten-rupee jezail—
The Crammer's boast, the Squadron's pride,
Shot like a rabbit in a ride!

No proposition Euclid wrote
　　No formulæ the text-books know,
Will turn the bullet from your coat,
　　Or ward the tulwar's downward blow.
Strike hard who cares—shoot straight who can—
The odds are on the cheaper man.

One sword-knot stolen from the camp
　　Will pay for all the school expenses
Of any Kurrum Valley scamp
　　Who knows no word of moods and tenses,
But, being blessed with perfect sight,
Picks off our messmates left and right.

With home-bred hordes the hillsides teem.
    The troopships bring us one by one,
At vast expense of time and steam,
    To slay Afridis where they run.
The 'captives of our bow and spear'
Are cheap, alas! as we are dear.

81   *Tommy*

I went into a public-'ouse to get a pint o' beer,
The publican 'e up an' sez, 'We serve no red-coats here.'
The girls be'ind the bar they laughed an' giggled fit to die,
I outs into the street again an' to myself sez I:
        O it's Tommy this, an' Tommy that, an' 'Tommy, go away';
        But it's 'Thank you, Mister Atkins,' when the band begins to
            play—
        The band begins to play, my boys, the band begins to play,
        O it's 'Thank you, Mister Atkins,' when the band begins to play.

I went into a theatre as sober as could be,
They gave a drunk civilian room, but 'adn't none for me;
They sent me to the gallery or round the music-'alls;
But when it comes to fightin', Lord! they'll shove me in the stalls!
        For it's Tommy this, an' Tommy that, an' 'Tommy wait outside';
        But it's 'Special train for Atkins' when the trooper's on the tide—
        The troopship's on the tide, my boys, the troopship's on the tide,
        O it's 'Special train for Atkins' when the trooper's on the tide.

Yes, makin' mock o' uniforms that guard you while you sleep
Is cheaper than them uniforms, an' they're starvation cheap;
An' hustlin' drunken soldiers when they're goin' large a bit
Is five times better business than paradin' in full kit.
        Then it's Tommy this, an' Tommy that, an' 'Tommy, 'ow's yer
            soul?'
        But it's 'Thin red line of 'eroes' when the drums begin to roll—
        The drums begin to roll, my boys, the drums begin to roll,
        O it's 'Thin red line of 'eroes' when the drums begin to roll.

We aren't no thin red 'eroes, nor we aren't no blackguards too,
But single men in barricks, most remarkable like you;
An' if sometimes our conduck isn't all your fancy paints,
Why, single men in barricks don't grow into plaster saints;

While it's Tommy this, an' Tommy that, an' 'Tommy, fall be'ind,'
But it's 'Please to walk in front, sir,' when there's trouble in the
     wind—
There's trouble in the wind, my boys, there's trouble in the wind,
O it's 'Please to walk in front, sir,' when there's trouble in the wind.

You talk o' better food for us, an' schools, an' fires, an' all:
We'll wait for extry rations if you treat us rational.
Don't mess about the cook-room slops, but prove it to our face
The Widow's Uniform is not the soldier-man's disgrace.
     For it's Tommy this, an' Tommy that, an' 'Chuck him out, the
          brute!'
     But it's 'Saviour of 'is country' when the guns begin to shoot;
     An' it's Tommy this, an' Tommy that, an' anything you please;
     An' Tommy ain't a bloomin' fool—you bet that Tommy sees!

SIR HENRY NEWBOLT

1862–1938

82   *He Fell among Thieves*

'Ye have robbed,' said he, 'ye have slaughtered and made an end,
     Take your ill-got plunder, and bury the dead:
What will ye more of your guest and sometime friend?'
     'Blood for our blood,' they said.

He laughed: 'If one may settle the score for five,
     I am ready; but let the reckoning stand till day:
I have loved the sunlight as dearly as any alive.'
     'You shall die at dawn,' said they.

He flung his empty revolver down the slope,
     He climbed alone to the Eastward edge of the trees;
All night long in a dream untroubled of hope
     He brooded, clasping his knees.

He did not hear the monotonous roar that fills
  The ravine where the Yassîn river sullenly flows;
He did not see the starlight on the Laspur hills,
  Or the far Afghan snows.

He saw the April noon on his books aglow,
  The wisteria trailing in at the window wide;
He heard his father's voice from the terrace below
  Calling him down to ride.

He saw the grey little church across the park,
  The mounds that hid the loved and honoured dead;
The Norman arch, the chancel softly dark,
  The brasses black and red.

He saw the School Close, sunny and green,
  The runner beside him, the stand by the parapet wall,
The distant tape, and the crowd roaring between,
  His own name over all.

He saw the dark wainscot and timbered roof,
  The long tables, and the faces merry and keen;
The College Eight and their trainer dining aloof,
  The Dons on the daïs serene.

He watched the liner's stem ploughing the foam,
  He felt her trembling speed and the thrash of her screw;
He heard her passengers' voices talking of home,
  He saw the flag she flew.

And now it was dawn. He rose strong on his feet,
  And strode to his ruined camp below the wood;
He drank the breath of the morning cool and sweet:
  His murderers round him stood.

Light on the Laspur hills was broadening fast,
  The blood-red snow-peaks chilled to a dazzling white:
He turned, and saw the golden circle at last,
  Cut by the Eastern height.

'O glorious Life, Who dwellest in earth and sun,
   I have lived, I praise and adore Thee.'
                        A sword swept.
Over the pass the voices one by one
   Faded, and the hill slept.

83   *Vitaï Lampada*

There's a breathless hush in the Close tonight—
   Ten to make and the match to win—
A bumping pitch and a blinding light,
   An hour to play and the last man in.
And it's not for the sake of a ribboned coat,
   Or the selfish hope of a season's fame,
But his Captain's hand on his shoulder smote—
   'Play up! play up! and play the game!'

The sand of the desert is sodden red,—
   Red with the wreck of a square that broke;—
The Gatling's jammed and the Colonel dead,
   And the regiment blind with dust and smoke.
The river of death has brimmed his banks,
   And England's far, and Honour a name,
But the voice of a schoolboy rallies the ranks:
   'Play up! play up! and play the game!'

This is the word that year by year,
   While in her place the School is set,
Every one of her sons must hear,
   And none that hears it dare forget.
This they all with a joyful mind
   Bear through life like a torch in flame,
And falling fling to the host behind—
   'Play up! play up! and play the game!'

THOMAS HARDY

1840–1928

84   *Embarcation**

(Southampton Docks: October 1899)

Here, where Vespasian's legions struck the sands,
And Cerdic with his Saxons entered in,
And Henry's army leapt afloat to win
Convincing triumphs over neighbour lands,

Vaster battalions press for further strands,
To argue in the selfsame bloody mode
Which this late age of thought, and pact, and code,
Still fails to mend.—Now deckward tramp the bands,

Yellow as autumn leaves, alive as spring;
And as each host draws out upon the sea
Beyond which lies the tragical To-be,
None dubious of the cause, none murmuring,

Wives, sisters, parents, wave white hands and smile,
As if they knew not that they weep the while.

85   *The Colonel's Soliloquy*

(Southampton Docks: October 1899)

'The quay recedes. Hurrah! Ahead we go! . . .
It's true I've been accustomed now to home,
And joints get rusty, and one's limbs may grow
          More fit to rest than roam.

* On 12 October 1899, following the dispatch of British troops into their territory,
Dutch settlers (Boers) in the Transvaal and the Orange Free State of South Africa
declared war on Great Britain. Despite ill health, Thomas Hardy bicycled 50 miles and
back to the pier in Southampton to watch the British soldiers embark.

'But I can stand as yet fair stress and strain;
There's not a little steel beneath the rust;
My years mount somewhat, but here's to't again!
    And if I fall, I must.

'God knows that for myself I have scanty care;
Past scrimmages have proved as much to all;
In Eastern lands and South I have had my share
    Both of the blade and ball.

'And where those villains ripped me in the flitch
With their old iron in my early time,
I'm apt at change of wind to feel a twitch,
    Or at a change of clime.

'And what my mirror shows me in the morning
Has more of blotch and wrinkle than of bloom;
My eyes, too, heretofore all glasses scorning,
    Have just a touch of rheum. . . .

'Now sounds "The Girl I've left behind me",—Ah,
The years, the ardours, wakened by that tune!
Time was when, with the crowd's farewell "Hurrah!"
    'Twould lift me to the moon.

'But now it's late to leave behind me one
Who if, poor soul, her man goes underground,
Will not recover as she might have done
    In days when hopes abound.

'She's waving from the wharfside, palely grieving,
As down we draw. . . . Her tears make little show,
Yet now she suffers more than at my leaving
    Some twenty years ago!

'I pray those left at home will care for her;
I shall come back; I have before; though when
The Girl you leave behind you is a grandmother,
    Things may not be as then.'

86   *A Christmas Ghost-Story*

South of the Line, inland from far Durban,
A mouldering soldier lies—your countryman.
Awry and doubled up are his gray bones,
And on the breeze his puzzled phantom moans
Nightly to clear Canopus: 'I would know
By whom and when the All-Earth-gladdening Law
Of Peace, brought in by that Man Crucified,
Was ruled to be inept, and set aside?
And what of logic or of truth appears
In tacking "Anno Domini" to the years?
Near twenty-hundred liveried thus have hied,
But tarries yet the Cause for which He died.'

                                        Christmas-eve 1899

87   *Drummer Hodge*

                              I

They throw in Drummer Hodge, to rest
        Uncoffined—just as found:
His landmark is a kopje-crest
        That breaks the veldt around;
And foreign constellations west
        Each night above his mound.

                              II

Young Hodge the Drummer never knew—
        Fresh from his Wessex home—
The meaning of the broad Karoo,
        The Bush, the dusty loam,
And why uprose to nightly view
        Strange stars amid the gloam.

                              III

Yet portion of that unknown plain
        Will Hodge for ever be;
His homely Northern breast and brain
        Grow to some Southern tree,
And strange-eyed constellations reign
        His stars eternally.

88   *A Wife in London*

(December 1899)

I

She sits in the tawny vapour
     That the Thames-side lanes have uprolled,
     Behind whose webby fold on fold
Like a waning taper
     The street-lamp glimmers cold.

A messenger's knock cracks smartly,
     Flashed news is in her hand
     Of meaning it dazes to understand
Though shaped so shortly:
     He—has fallen—in the far South Land. . . .

II

'Tis the morrow; the fog hangs thicker,
     The postman nears and goes:
     A letter is brought whose lines disclose
By the firelight flicker
     His hand, whom the worm now knows:

Fresh—firm—penned in highest feather—
     Page-full of his hoped return,
     And of home-planned jaunts by brake and burn
In the summer weather,
     And of new love that they would learn.

89   *The Man He Killed*

'Had he and I but met
     By some old ancient inn,
We should have sat us down to wet
     Right many a nipperkin!

'But ranged as infantry,
     And staring face to face,
I shot at him as he at me,
     And killed him in his place.

'I shot him dead because—
Because he was my foe,
Just so: my foe of course he was;
    That's clear enough; although

'He thought he'd 'list, perhaps,
    Off-hand like—just as I—
Was out of work—had sold his traps—
    No other reason why.

'Yes; quaint and curious war is!
    You shoot a fellow down
You'd treat if met where any bar is,
    Or help to half-a-crown.'

1902

A. E. HOUSMAN
1859–1936

90

On the idle hill of summer,
    Sleepy with the flow of streams,
Far I hear the steady drummer
    Drumming like a noise in dreams.

Far and near and low and louder
    On the roads of earth go by,
Dear to friends and food for powder,
    Soldiers marching, all to die.

East and west on fields forgotten
    Bleach the bones of comrades slain,
Lovely lads and dead and rotten;
    None that go return again.

Far the calling bugles hollo,
    High the screaming fife replies,
Gay the files of scarlet follow:
    Woman bore me, I will rise.

91

Soldier from the wars returning,
  Spoiler of the taken town,
Here is ease that asks not earning;
  Turn you in and sit you down.

Peace is come and wars are over,
  Welcome you and welcome all,
While the charger crops the clover
  And his bridle hangs in stall.

Now no more of winters biting,
  Filth in trench from fall to spring,
Summers full of sweat and fighting
  For the Kesar or the King.

Rest you, charger, rust you, bridle;
  Kings and kesars, keep your pay;
Soldier, sit you down and idle
  At the inn of night for aye.

92   *Grenadier*

The Queen she sent to look for me,
  The sergeant he did say,
'Young man, a soldier will you be
  For thirteen pence a day?'

For thirteen pence a day did I
  Take off the things I wore,
And I have marched to where I lie,
  And I shall march no more.

My mouth is dry, my shirt is wet,
  My blood runs all away,
So now I shall not die in debt
  For thirteen pence a day.

Tomorrow after new young men
  The sergeant he must see,
For things will all be over then
  Between the Queen and me.

And I shall have to bate my price,
  For in the grave, they say,
Is neither knowledge nor device
  Nor thirteen pence a day.

93   *Lancer*

I 'listed at home for a lancer,
  Oh who would not sleep with the brave?
I 'listed at home for a lancer
  To ride on a horse to my grave.

And over the seas we were bidden
  A country to take and to keep;
And far with the brave I have ridden,
  And now with the brave I shall sleep.

For round me the men will be lying
  That learned me the way to behave,
And showed me my business of dying:
  Oh who would not sleep with the brave?

They ask and there is not an answer;
Says I, I will 'list for a lancer,
  Oh who would not sleep with the brave?

And I with the brave shall be sleeping
  At ease on my mattress of loam,
When back from their taking and keeping
  The squadron is riding at home.

The wind with the plumes will be playing,
  The girls will stand watching them wave,
And eyeing my comrades and saying
  Oh who would not sleep with the brave?

They ask and there is not an answer;
Says you, I will 'list for a lancer,
  Oh who would not sleep with the brave?

94 *Astronomy*

The Wain upon the northern steep
    Descends and lifts away.
Oh I will sit me down and weep
    For bones in Africa.

For pay and medals, name and rank,
    Things that he has not found,
He hove the Cross to heaven and sank
    The pole-star underground.

And now he does not even see
    Signs of the nadir roll
At night over the ground where he
    Is buried with the pole.

T. W. H. CROSLAND
1865–1924

95 *Slain*

'Dulce et decorum est pro patria mori'

You who are still and white
    And cold like stone;
For whom the unfailing light
    Is spent and done;

For whom no more the breath
    Of dawn, nor evenfall,
Nor Spring nor love nor death
    Matter at all;

Who were so strong and young,
    And brave and wise,
And on the dark are flung
    With darkened eyes;

Who roystered and caroused
    But yesterday,
And now are dumbly housed
    In stranger clay;

Who valiantly led,
  Who followed valiantly,
Who knew no touch of dread
  Of that which was to be;

Children that were as nought
  Ere ye were tried,
How have ye dared and fought,
  Triumphed and died!

    .   .   .

Yea, it is very sweet
  And decorous
The omnipotent Shade to meet
  And flatter thus.

EDGAR WALLACE

1875–1932

96   *War*

I

A tent that is pitched at the base:
  A wagon that comes from the night:
A stretcher—and on it a Case:
  A surgeon, who's holding a light.
The Infantry's bearing the brunt—
  O hark to the wind-carried cheer!
A mutter of guns at the front:
  A whimper of sobs at the rear.
And it's *War*! 'Orderly, hold the light.
  You can lay him down on the table: so.
Easily—gently! Thanks—you may go.'
  And it's *War*! but the part that is not for show.

II

A tent, with a table athwart,
  A table that's laid out for one;
A waterproof cover—and nought
  But the limp, mangled work of a gun.

A bottle that's stuck by the pole,
  A guttering dip in its neck;
The flickering light of a soul
  On the wondering eyes of The Wreck,
And it's *War*! 'Orderly, hold his hand.
  I'm not going to hurt you, so don't be afraid.
A richochet! God! what a mess it has made!'
  And it's *War*! and a very unhealthy trade.

III

The clink of a stopper and glass:
  A sigh as the chloroform drips:
A trickle of—what? on the grass,
  And bluer and bluer the lips.
The lashes have hidden the stare . . .
  A rent, and the clothes fall away . . .
A touch, and the wound is laid bare . . .
  A cut, and the face has turned grey . . .
And it's *War*! 'Orderly, take It out.
  It's hard for his child, and it's rough on his wife,
There might have been—sooner—a chance for his life.
  But it's *War*! And—Orderly, clean this knife!'

RUDYARD KIPLING

1865–1936

97   *Bridge-Guard in the Karroo*

1901

'. . . and will supply details to guard the Blood River Bridge.'
             District Orders: Lines of Communication—
             South African War.

Sudden the desert changes,
  The raw glare softens and clings,
Till the aching Oudtshoorn ranges
  Stand up like the thrones of Kings—

Ramparts of slaughter and peril—
  Blazing, amazing, aglow—
'Twixt the sky-line's belting beryl
  And the wine-dark flats below.

Royal the pageant closes,
  Lit by the last of the sun—
Opal and ash-of-roses,
  Cinnamon, umber, and dun.

The twilight swallows the thicket,
  The starlight reveals the ridge.
The whistle shrills to the picket—
  We are changing guard on the bridge. .

(Few, forgotten and lonely,
  Where the empty metals shine—
No, not combatants—only
  Details guarding the line.)

We slip through the broken panel
  Of fence by the ganger's shed;
We drop to the waterless channel
  And the lean track overhead;

We stumble on refuse of rations,
  The beef and the biscuit-tins;
We take our appointed stations,
  And the endless night begins.

We hear the Hottentot herders
  As the sheep click past to the fold—
And the click of the restless girders
  As the steel contracts in the cold—

Voices of jackals calling
  And, loud in the hush between,
A morsel of dry earth falling
  From the flanks of the scarred ravine.

And the solemn firmament marches,
  And the hosts of heaven rise
Framed through the iron arches—
  Banded and barred by the ties,

Till we feel the far track humming,
　And we see her headlight plain,
And we gather and wait her coming—
　The wonderful north-bound train.

(Few, forgotten and lonely,
　Where the white car-windows shine—
No, not combatants—only
　Details guarding the line.)

Quick, ere the gift escape us!
　Out of the darkness we reach
For a handful of week-old papers
　And a mouthful of human speech.

And the monstrous heaven rejoices,
　And the earth allows again
Meetings, greetings, and voices
　Of women talking with men.

So we return to our places,
　As out on the bridge she rolls;
And the darkness covers our faces,
　And the darkness re-enters our souls.

More than a little lonely
　Where the lessening tail-lights shine.
No—not combatants—only
　Details guarding the line!

98　　　　　　　　　*The Dykes*

1902

We have no heart for the fishing—we have no hand for the oar—
All that our fathers taught us of old pleases us now no more.
All that our own hearts bid us believe we doubt where we do not deny—
There is no proof in the bread we eat nor rest in the toil we ply.

Look you, our foreshore stretches far through sea-gate, dyke, and
　　groin—
Made land all, that our fathers made, where the flats and the fairway
　　join.

They forced the sea a sea-league back. They died, and their work stood
    fast.
We were born to peace in the lee of the dykes, but the time of our peace
    is past.

Far off, the full tide clambers and slips, mouthing and testing all,
Nipping the flanks of the water-gates, baying along the wall;
Turning the shingle, returning the shingle, changing the set of the
    sand . . .
We are too far from the beach, men say, to know how the outworks
    stand.

So we come down, uneasy, to look; uneasily pacing the beach.
These are the dykes our fathers made: we have never known a breach.
Time and again has the gale blown by and we were not afraid;
Now we come only to look at the dykes—at the dykes our fathers made.

O'er the marsh where the homesteads cower apart the harried sunlight
    flies,
Shifts and considers, wanes and recovers, scatters and sickens and
    dies—
An evil ember bedded in ash—a spark blown west by the wind . . .
We are surrendered to night and the sea—the gale and the tide behind!

At the bridge of the lower saltings the cattle gather and blare,
Roused by the feet of running men, dazed by the lantern-glare.
Unbar and let them away for their lives—the levels drown as they stand,
Where the flood-wash forces the sluices aback and the ditches deliver
    inland.

Ninefold deep to the top of the dykes the galloping breakers stride,
And their overcarried spray is a sea—a sea on the landward side.
Coming, like stallions they paw with their hooves, going they snatch with
    their teeth,
Till the bents and the furze and the sand are dragged out, and the
    old-time hurdles beneath.

Bid men gather fuel for fire, the tar, the oil, and the tow—
Flame we shall need, not smoke, in the dark if the riddled sea-banks go.
Bid the ringers watch in the tower (who knows how the dawn shall
    prove?)
Each with his rope between his feet and the trembling bells above.

Now we can only wait till the day, wait and apportion our shame.
These are the dykes our fathers left, but we would not look to the same.
Time and again were we warned of the dykes, time and again we
    delayed:
Now, it may fall, we have slain our sons, as our fathers we have betrayed.

.   .   .

Walking along the wreck of the dykes, watching the work of the seas!
These were the dykes our fathers made to our great profit and ease.
But the peace is gone and the profit is gone, with the old sure days
    withdrawn . . .
That our own houses show as strange when we come back in the dawn!

THOMAS HARDY

1840–1928

99   *Men Who March Away*

(*Song of the Soldiers*)

What of the faith and fire within us
        Men who march away
        Ere the barn-cocks say
        Night is growing gray,
Leaving all that here can win us;
What of the faith and fire within us
        Men who march away?

Is it a purblind prank, O think you,
        Friend with the musing eye,
        Who watch us stepping by
        With doubt and dolorous sigh?
Can much pondering so hoodwink you!
Is it a purblind prank, O think you,
        Friend with the musing eye?

Nay. We well see what we are doing,
        Though some may not see—
        Dalliers as they be—
        England's need are we;
Her distress would leave us rueing:
Nay. We well see what we are doing,
        Though some may not see!

In our heart of hearts believing
    Victory crowns the just,
    And that braggarts must
    Surely bite the dust,
Press we to the field ungrieving,
In our heart of hearts believing
    Victory crowns the just.

Hence the faith and fire within us
    Men who march away
    Ere the barn-cocks say
    Night is growing gray,
Leaving all that here can win us;
Hence the faith and fire within us
    Men who march away.

5 September 1914

100   *In Time of 'The Breaking of Nations'*

I

Only a man harrowing clods
    In a slow silent walk
With an old horse that stumbles and nods
    Half asleep as they stalk.

II

Only thin smoke without flame
    From the heaps of couch-grass;
Yet this will go onward the same
    Though Dynasties pass.

III

Yonder a maid and her wight
    Come whispering by:
War's annals will cloud into night
    Ere their story die.

1915

RUPERT BROOKE
1887–1915

101 *Peace*

Now, God be thanked Who has matched us with His hour,
  And caught our youth, and wakened us from sleeping,
With hand made sure, clear eye, and sharpened power,
  To turn, as swimmers into cleanness leaping,
Glad from a world grown old and cold and weary,
  Leave the sick hearts that honour could not move,
And half-men, and their dirty songs and dreary,
  And all the little emptiness of love!

Oh! we, who have known shame, we have found release there,
  Where there's no ill, no grief, but sleep has mending.
    Naught broken save this body, lost but breath;
Nothing to shake the laughing heart's long peace there
  But only agony, and that has ending;
    And the worst friend and enemy is but Death.

102 *The Dead*

Blow out, you bugles, over the rich Dead!
  There's none of these so lonely and poor of old,
  But, dying, has made us rarer gifts than gold.
These laid the world away; poured out the red
Sweet wine of youth; gave up the years to be
  Of work and joy, and that unhoped serene,
  That men call age; and those who would have been,
Their sons, they gave, their immortality.

Blow, bugles, blow! They brought us, for our dearth,
  Holiness, lacked so long, and Love, and Pain.
Honour has come back, as a king, to earth,
  And paid his subjects with a royal wage;
And Nobleness walks in our ways again;
  And we have come into our heritage.

103 *The Soldier*

If I should die, think only this of me:
    That there's some corner of a foreign field
That is for ever England. There shall be
    In that rich earth a richer dust concealed;
A dust whom England bore, shaped, made aware,
    Gave, once, her flowers to love, her ways to roam,
A body of England's, breathing English air,
    Washed by the rivers, blest by suns of home.

And think, this heart, all evil shed away,
    A pulse in the eternal mind, no less
        Gives somewhere back the thoughts by England given;
Her sights and sounds; dreams happy as her day;
    And laughter, learnt of friends; and gentleness,
        In hearts at peace, under an English heaven.

HERBERT ASQUITH

1881–1947

104 *The Volunteer*

Here lies a clerk who half his life had spent
Toiling at ledgers in a city grey,
Thinking that so his days would drift away
With no lance broken in life's tournament.
Yet ever 'twixt the books and his bright eyes
The gleaming eagles of the legions came,
And horsemen, charging under phantom skies,
Went thundering past beneath the oriflamme.

And now those waiting dreams are satisfied;
From twilight to the halls of dawn he went;
His lance is broken; but he lies content
With that high hour, in which he lived and died.
And falling thus he wants no recompense,
Who found his battle in the last resort;
Nor need he any hearse to bear him hence,
Who goes to join the men of Agincourt.

JULIAN GRENFELL
1888–1915

Into Battle

(Flanders, April 1915)

The naked earth is warm with Spring,
   And with green grass and bursting trees
Leans to the sun's gaze glorying,
   And quivers in the sunny breeze;

And life is colour and warmth and light,
   And a striving evermore for these;
And he is dead who will not fight;
   And who dies fighting has increase.

The fighting man shall from the sun
   Take warmth, and life from the glowing earth;
Speed with the light-foot winds to run,
   And with the trees to newer birth;
And find, when fighting shall be done,
   Great rest, and fullness after dearth.

All the bright company of Heaven
   Hold him in their high comradeship,
The Dog-Star, and the Sisters Seven,
   Orion's Belt and sworded hip.

The woodland trees that stand together,
   They stand to him each one a friend;
They gently speak in the windy weather;
   They guide to valley and ridge's end.

The kestrel hovering by day,
   And the little owls that call by night,
Bid him be swift and keen as they,
   As keen of ear, as swift of sight.

The blackbird sings to him, 'Brother, brother,
   If this be the last song you shall sing,
Sing well, for you may not sing another;
   Brother, sing.'

In dreary, doubtful waiting hours,
　Before the brazen frenzy starts,
The horses show him nobler powers;
　O patient eyes, courageous hearts!

And when the burning moment breaks,
　And all things else are out of mind,
And only joy of battle takes
　Him by the throat, and makes him blind,

Through joy and blindness he shall know,
　Not caring much to know, that still
Nor lead nor steel shall reach him, so
　That it be not the Destined Will.

The thundering line of battle stands,
　And in the air Death moans and sings;
But Day shall clasp him with strong hands,
　And Night shall fold him in soft wings.

JOHN McCRAE

1872–1918

106　　　　　　*In Flanders Fields*

In Flanders fields the poppies blow
Between the crosses, row on row,
　That mark our place; and in the sky
　The larks, still bravely singing, fly
Scarce heard amid the guns below.

We are the Dead. Short days ago
We lived, felt dawn, saw sunset glow,
　Loved and were loved, and now we lie
　In Flanders fields.

Take up our quarrel with the foe:
To you from failing hands we throw
　The torch; be yours to hold it high.
　If ye break faith with us who die
We shall not sleep, though poppies grow
　In Flanders fields.

CHARLES SORLEY

1895–1915

107   All the hills and vales along
Earth is bursting into song,
And the singers are the chaps
Who are going to die perhaps.
  O sing, marching men,
  Till the valleys ring again.
  Give your gladness to earth's keeping,
  So be glad, when you are sleeping.

Cast away regret and rue,
Think what you are marching to.
Little live, great pass.
Jesus Christ and Barabbas
Were found the same day.
This died, that went his way.
  So sing with joyful breath,
  For why, you are going to death.
  Teeming earth will surely store
  All the gladness that you pour.

Earth that never doubts nor fears,
Earth that knows of death, not tears,
Earth that bore with joyful ease
Hemlock for Socrates,
Earth that blossomed and was glad
'Neath the cross that Christ had,
Shall rejoice and blossom too
When the bullet reaches you.
  Wherefore, men marching
  On the road to death, sing!
  Pour your gladness on earth's head,
  So be merry, so be dead.

From the hills and valleys earth
Shouts back the sound of mirth,
Tramp of feet and lilt of song
Ringing all the road along.

All the music of their going,
Ringing swinging glad song-throwing,
Earth will echo still, when foot
Lies numb and voice mute.
    On, marching men, on
    To the gates of death with song.
    Sow your gladness for earth's reaping,
    So you may be glad, though sleeping.
    Strew your gladness on earth's bed,
    So be merry, so be dead.

108   When you see millions of the mouthless dead
Across your dreams in pale battalions go,
Say not soft things as other men have said,
That you'll remember. For you need not so.
Give them not praise. For, deaf, how should they know
It is not curses heaped on each gashed head?
Nor tears. Their blind eyes see not your tears flow.
Nor honour. It is easy to be dead.
Say only this, 'They are dead.' Then add thereto,
'Yet many a better one has died before.'
Then, scanning all the o'ercrowded mass, should you
Perceive one face that you loved heretofore,
It is a spook. None wears the face you knew.
Great death has made all his for evermore.

A. E. HOUSMAN

1859–1936

109   *Epitaph on an Army of Mercenaries*

These, in the day when heaven was falling,
    The hour when earth's foundations fled,
Followed their mercenary calling
    And took their wages and are dead.

Their shoulders held the sky suspended;
    They stood, and earth's foundations stay;
What God abandoned, these defended,
    And saved the sum of things for pay.

HUGH MacDIARMID

1892–1978

110   *Another Epitaph on an Army of Mercenaries*

It is a God-damned lie to say that these
Saved, or knew, anything worth any man's pride.
They were professional murderers and they took
Their blood money and impious risks and died.
In spite of all their kind some elements of worth
With difficulty persist here and there on earth.

CARL SANDBURG

1878–1967

111   *Grass*

Pile the bodies high at Austerlitz and Waterloo.
Shovel them under and let me work—
              I am the grass; I cover all.

And pile them high at Gettysburg
And pile them high at Ypres and Verdun.
Shovel them under and let me work.
Two years, ten years, and passengers ask the conductor:
              What place is this?
              Where are we now?

              I am the grass.
              Let me work.

ROBERT FROST

1874–1963

112

Range-Finding

The battle rent a cobweb diamond-strung
And cut a flower beside a ground bird's nest
Before it stained a single human breast.
The stricken flower bent double and so hung.
And still the bird revisited her young.
A butterfly its fall had dispossessed
A moment sought in air his flower of rest,
Then lightly stooped to it and fluttering clung.

On the bare upland pasture there had spread
O'ernight 'twixt mullein stalks a wheel of thread
And straining cables wet with silver dew.
A sudden passing bullet shook it dry.
The indwelling spider ran to greet the fly,
But finding nothing, sullenly withdrew.

WALLACE STEVENS

1879–1955

113

The Death of a Soldier

Life contracts and death is expected,
As in a season of autumn.
The soldier falls.

He does not become a three-days personage,
Imposing his separation,
Calling for pomp.

Death is absolute and without memorial,
As in a season of autumn,
When the wind stops,

When the wind stops and, over the heavens,
The clouds go, nevertheless,
In their direction.

GUILLAUME APOLLINAIRE

1880–1918

114

Calligram, 15 May 1915

The sky's as blue and black as ink
My eyes drown in it and sink

Darkness a shell whines over me
I write this under a willow tree

The evening star a punctual gem shines

[The words of the poem are arranged in the shape of a star and a spray of light:]

The eveni · ctual gem

r
a
t a
s p
g u
n n
Shines c
dem
a
l i
i r a j a d
k a h s
e

look some lovely she
or like the sends
shi ning
on our
battery

Translated from the French by O. Bernard

170

BENJAMIN PÉRET

1899–1959

115 *Little Song of the Maimed*

Lend me your arm
to replace my leg
The rats ate it for me
at Verdun
at Verdun
I ate lots of rats
but they didn't give me back my leg
and that's why I was given the CROIX DE GUERRE
and a wooden leg
and a wooden leg

Translated from the French by David Gascoyne

W. B. YEATS

1865–1939

116 *On Being Asked for a War Poem*

I think it better that in times like these
A poet's mouth be silent, for in truth
We have no gift to set a statesman right;
He has had enough of meddling who can please
A young girl in the indolence of her youth,
Or an old man upon a winter's night.

117 *Easter 1916**

I have met them at close of day
Coming with vivid faces
From counter or desk among grey
Eighteenth-century houses.

* On Easter Sunday 1916, Irish republicans seized and occupied the Post Office at the centre of Dublin in an unsuccessful attempt to overthrow British rule. A week of fighting ensued; by 29 April the insurgents had been captured or killed, and in May the leaders were executed.

I have passed with a nod of the head
Or polite meaningless words,
Or have lingered awhile and said
Polite meaningless words,
And thought before I had done
Of a mocking tale or a gibe
To please a companion
Around the fire at the club,
Being certain that they and I
But lived where motley is worn:
All changed, changed utterly:
A terrible beauty is born.

That woman's days were spent
In ignorant good-will,
Her nights in argument
Until her voice grew shrill.
What voice more sweet than hers
When, young and beautiful,
She rode to harriers?
This man had kept a school
And rode our wingèd horse;
This other his helper and friend
Was coming into his force;
He might have won fame in the end,
So sensitive his nature seemed,
So daring and sweet his thought.
This other man I had dreamed
A drunken, vainglorious lout.
He had done most bitter wrong
To some who are near my heart,
Yet I number him in the song;
He, too, has resigned his part
In the casual comedy;
He, too, has been changed in his turn,
Transformed utterly:
A terrible beauty is born.

Hearts with one purpose alone
Through summer and winter seem
Enchanted to a stone
To trouble the living stream.

The horse that comes from the road,
The rider, the birds that range
From cloud to tumbling cloud,
Minute by minute they change;
A shadow of cloud on the stream
Changes minute by minute;
A horse-hoof slides on the brim,
And a horse plashes within it;
The long-legged moor-hens dive,
And hens to moor-cocks call;
Minute by minute they live:
The stone's in the midst of all.

Too long a sacrifice
Can make a stone of the heart.
O when may it suffice?
That is Heaven's part, our part
To murmur name upon name,
As a mother names her child
When sleep at last has come
On limbs that had run wild.
What is it but nightfall?
No, no, not night but death;
Was it needless death after all?
For England may keep faith
For all that is done and said.
We know their dream; enough
To know they dreamed and are dead;
And what if excess of love
Bewildered them till they died?
I write it out in a verse—
MacDonagh and MacBride
And Connolly and Pearse
Now and in time to be,
Wherever green is worn,
Are changed, changed utterly:
A terrible beauty is born.

25 *September* 1916

118 ## *Sixteen Dead Men*

O but we talked at large before
The sixteen men were shot,
But who can talk of give and take,
What should be and what not
While those dead men are loitering there
To stir the boiling pot?

You say that we should still the land
Till Germany's overcome;
But who is there to argue that
Now Pearse is deaf and dumb?
And is their logic to outweigh
MacDonagh's bony thumb?

How could you dream they'd listen
That have an ear alone
For those new comrades they have found,
Lord Edward and Wolfe Tone,
Or meddle with our give and take
That converse bone to bone?

119 ## *An Irish Airman Foresees His Death**

I know that I shall meet my fate
Somewhere among the clouds above;
Those that I fight I do not hate,
Those that I guard I do not love;
My country is Kiltartan Cross,
My countrymen Kiltartan's poor,
No likely end could bring them loss
Or leave them happier than before.
Nor law, nor duty bade me fight,
Nor public men, nor cheering crowds,

---

* Major Robert Gregory, recipient of the Military Cross and the Légion d'Honneur, was killed in action when his plane was shot down on the Italian front on 23 January 1918.

A lonely impulse of delight
Drove to this tumult in the clouds;
I balanced all, brought all to mind,
The years to come seemed waste of breath,
A waste of breath the years behind
In balance with this life, this death.

120

Reprisals

Some nineteen German planes, they say,
You had brought down before you died.
We called it a good death. Today
Can ghost or man be satisfied?
Although your last exciting year
Outweighed all other years, you said,
Though battle joy may be so dear
A memory, even to the dead,
It chases other thought away,
Yet rise from your Italian tomb,
Flit to Kiltartan Cross and stay
Till certain second thoughts have come
Upon the cause you served, that we
Imagined such a fine affair:
Half-drunk or whole-mad soldiery
Are murdering your tenants there.
Men that revere your father yet
Are shot at on the open plain.
Where may new-married women sit
And suckle children now? Armed men
May murder them in passing by
Nor law nor parliament take heed.
Then close your ears with dust and lie
Among the other cheated dead.

SIEGFRIED SASSOON
1886–1967

121   *'They'*

The Bishop tells us: 'When the boys come back
They will not be the same; for they'll have fought
In a just cause: they lead the last attack
On Anti-Christ; their comrades' blood has bought
New right to breed an honourable race,
They have challenged Death and dared him face to face.'

'We're none of us the same!' the boys reply.
'For George lost both his legs; and Bill's stone blind;
Poor Jim's shot through the lungs and like to die;
And Bert's gone syphilitic: you'll not find
A chap who's served that hasn't found *some* change.'
And the Bishop said: 'The ways of God are strange!'

122   *The Hero*

'Jack fell as he'd have wished,' the Mother said,
And folded up the letter that she'd read.
'The Colonel writes so nicely.' Something broke
In the tired voice that quavered to a choke.
She half looked up. 'We mothers are so proud
Of our dead soldiers.' Then her face was bowed.

Quietly the Brother Officer went out.
He'd told the poor old dear some gallant lies
That she would nourish all her days, no doubt.
For while he coughed and mumbled, her weak eyes
Had shone with gentle triumph, brimmed with joy,
Because he'd been so brave, her glorious boy.

He thought how 'Jack', cold-footed, useless swine,
Had panicked down the trench that night the mine
Went up at Wicked Corner; how he'd tried
To get sent home, and how, at last, he died,
Blown to small bits. And no one seemed to care
Except that lonely woman with white hair.

123 ## *The Rear-Guard*

(Hindenburg Line, April 1917)

Groping along the tunnel, step by step,
He winked his prying torch with patching glare
From side to side, and sniffed the unwholesome air.

Tins, boxes, bottles, shapes too vague to know;
A mirror smashed, the mattress from a bed;
And he, exploring fifty feet below
The rosy gloom of battle overhead.

Tripping, he grabbed the wall; saw someone lie
Humped at his feet, half-hidden by a rug,
And stooped to give the sleeper's arm a tug.
'I'm looking for headquarters.' No reply.
'God blast your neck!' (For days he'd had no sleep,)
'Get up and guide me through this stinking place.'

Savage, he kicked a soft, unanswering heap,
And flashed his beam across the livid face
Terribly glaring up, whose eyes yet wore
Agony dying hard ten days before;
And fists of fingers clutched a blackening wound.

Alone he staggered on until he found
Dawn's ghost that filtered down a shafted stair
To the dazed, muttering creatures underground
Who hear the boom of shells in muffled sound.
At last, with sweat of horror in his hair,
He climbed through darkness to the twilight air,
Unloading hell behind him step by step.

124 ## *The General*

'Good-morning; good-morning!' the General said
When we met him last week on our way to the line.
Now the soldiers he smiled at are most of 'em dead,
And we're cursing his staff for incompetent swine.

'He's a cheery old card,' grunted Harry to Jack
As they slogged up to Arras with rifle and pack.

.   .   .

But he did for them both by his plan of attack.

125   *Glory of Women*

You love us when we're heroes, home on leave,
Or wounded in a mentionable place.
You worship decorations; you believe
That chivalry redeems the war's disgrace.
You make us shells. You listen with delight,
By tales of dirt and danger fondly thrilled.
You crown our distant ardours while we fight,
And mourn our laurelled memories when we're killed.
You can't believe that British troops 'retire'
When hell's last horror breaks them, and they run,
Trampling the terrible corpses—blind with blood.
    O German mother dreaming by the fire,
    While you are knitting socks to send your son
    His face is trodden deeper in the mud.

126   *Everyone Sang*

Everyone suddenly burst out singing;
And I was filled with such delight
As prisoned birds must find in freedom,
Winging wildly across the white
Orchards and dark-green fields; on—on—and out of sight.

Everyone's voice was suddenly lifted;
And beauty came like the setting sun:
My heart was shaken with tears; and horror
Drifted away . . . O, but Everyone
Was a bird; and the song was wordless; the singing will
    never be done.

EDWARD THOMAS

1878–1917

127   *In Memoriam (Easter 1915)*

The flowers left thick at nightfall in the wood
This Eastertide call into mind the men,
Now far from home, who, with their sweethearts, should
Have gathered them and will do never again.

128   *The Cherry Trees*

The cherry trees bend over and are shedding
On the old road where all that passed are dead,
Their petals, strewing the grass as for a wedding
This early May morn when there is none to wed.

129   *Rain*

Rain, midnight rain, nothing but the wild rain
On this bleak hut, and solitude, and me
Remembering again that I shall die
And neither hear the rain nor give it thanks
For washing me cleaner than I have been
Since I was born into this solitude.
Blessed are the dead that the rain rains upon:
But here I pray that none whom once I loved
Is dying tonight or lying still awake
Solitary, listening to the rain,
Either in pain or thus in sympathy
Helpless among the living and the dead,
Like a cold water among broken reeds,
Myriads of broken reeds all still and stiff,
Like me who have no love which this wild rain
Has not dissolved except the love of death,
If love it be towards what is perfect and
Cannot, the tempest tells me, disappoint.

130 *As the team's head brass*

As the team's head brass flashed out on the turn
The lovers disappeared into the wood.
I sat among the boughs of the fallen elm
That strewed an angle of the fallow, and
Watched the plough narrowing a yellow square
Of charlock. Every time the horses turned
Instead of treading me down, the ploughman leaned
Upon the handles to say or ask a word,
About the weather, next about the war.
Scraping the share he faced towards the wood,
And screwed along the furrow till the brass flashed
Once more.
       The blizzard felled the elm whose crest
I sat in, by a woodpecker's round hole,
The ploughman said. 'When will they take it away?'
'When the war's over.' So the talk began—
One minute and an interval of ten,
A minute more and the same interval.
'Have you been out?' 'No.' 'And don't want to, perhaps?'
'If I could only come back again, I should.
I could spare an arm. l shouldn't want to lose
A leg. If I should lose my head, why, so,
I should want nothing more. . . . Have many gone
From here?' 'Yes.' 'Many lost?' 'Yes, a good few.
Only two teams work on the farm this year.
One of my mates is dead. The second day
In France they killed him. It was back in March,
The very night of the blizzard, too. Now if
He had stayed here we should have moved the tree.'
'And I should not have sat here. Everything
Would have been different. For it would have been
Another world.' 'Ay, and a better, though
If we could see all all might seem good.' Then
The lovers came out of the wood again:
The horses started and for the last time
I watched the clods crumble and topple over
After the ploughshare and the stumbling team.

IVOR GURNEY

1890–1937

131   *To His Love*

He's gone, and all our plans
   Are useless indeed.
We'll walk no more on Cotswold
   Where the sheep feed
   Quietly and take no heed.

His body that was so quick
   Is not as you
Knew it, on Severn river
   Under the blue
   Driving our small boat through.

You would not know him now . . .
   But still he died
Nobly, so cover him over
   With violets of pride
   Purple from Severn side.

Cover him, cover him soon!
   And with thick-set
Masses of memoried flowers—
   Hide that red wet
   Thing I must somehow forget.

132   *Ballad of the Three Spectres*

As I went up by Ovillers
   In mud and water cold to the knee,
There went three jeering, fleering spectres,
   That walked abreast and talked of me.

The first said, 'Here's a right brave soldier
   That walks the dark unfearingly;
Soon he'll come back on a fine stretcher,
   And laughing for a nice Blighty.'

The second, 'Read his face, old comrade,
    No kind of lucky chance I see;
One day he'll freeze in mud to the marrow,
    Then look his last on Picardie.'

Though bitter the word of these first twain
    Curses the third spat venomously;
'He'll stay untouched till the war's last dawning
    Then live one hour of agony.'

Liars the first two were. Behold me
    At sloping arms by one—two—three;
Waiting the time I shall discover
    Whether the third spake verity.

133   *The Silent One*

Who died on the wires, and hung there, one of two—
Who for his hours of life had chattered through
Infinite lovely chatter of Bucks accent:
Yet faced unbroken wires; stepped over, and went
A noble fool, faithful to his stripes—and ended.
But I weak, hungry, and willing only for the chance
Of line—to fight in the line, lay down under unbroken
Wires, and saw the flashes and kept unshaken,
Till the politest voice—a finicking accent, said:
'Do you think you might crawl through there: there's a hole.'
Darkness, shot at: I smiled, as politely replied—
'I'm afraid not, Sir.' There was no hole no way to be seen,
Nothing but chance of death, after tearing of clothes.
Kept flat, and watched the darkness, hearing bullets whizzing—
And thought of music—and swore deep heart's deep oaths
(Polite to God) and retreated and came on again,
Again retreated—and a second time faced the screen.

ISAAC ROSENBERG

1890–1918

134 *On Receiving News of the War*

Snow is a strange white word;
No ice or frost
Have asked of bud or bird
For Winter's cost.

Yet ice and frost and snow
From earth to sky
This Summer land doth know,
No man knows why.

In all men's hearts it is.
Some spirit old
Hath turned with malign kiss
Our lives to mould.

Red fangs have torn His face.
God's blood is shed.
He mourns from His lone place
His children dead.

O! ancient crimson curse!
Corrode, consume.
Give back this universe
Its pristine bloom.

Cape Town, 1914

135 *August 1914*

What in our lives is burnt
In the fire of this?
The heart's dear granary?
The much we shall miss?

183

Three lives hath one life—
Iron, honey, gold.
The gold, the honey gone—
Left is the hard and cold.

Iron are our lives
Molten right through our youth.
A burnt space through ripe fields,
A fair mouth's broken tooth.

1916

136   *Break of Day in the Trenches*

The darkness crumbles away.
It is the same old druid Time as ever,
Only a live thing leaps my hand,
A queer sardonic rat,
As I pull the parapet's poppy
To stick behind my ear.
Droll rat, they would shoot you if they knew
Your cosmopolitan sympathies.
Now you have touched this English hand
You will do the same to a German
Soon, no doubt, if it be your pleasure
To cross the sleeping green between.
It seems you inwardly grin as you pass
Strong eyes, fine limbs, haughty athletes,
Less chanced than you for life,
Bonds to the whims of murder,
Sprawled in the bowels of the earth,
The torn fields of France.
What do you see in our eyes
At the shrieking iron and flame
Hurled through still heavens?
What quaver—what heart aghast?
Poppies whose roots are in man's veins
Drop, and are ever dropping;
But mine in my ear is safe—
Just a little white with the dust.

June 1916

137 *Dead Man's Dump*

The plunging limbers over the shattered track
Racketed with their rusty freight,
Stuck out like many crowns of thorns,
And the rusty stakes like sceptres old
To stay the flood of brutish men
Upon our brothers dear.

The wheels lurched over sprawled dead
But pained them not, though their bones crunched,
Their shut mouths made no moan,
They lie there huddled, friend and foeman,
Man born of man, and born of woman,
And shells go crying over them
From night till night and now.

Earth has waited for them
All the time of their growth
Fretting for their decay:
Now she has them at last!
In the strength of their strength
Suspended—stopped and held.

What fierce imaginings their dark souls lit?
Earth! have they gone into you?
Somewhere they must have gone,
And flung on your hard back
Is their souls' sack,
Emptied of God-ancestralled essences.
Who hurled them out? Who hurled?

None saw their spirits' shadow shake the grass,
Or stood aside for the half-used life to pass
Out of those doomed nostrils and the doomed mouth,
When the swift iron burning bee
Drained the wild honey of their youth.

What of us, who flung on the shrieking pyre,
Walk, our usual thoughts untouched,
Our lucky limbs as on ichor fed,
Immortal seeming ever?

Perhaps when the flames beat loud on us,
A fear may choke in our veins
And the startled blood may stop.

The air is loud with death,
The dark air spurts with fire
The explosions ceaseless are.
Timelessly now, some minutes past,
These dead strode time with vigorous life,
Till the shrapnel called 'an end!'
But not to all. In bleeding pangs
Some borne on stretchers dreamed of home,
Dear things, war-blotted from their hearts.

A man's brains splattered on
A stretcher-bearer's face;
His shook shoulders slipped their load,
But when they bent to look again
The drowning soul was sunk too deep
For human tenderness.

They left this dead with the older dead,
Stretched at the cross roads.
Burnt black by strange decay,
Their sinister faces lie;
The lid over each eye,
The grass and coloured clay
More motions have then they,
Joined to the great sunk silences.

Here is one not long dead;
His dark hearing caught our far wheels,
And the choked soul stretched weak hands
To reach the living word the far wheels said,
The blood-dazed intelligence beating for light,
Crying through the suspense of the far torturing wheels
Swift for the end to break,
Or the wheels to break,
Cried as the tide of the world broke over his sight.

Will they come? Will they ever come?
Even as the mixed hoofs of the mules,
The quivering-bellied mules,

And the rushing wheels all mixed
With his tortured upturned sight,
So we crashed round the bend,
We heard his weak scream,
We heard his very last sound,
And our wheels grazed his dead face.

1917

138   *Returning, We Hear the Larks*

Sombre the night is.
And though we have our lives, we know
What sinister threat lurks there.

Dragging these anguished limbs, we only know
This poison-blasted track opens on our camp—
On a little safe sleep.

But hark! joy—joy—strange joy.
Lo! heights of night ringing with unseen larks.
Music showering our upturned list'ning faces.

Death could drop from the dark
As easily as song—
But song only dropped,
Like a blind man's dreams on the sand
By dangerous tides,
Like a girl's dark hair for she dreams no ruin lies there,
Or her kisses where a serpent hides.

1917

WILFRED OWEN

1893–1918

139   *Anthem for Doomed Youth*

What passing-bells for these who die as cattle?
  —Only the monstrous anger of the guns.
  Only the stuttering rifles' rapid rattle
Can patter out their hasty orisons.
No mockeries now for them; no prayers nor bells;
  Nor any voice of mourning save the choirs,—
The shrill, demented choirs of wailing shells;
  And bugles calling for them from sad shires.

What candles may be held to speed them all?
  Not in the hands of boys but in their eyes
Shall shine the holy glimmers of goodbyes.
  The pallor of girls' brows shall be their pall;
Their flowers the tenderness of patient minds,
And each slow dusk a drawing-down of blinds.

140   *Dulce Et Decorum Est*

Bent double, like old beggars under sacks,
Knock-kneed, coughing like hags, we cursed through sludge,
Till on the haunting flares we turned our backs
And towards our distant rest began to trudge.
Men marched asleep. Many had lost their boots
But limped on, blood-shod. All went lame; all blind;
Drunk with fatigue; deaf even to the hoots
Of tired, outstripped Five-Nines that dropped behind.

Gas! GAS! Quick, boys!—An ecstasy of fumbling,
Fitting the clumsy helmets just in time;
But someone still was yelling out and stumbling,
And flound'ring like a man in fire or lime . . .
Dim, through the misty panes and thick green light,
As under a green sea, I saw him drowning.

In all my dreams, before my helpless sight,
He plunges at me, guttering, choking, drowning.

If in some smothering dreams you too could pace
Behind the wagon that we flung him in,
And watch the white eyes writhing in his face,
His hanging face, like a devil's sick of sin;
If you could hear, at every jolt, the blood
Come gargling from the froth-corrupted lungs,
Obscene as cancer, bitter as the cud
Of vile, incurable sores on innocent tongues,—
My friend, you would not tell with such high zest
To children ardent for some desperate glory,
The old Lie: Dulce et decorum est
Pro patria mori.

141 *Exposure*

Our brains ache, in the merciless iced east winds that knive us . . .
Wearied we keep awake because the night is silent . . .
Low, drooping flares confuse our memory of the salient . . .
Worried by silence, sentries whisper, curious, nervous,
     But nothing happens.

Watching, we hear the mad gusts tugging on the wire,
Like twitching agonies of men among its brambles.
Northward, incessantly, the flickering gunnery rumbles,
Far off, like a dull rumour of some other war.
     What are we doing here?

The poignant misery of dawn begins to grow . . .
We only know war lasts, rain soaks, and clouds sag stormy.
Dawn massing in the east her melancholy army
Attacks once more in ranks on shivering ranks of grey,
     But nothing happens.

Sudden successive flights of bullets streak the silence.
Less deathly than the air that shudders black with snow,
With sidelong flowing flakes that flock, pause, and renew;
We watch them wandering up and down the wind's nonchalance,
     But nothing happens.

Pale flakes with fingering stealth come feeling for our faces—
We cringe in holes, back on forgotten dreams, and stare, snow-dazed,
Deep into grassier ditches. So we drowse, sun-dozed,
Littered with blossoms trickling where the blackbird fusses,
    —Is it that we are dying?

Slowly our ghosts drag home: glimpsing the sunk fires, glozed
With crusted dark-red jewels; crickets jingle there;
For hours the innocent mice rejoice: the house is theirs;
Shutters and doors, all closed: on us the doors are closed,—
    We turn back to our dying.

Since we believe not otherwise can kind fires burn;
Nor ever suns smile true on child, or field, or fruit.
For God's invincible spring our love is made afraid;
Therefore, not loath, we lie out here; therefore were born,
    For love of God seems dying.

Tonight, this frost will fasten on this mud and us,
Shrivelling many hands, puckering foreheads crisp.
The burying-party, picks and shovels in shaking grasp,
Pause over half-known faces. All their eyes are ice,
    But nothing happens.

142   *Insensibility*

I

Happy are men who yet before they are killed
Can let their veins run cold.
Whom no compassion fleers
Or makes their feet
Sore on the alleys cobbled with their brothers.
The front line withers.
But they are troops who fade, not flowers,
For poets' tearful fooling:
Men, gaps for filling:
Losses, who might have fought
Longer; but no one bothers.

II

And some cease feeling
Even themselves or for themselves.
Dullness best solves
The tease and doubt of shelling,
And Chance's strange arithmetic
Comes simpler than the reckoning of their shilling.
They keep no check on armies' decimation.

III

Happy are these who lose imagination:
They have enough to carry with ammunition.
Their spirit drags no pack.
Their old wounds, save with cold, can not more ache.
Having seen all things red,
Their eyes are rid
Of the hurt of the colour of blood for ever.
And terror's first constriction over,
Their hearts remain small-drawn.
Their senses in some scorching cautery of battle
Now long since ironed,
Can laugh among the dying, unconcerned.

IV

Happy the soldier home, with not a notion
How somewhere, every dawn, some men attack,
And many sighs are drained.
Happy the lad whose mind was never trained:
His days are worth forgetting more than not.
He sings along the march
Which we march taciturn, because of dusk,
The long, forlorn, relentless trend
From larger day to huger night.

V

We wise, who with a thought besmirch
Blood over all our soul,
How should we see our task
But through his blunt and lashless eyes?

Alive, he is not vital overmuch;
Dying, not mortal overmuch;
Nor sad, nor proud,
Nor curious at all.
He cannot tell
Old men's placidity from his.

VI

But cursed are dullards whom no cannon stuns,
That they should be as stones.
Wretched are they, and mean
With paucity that never was simplicity.
By choice they made themselves immune
To pity and whatever moans in man
Before the last sea and the hapless stars;
Whatever mourns when many leave these shores;
Whatever shares
The eternal reciprocity of tears.

143   *The Send-Off*

Down the close darkening lanes they sang their way
To the siding-shed,
And lined the train with faces grimly gay.

Their breasts were stuck all white with wreath and spray
As men's are, dead.

Dull porters watched them, and a casual tramp
Stood staring hard,
Sorry to miss them from the upland camp.

Then, unmoved, signals nodded, and a lamp
Winked to the guard.

So secretly, like wrongs hushed-up, they went.
They were not ours:
We never heard to which front these were sent;

Nor there if they yet mock what women meant
Who gave them flowers.

Shall they return to beating of great bells
In wild train-loads?
A few, a few, too few for drums and yells,

May creep back, silent, to village wells,
Up half-known roads.

144   *Futility*

Move him into the sun—
Gently its touch awoke him once,
At home, whispering of fields half-sown.
Always it woke him, even in France,
Until this morning and this snow.
If anything might rouse him now
The kind old sun will know.

Think how it wakes the seeds—
Woke once the clays of a cold star.
Are limbs, so dear achieved, are sides
Full-nerved, still warm, too hard to stir?
Was it for this the clay grew tall?
—O what made fatuous sunbeams toil
To break earth's sleep at all?

145   *Strange Meeting*

It seemed that out of battle I escaped
Down some profound dull tunnel, long since scooped
Through granites which titanic wars had groined.

Yet also there encumbered sleepers groaned,
Too fast in thought or death to be bestirred.
Then, as I probed them, one sprang up, and stared
With piteous recognition in fixed eyes,
Lifting distressful hands, as if to bless.
And by his smile, I knew that sullen hall,—
By his dead smile I knew we stood in Hell.

With a thousand pains that vision's face was grained;
Yet no blood reached there from the upper ground,
And no guns thumped, or down the flues made moan.
'Strange friend,' I said, 'here is no cause to mourn.'
'None,' said that other, 'save the undone years,
The hopelessness. Whatever hope is yours,
Was my life also; I went hunting wild
After the wildest beauty in the world,
Which lies not calm in eyes, or braided hair,
But mocks the steady running of the hour,
And if it grieves, grieves richlier than here.
For by my glee might many men have laughed,
And of my weeping something had been left,
Which must die now. I mean the truth untold,
The pity of war, the pity war distilled.
Now men will go content with what we spoiled,
Or, discontent, boil bloody, and be spilled.
They will be swift with swiftness of the tigress.
None will break ranks, though nations trek from progress.
Courage was mine, and I had mystery,
Wisdom was mine, and I had mastery:
To miss the march of this retreating world
Into vain citadels that are not walled.
Then, when much blood had clogged their chariot-wheels,
I would go up and wash them from sweet wells,
Even with truths that lie too deep for taint.
I would have poured my spirit without stint
But not through wounds; not on the cess of war.
Foreheads of men have bled where no wounds were.

'I am the enemy you killed, my friend.
I knew you in this dark: for so you frowned
Yesterday through me as you jabbed and killed.
I parried; but my hands were loath and cold.
Let us sleep now. . . .'

ROBERT GRAVES

1895–1985

146

Sergeant-Major Money

(1917)

It wasn't our battalion, but we lay alongside it,
　So the story is as true as the telling is frank.
They hadn't one Line-officer left, after Arras,
　Except a batty major and the Colonel, who drank.

'B' Company Commander was fresh from the Depot,
　An expert on gas drill, otherwise a dud;
So Sergeant-Major Money carried on, as instructed,
　And that's where the swaddies began to sweat blood.

His Old Army humour was so well-spiced and hearty
　That one poor sod shot himself, and one lost his wits;
But discipline's maintained, and back in rest-billets
　The Colonel congratulates 'B' company on their kits.

The subalterns went easy, as was only natural
　With a terror like Money driving the machine,
Till finally two Welshmen, butties from the Rhondda,
　Bayoneted their bugbear in a field-canteen.

Well, we couldn't blame the officers, they relied on Money;
　We couldn't blame the pitboys, their courage was grand;
Or, least of all, blame Money, an old stiff surviving
　In a New (bloody) Army he couldn't understand.

147

Recalling War

Entrance and exit wounds are silvered clean,
The track aches only when the rain reminds.
The one-legged man forgets his leg of wood,
The one-armed man his jointed wooden arm.
The blinded man sees with his ears and hands
As much or more than once with both his eyes.
Their war was fought these twenty years ago

And now assumes the nature-look of time,
As when the morning traveller turns and views
His wild night-stumbling carved into a hill.

What, then, was war? No mere discord of flags
But an infection of the common sky
That sagged ominously upon the earth
Even when the season was the airiest May.
Down pressed the sky, and we, oppressed, thrust out
Boastful tongue, clenched fist and valiant yard.
Natural infirmities were out of mode,
For Death was young again: patron alone
Of healthy dying, premature fate-spasm.

Fear made fine bed-fellows. Sick with delight
At life's discovered transitoriness,
Our youth became all-flesh and waived the mind.
Never was such antiqueness of romance,
Such tasty honey oozing from the heart.
And old importances came swimming back—
Wine, meat, log-fires, a roof over the head,
A weapon at the thigh, surgeons at call.
Even there was a use again for God—
A word of rage in lack of meat, wine, fire,
In ache of wounds beyond all surgeoning.

War was return of earth to ugly earth,
War was foundering of sublimities,
Extinction of each happy art and faith
By which the world had still kept head in air.
Protesting logic or protesting love,
Until the unendurable moment struck—
The inward scream, the duty to run mad.

And we recall the merry ways of guns—
Nibbling the walls of factory and church
Like a child, piecrust; felling groves of trees
Like a child, dandelions with a switch!
Machine-guns rattle toy-like from a hill,
Down in a row the brave tin-soldiers fall:
A sight to be recalled in elder days
When learnedly the future we devote
To yet more boastful visions of despair.

148 *The Persian Version*

Truth-loving Persians do not dwell upon
The trivial skirmish fought near Marathon.
As for the Greek theatrical tradition
Which represents that summer's expedition
Not as a mere reconnaissance in force
By three brigades of foot and one of horse
(Their left flank covered by some obsolete
Light craft detached from the main Persian fleet)
But as a grandiose, ill-starred attempt
To conquer Greece—they treat it with contempt;
And only incidentally refute
Major Greek claims, by stressing what repute
The Persian monarch and the Persian nation
Won by this salutary demonstration:
Despite a strong defence and adverse weather
All arms combined magnificently together.

EDMUND BLUNDEN
1896–1974

149 *Two Voices*

'There's something in the air,' he said
    In the large parlour cool and bare;
The plain words in his hearers bred
    A tumult, yet in silence there
All waited; wryly gay, he left the phrase,
Ordered the march and bade us go our ways.

'We're going South, man'; as he spoke
    The howitzer with huge ping-bang
Racked the light hut; as thus he broke
    The death-news, bright the skylarks sang;
He took his riding-crop and humming went
Among the apple-trees all bloom and scent.

Now far withdraws the roaring night
  Which wrecked our flower after the first
Of those two voices; misty light
  Shrouds Thiepval Wood and all its worst:
But still 'There's something in the air' I hear,
And still 'We're going South, man,' deadly near.

150   *The Zonnebeke Road*

Morning, if this late withered light can claim
Some kindred with that merry flame
Which the young day was wont to fling through space!
Agony stares from each gray face.
And yet the day is come; stand down! stand down!
Your hands unclasp from rifles while you can;
The frost has pierced them to the bended bone?
Why, see old Stevens there, that iron man,
Melting the ice to shave his grotesque chin:
Go ask him, shall we win?
I never liked this bay, some foolish fear
Caught me the first time that I came in here;
That dugout fallen in awakes, perhaps,
Some formless haunting of some corpse's chaps.
True, and wherever we have held the line,
There were such corners, seeming-saturnine
For no good cause.
                    Now where Haymarket starts,
That is no place for soldiers with weak hearts;
The minenwerfers have it to the inch.
Look, how the snow-dust whisks along the road,
Piteous and silly; the stones themselves must flinch
In this east wind; the low sky like a load
Hangs over—a dead-weight. But what a pain
Must gnaw where its clay cheek
Crushes the shell-chopped trees that fang the plain—
The ice-bound throat gulps out a gargoyle shriek.
The wretched wire before the village line
Rattles like rusty brambles or dead bine,
And then the daylight oozes into dun;
Black pillars, those are trees where roadways run.
Even Ypres now would warm our souls; fond fool,
Our tour's but one night old, seven more to cool!

O screaming dumbness, O dull clashing death,
Shreds of dead grass and willows, homes and men,
Watch as you will, men clench their chattering teeth
And freeze you back with that one hope, disdain.

151 ## *Vlamertinghe: Passing the Château,*
July 1917

'And all her silken flanks with garlands drest'—
But we are coming to the sacrifice.
Must those have flowers who are not yet gone West?
May those have flowers who live with death and lice?
This must be the floweriest place
That earth allows; the queenly face
Of the proud mansion borrows grace for grace
Spite of those brute guns lowing at the skies.

Bold great daisies, golden lights,
Bubbling roses' pinks and whites—
Such a gay carpet! poppies by the million;
Such damask! such vermilion!
But if you ask me, mate, the choice of colour
Is scarcely right; this red should have been much duller.

152 ## *Report on Experience*

I have been young, and now am not too old;
And I have seen the righteous forsaken,
His health, his honour and his quality taken.
    This is not what we were formerly told.

I have seen a green country, useful to the race,
Knocked silly with guns and mines, its villages vanished,
Even the last rat and last kestrel banished—
    God bless us all, this was peculiar grace.

I knew Seraphina; Nature gave her hue,
Glance, sympathy, note, like one from Eden.
I saw her smile warp, heard her lyric deaden;
    She turned to harlotry;—this I took to be new.

Say what you will, our God sees how they run.
These disillusions are His curious proving
That He loves humanity and will go on loving;
Over these are faith, life, virtue in the sun.

RICHARD ALDINGTON

1892–1962

153   *Battlefield*

The wind is piercing chill
And blows fine grains of snow
Over this shell-rent ground;
Every house in sight
Is smashed and desolate.

But in this fruitless land,
Thorny with wire
And foul with rotting clothes and sacks,
The crosses flourish—
Ci-gît, ci-gît, ci-gît . . .
'Ci-gît 1 soldat Allemand,
Priez pour lui.'

EDGELL RICKWORD

1898–1982

154   *Winter Warfare*

Colonel Cold strode up the Line
   (tabs of rime and spurs of ice);
stiffened all that met his glare:
   horses, men, and lice.

Visited a forward post,
   left them burning, ear to foot;
fingers stuck to biting steel,
   toes to frozen boot.

Stalked on into No Man's Land,
   turned the wire to fleecy wool,
iron stakes to sugar sticks
   snapping at a pull.

Those who watched with hoary eyes
   saw two figures gleaming there;
Hauptmann Kälte, Colonel Cold,
   gaunt in the grey air.

Stiffly, tinkling spurs they moved,
   glassy-eyed, with glinting heel
stabbing those who lingered there
   torn by screaming steel.

E. E. CUMMINGS

1894–1962

155   my sweet old etcetera
aunt lucy during the recent

war could and what
is more did tell you just
what everybody was fighting

for,
my sister

isabel created hundreds
(and
hundreds)of socks not to
mention shirts fleaproof earwarmers

etcetera wristers etcetera, my
mother hoped that

i would die etcetera
bravely of course my father used
to become hoarse talking about how it was
a privilege and if only he
could meanwhile my

self etcetera lay quietly
in the deep mud et

cetera
(dreaming,
et
  cetera, of
Your smile
eyes knees and of your Etcetera)

156   'next to of course god america i
love you land of the pilgrims' and so forth oh
say can you see by the dawn's early my
country 'tis of centuries come and go
and are no more what of it we should worry
in every language even deafanddumb
thy sons acclaim your glorious name by gorry
by jingo by gee by gosh by gum
why talk of beauty what could be more beaut-
iful than these heroic happy dead
who rushed like lions to the roaring slaughter
they did not stop to think they died instead
then shall the voice of liberty be mute?'

He spoke.   And drank rapidly a glass of water

157   i sing of Olaf glad and big
whose warmest heart recoiled at war:
a conscientious object-or

his wellbelovéd colonel(trig
westpointer most succinctly bred)
took erring Olaf soon in hand;
but—though an host of overjoyed
noncoms(first knocking on the head
him)do through icy waters roll
that helplessness which others stroke
with brushes recently employed
anent this muddy toiletbowl,
while kindred intellects evoke
allegiance per blunt instruments—

Olaf(being to all intents
a corpse and wanting any rag
upon what God unto him gave)
responds, without getting annoyed
'I will not kiss your f.ing flag'

straightway the silver bird looked grave
(departing hurriedly to shave)

but—though all kinds of officers
(a yearning nation's blueeyed pride)
their passive prey did kick and curse
until for wear their clarion
voices and boots were much the worse,
and egged the firstclassprivates on
his rectum wickedly to tease
by means of skilfully applied
bayonets roasted hot with heat—
Olaf(upon what were once knees)
does almost ceaselessly repeat
'there is some s. I will not eat'

our president, being of which
assertions duly notified
threw the yellowsonofabitch
into a dungeon, where he died

Christ(of His mercy infinite)
i pray to see;and Olaf,too

preponderatingly because
unless statistics lie he was
more brave than me:more blond than you.

JOHN PEALE BISHOP

1892–1944

158

In the Dordogne

We stood up before day
And shaved by metal mirrors
In the faint flame of a faulty candle.

And we hurried down the wide stone stairs
With a clirr of spur chains
On stone. And we thought
When the cocks crew
That the ghosts of a dead dawn
Would rise and be off. But they stayed
Under the window, crouched on the staircase,
The windows now the color of morning.

The colonel slept in the bed of Sully
Slept on: but we descended
And saw in a niche in the white wall
A Virgin and Child, serene
Who were stone: we saw sycamores:
Three aged mages
Scattering gifts of gold.
But when the wind blew, there were autumn odors
And the shadowed trees
Had the dapplings of young fawns.

And each day one died or another
Died: each week we sent out thousands
That returned by hundreds
Wounded or gassed. And those that died
We buried close to the old wall
Within a stone's throw of Périgord
Under the tower of the troubadours.

And because we had courage;
Because there was courage and youth
Ready to be wasted; because we endured
And were prepared for all endurance;
We thought something must come of it:
That the Virgin would raise her Child and smile;
The trees gather up their gold and go;
That courage would avail something
And something we had never lost
Be regained through wastage, by dying,
By burying the others under the English tower.

The colonel slept on in the bed of Sully
Under the ravelling curtains; the leaves fell
And were blown away; the young men rotted

Under the shadow of the tower
In a land of small clear silent streams
Where the coming on of evening is
The letting down of blue and azure veils
Over the clear and silent streams
Delicately bordered by poplars.

DAVID JONES

1895–1974

159   from *In Parenthesis*

But sweet sister death has gone debauched today and stalks
on this high ground with strumpet confidence, makes no coy
veiling of her appetite but leers from you to me with all her
parts discovered.
    By one and one the line gaps, where her fancy will—how-
soever they may howl for their virginity
she holds them—who impinge less on space
sink limply to a heap
nourish a lesser category of being
like those other who fructify the land
like Tristram
Lamorak de Galis
Alisand le Orphelin
Beaumains who was youngest
or all of them in shaft-shade
at strait Thermopylae
or the sweet brothers Balin and Balan
embraced beneath their single monument.
    Jonathan my lovely one
on Gelboe mountain
and the young man Absalom.
White Hart transfixed in his dark lodge.
Peredur of steel arms
and he who with intention took grass of that field to be for
him the Species of Bread.
    Taillefer the maker,
and on the same day,

thirty thousand other ranks.
And in the country of Béarn—Oliver
and all the rest—so many without memento
beneath the tumuli on the high hills
and under the harvest places.[1]

But how intolerably bright the morning is where we who are
alive and remain, walk lifted up, carried forward by an effec-
tive word.

But red horses now—blare every trump without economy,
burn boat and sever every tie every held thing goes west and
tethering snapt, bolts unshot and brass doors flung wide and
you go forward, foot goes another step further.

The immediate foreground sheers up, tilts toward,
like an high wall falling.
There she breaches black perpendiculars
where the counter-barrage warms to the seventh power where
the Three Children walk under the fair morning
and the Twin Brother[2]
and the high grass soddens through your puttees
and dew asperges the freshly dead.

There doesn't seem a soul about yet surely we walk already
near his preserves; there goes old Dawes as large as life and
there is Lazarus Cohen like on field-days, he always would
have his entrenching-tool-blade-carrier hung low, jogging
on his fat arse.
    They pass a quite ordinary message about keeping aligned
with No. 8.

You drop apprehensively—the sun gone out,
strange airs smite your body
and muck rains straight from heaven
and everlasting doors lift up for 'o2 Weavel.
    You cant see anything but sheen on drifting particles and
you move forward in your private bright cloud like
one assumed
who is borne up by an exterior volition.

You stumble on a bunch of six with Sergeant Quilter getting
them out again to the proper interval, and when the chemical

thick air dispels you see briefly and with great clearness what
kind of a show this is.

The gentle slopes are green to remind you
of South English places, only far wider and flatter spread and
grooved and harrowed criss-cross whitely and the disturbed
subsoil heaped up albescent.

Across upon this undulated board of verdure chequered
bright
when you look to left and right
small, drab, bundled pawns severally make effort
moved in tenuous line
and if you looked behind—the next wave came slowly, as suc-
cessive surfs creep in to dissipate on flat shore;
and to your front, stretched long laterally,
and receded deeply,
the dark wood.

And now the gradient runs more flatly toward the separate
scared saplings, where they make fringe for the interior thicket
and you take notice.
    There between the thinning uprights
at the margin
straggle tangled oak and flayed sheeny beech-bole, and fragile
birch whose silver queenery is draggled and ungraced
and June shoots lopt
and fresh stalks bled
            runs the Jerry trench.
And cork-screw stapled trip-wire
to snare among the briars
and iron warp with bramble weft
with meadow-sweet and lady-smock
for a fair camouflage.

Mr Jenkins half inclined his head to them—he walked just
barely in advance of his platoon and immediately to the left of
Private Ball.

    He makes the conventional sign
and there is the deeply inward effort of spent men who would
make response for him,
and take it at the double.

He sinks on one knee
and now on the other,
his upper body tilts in rigid inclination
this way and back;
weighted lanyard runs to full tether,
        swings like a pendulum
        and the clock run down.
Lurched over, jerked iron saucer over tilted brow,
clampt unkindly over lip and chin
nor no ventaille to this darkening
        and masked face lifts to grope the air
and so disconsolate;
enfeebled fingering at a paltry strap—
buckle holds,
holds him blind against the morning.
   Then stretch still where weeds pattern the chalk predella
—where it rises to his wire[3]—and Sergeant T. Quilter takes
over.

NOTES

[1] *shaft-shade.* Cf. Herodotus, book vii, *Polymnia*, Dieneces' speech.

sweet brothers . . . monument. Cf. Malory, book ii, ch. 19.

White Hart transfixed. Cf. *Richard II*, Act v, Sc. vi.

Peredur of steel arms. Peredur. The *Percivale* of the romances called 'of steel arms' in the Triads, and by the Gododdin poet: 'Peredur with arms of steel ...' (he commemorates other warriors, and proceeds) '. . . though men might have slain them, they too were slayers, none returned to their homes.'

with intention . . . Species of Bread. In some battle of the Welsh, all reference to which escapes me, a whole army ate grass in token of the Body of the Lord. Also somewhere in the Malory, a single knight feeling himself at the point of death makes this same act.

Taillefer . . . other ranks. Cf. Wace, *Roman de Rou:* 'Then Taillefer, who sang right well, rode before the duke singing of Carlemaine and of Rollant, of Oliver and the vassals who died at Renchevals.'

country of Béarn . . . harvest places. Not that Roncesvalles is in the Béarn country, but I associate it with Béarn because, once, looking from a window in Salies-de-Béarn I could see a gap in the hills, which my hostess told me was indeed the pass where Roland fell. [DJ]

[2] *seventh power . . . Three Children . . . Twin Brother.* Cf. Book of Daniel, ch. iii. Here I identify 'The Great Twin Brethren' at the battle of Lake Regillus with the Second Person of the Blessed Trinity—who walked with the Three Children in the fiery furnace. [DJ]

[3] *chalk predella . . . his wire.* The approach to the German trenches here rose slightly, in low chalk ridges. [DJ]

LAURENCE BINYON
1869–1943

For the Fallen

(September 1914)

With proud thanksgiving, a mother for her children,
England mourns for her dead across the sea.
Flesh of her flesh they were, spirit of her spirit,
Fallen in the cause of the free.

Solemn the drums thrill: Death august and royal
Sings sorrow up into immortal spheres.
There is music in the midst of desolation
And a glory that shines upon our tears.

They went with songs to the battle, they were young,
Straight of limb, true of eye, steady and aglow.
They were staunch to the end against odds uncounted,
They fell with their faces to the foe.

They shall grow not old, as we that are left grow old:
Age shall not weary them, nor the years condemn.
At the going down of the sun and in the morning
We will remember them.

They mingle not with their laughing comrades again;
They sit no more at familiar tables of home;
They have no lot in our labour of the day-time;
They sleep beyond England's foam.

But where our desires are and our hopes profound,
Felt as a well-spring that is hidden from sight,
To the innermost heart of their own land they are known
As the stars are known to the Night;

As the stars that shall be bright when we are dust,
Moving in marches upon the heavenly plain,
As the stars that are starry in the time of our darkness,
To the end, to the end, they remain.

EZRA POUND

1885–1972

from *Hugh Selwyn Mauberley*

(*Life and contacts*)

These fought in any case,
and some believing,
          pro domo, in any case . . .

Some quick to arm,
some for adventure,
some from fear of weakness,
some from fear of censure,
some for love of slaughter, in imagination,
learning later . . .
some in fear, learning love of slaughter;
Died some, pro patria,
          non 'dulce' non 'et decor' . . .
walked eye-deep in hell
believing in old men's lies, then unbelieving
came home, home to a lie,
home to many deceits,
home to old lies and new infamy;
usury age-old and age-thick
and liars in public places.

Daring as never before, wastage as never before.
Young blood and high blood,
fair cheeks, and fine bodies;

fortitude as never before

frankness as never before,
disillusions as never told in the old days,
hysterias, trench confessions,
laughter out of dead bellies.

*

There died a myriad,
And of the best, among them,
For an old bitch gone in the teeth,
For a botched civilization,

Charm, smiling at the good mouth,
Quick eyes gone under earth's lid,

For two gross of broken statues,
For a few thousand battered books.

T. S. ELIOT

1888–1965

162   *Triumphal March*

Stone, bronze, stone, steel, stone, oakleaves, horses' heels
Over the paving.
And the flags. And the trumpets. And so many eagles.
How many? Count them. And such a press of people.
We hardly knew ourselves that day, or knew the City.
This is the way to the temple, and we so many crowding the way.
So many waiting, how many waiting? what did it matter, on such a day?
Are they coming? No, not yet. You can see some eagles.
   And hear the trumpets.
Here they come. Is he coming?
The natural wakeful life of our Ego is a perceiving.
We can wait with our stools and our sausages.
What comes first? Can you see? Tell us. It is

   5,800,000 rifles and carbines,
     102,000 machine guns,
      28,000 trench mortars,
      53,000 field and heavy guns,
I cannot tell how many projectiles, mines and fuses,
      13,000 aeroplanes,
      24,000 aeroplane engines,
      50,000 ammunition waggons,
now 55,000 army waggons,
      11,000 field kitchens,
       1,150 field bakeries.

What a time that took. Will it be he now? No,
Those are the golf club Captains, these the Scouts,
And now the *société gymnastique de Poissy*
And now come the Mayor and the Liverymen. Look
There he is now, look:
There is no interrogation in his eyes
Or in the hands, quiet over the horse's neck,
And the eyes watchful, waiting, perceiving, indifferent.
O hidden under the dove's wing, hidden in the turtle's breast,
Under the palmtree at noon, under the running water
At the still point of the turning world. O hidden.

Now they go up to the temple. Then the sacrifice.
Now come the virgins bearing urns, urns containing
Dust
Dust
Dust of dust, and now
Stone, bronze, stone, steel, stone, oakleaves, horses' heels
Over the paving.

That is all we could see. But how many eagles! and how many trumpets!
(And Easter Day, we didn't get to the country,
So we took young Cyril to church. And they rang a bell
And he said right out loud, *crumpets*.)
                              Don't throw away that sausage,
It'll come in handy. He's artful. Please, will you
Give us a light?
Light
Light
Et les soldats faisaient la haie? ILS LA FAISAIENT.

G. K. CHESTERTON
1874–1936

163   *Elegy in a Country Churchyard*

The men that worked for England
They have their graves at home:
And bees and birds of England
About the cross can roam.

But they that fought for England,
Following a falling star,
Alas, alas for England
They have their graves afar.

And they that rule in England,
In stately conclave met,
Alas, alas for England
They have no graves as yet.

RUDYARD KIPLING
1865–1936

164   *Epitaphs of the War*

1914–18

'EQUALITY OF SACRIFICE'

A. 'I was a Have.'   B. 'I was a "have-not."'
(*Together.*) 'What hast thou given which I gave not?'

A SERVANT

We were together since the War began.
He was my servant—and the better man.

A SON

My son was killed while laughing at some jest. I would I knew
What it was, and it might serve me in a time when jests are few.

AN ONLY SON

I have slain none except my Mother. She
(Blessing her slayer) died of grief for me.

RUDYARD KIPLING

EX-CLERK

Pity not! The Army gave
Freedom to a timid slave:
In which Freedom did he find
Strength of body, will, and mind:
By which strength he came to prove
Mirth, Companionship, and Love:
For which Love to Death he went:
In which Death he lies content.

THE WONDER

Body and Spirit I surrendered whole
To harsh Instructors—and received a soul . . .
If mortal man could change me through and through
From all I was—what may The God not do?

HINDU SEPOY IN FRANCE

This man in his own country prayed we know not to what Powers.
We pray Them to reward him for his bravery in ours.

THE COWARD

I could not look on Death, which being known,
Men led me to him, blindfold and alone.

SHOCK

My name, my speech, my self I had forgot.
My wife and children came—I knew them not.
I died. My Mother followed. At her call
And on her bosom I remembered all.

A GRAVE NEAR CAIRO

Gods of the Nile, should this stout fellow here
Get out—get out! He knows not shame nor fear.

RUDYARD KIPLING

PELICANS IN THE WILDERNESS
A Grave near Halfa

The blown sand heaps on me, that none may learn
  Where I am laid for whom my children grieve. . . .
O wings that beat at dawning, ye return
  Out of the desert to your young at eve!

TWO CANADIAN MEMORIALS

I

We giving all gained all.
  Neither lament us nor praise.
Only in all things recall,
  It is Fear, not Death that slays.

II

From little towns in a far land we came,
  To save our honour and a world aflame.
By little towns in a far land we sleep;
  And trust that world we won for you to keep!

THE FAVOUR

Death favoured me from the first, well knowing I could not endure
  To wait on him day by day. He quitted my betters and came
Whistling over the fields, and, when he had made all sure,
  'Thy line is at end,' he said, 'but at least I have saved its name.'

THE BEGINNER

On the first hour of my first day
  In the front trench I fell.
(Children in boxes at a play
  Stand up to watch it well.)

R.A.F. (AGED EIGHTEEN)

Laughing through clouds, his milk-teeth still unshed,
Cities and men he smote from overhead.
His deaths delivered, he returned to play
Childlike, with childish things not put away.

RUDYARD KIPLING

THE REFINED MAN

I was of delicate mind. I stepped aside for my needs,
   Disdaining the common office. I was seen from afar and killed....
How is this matter for mirth? Let each man be judged by his deeds.
   I have paid my price to live with myself on the terms that I willed.

NATIVE WATER-CARRIERS (M.E.F.)

Prometheus brought down fire to men.
   This brought up water.
The Gods are jealous—now, as then,
   Giving no quarter.

BOMBED IN LONDON

On land and sea I strove with anxious care
To escape conscription. It was in the air!

THE SLEEPY SENTINEL

Faithless the watch that I kept: now I have none to keep.
I was slain because I slept: now I am slain I sleep.
Let no man reproach me again, whatever watch is unkept—
I sleep because I am slain. They slew me because I slept.

BATTERIES OUT OF AMMUNITION

If any mourn us in the workshop, say
We died because the shift kept holiday.

COMMON FORM

If any question why we died,
Tell them, because our fathers lied.

A DEAD STATESMAN

I could not dig: I dared not rob:
Therefore I lied to please the mob.
Now all my lies are proved untrue
And I must face the men I slew.
What tale shall serve me here among
Mine angry and defrauded young?

RUDYARD KIPLING

THE REBEL

If I had clamoured at Thy Gate
    For gift of Life on Earth,
And, thrusting through the souls that wait,
    Flung headlong into birth—
Even then, even then, for gin and snare
    About my pathway spread,
Lord, I had mocked Thy thoughtful care
    Before I joined the Dead!
But now? . . . I was beneath Thy Hand
    Ere yet the Planets came.
And now—though Planets pass, I stand
    The witness to Thy shame!

THE OBEDIENT

Daily, though no ears attended,
    Did my prayers arise.
Daily, though no fire descended,
    Did I sacrifice.
Though my darkness did not lift,
    Though I faced no lighter odds,
Though the Gods bestowed no gift,
        None the less,
  None the less, I served the Gods!

A DRIFTER OFF TARENTUM

He from the wind-bitten North with ship and companions descended,
    Searching for eggs of death spawned by invisible hulls.
Many he found and drew forth. Of a sudden the fishery ended
    In flame and a clamorous breath known to the eye-pecking gulls.

DESTROYERS IN COLLISION

For Fog and Fate no charm is found
    To lighten or amend.
I, hurrying to my bride, was drowned—
    Cut down by my best friend.

RUDYARD KIPLING

CONVOY ESCORT

I was a shepherd to fools
    Causelessly bold or afraid.
They would not abide by my rules.
    Yet they escaped. For I stayed.

UNKNOWN FEMALE CORPSE

Headless, lacking foot and hand,
Horrible I come to land.
I beseech all women's sons
Know I was a mother once.

RAPED AND REVENGED

One used and butchered me: another spied
Me broken—for which thing an hundred died.
So it was learned among the heathen hosts
How much a freeborn woman's favour costs.

SALONIKAN GRAVE

I have watched a thousand days
Push out and crawl into night
Slowly as tortoises.
Now I, too, follow these.
It is fever, and not the fight—
Time, not battle,—that slays.

THE BRIDEGROOM

Call me not false, beloved,
    If, from thy scarce-known breast
So little time removed,
    In other arms I rest.

For this more ancient bride,
    Whom coldly I embrace,
Was constant at my side
    Before I saw thy face.

Our marriage, often set—
    By miracle delayed—
At last is consummate,
    And cannot be unmade.

Live, then, whom Life shall cure,
Almost, of Memory,
And leave us to endure
Its immortality.

V.A.D. (MEDITERRANEAN)

Ah, would swift ships had never been, for then we ne'er had found,
These harsh Ægean rocks between, this little virgin drowned,
Whom neither spouse nor child shall mourn, but men she nursed
      through pain
And—certain keels for whose return the heathen look in vain.

ACTORS

On a Memorial Tablet in Holy Trinity Church,
Stratford-on-Avon

We counterfeited once for your disport
   Men's joy and sorrow: but our day has passed.
We pray you pardon all where we fell short—
   Seeing we were your servants to this last.

JOURNALISTS

On a Panel in the Hall of the Institute of Journalists
We have served our day.

ELIZABETH DARYUSH

1887–1977

165   *Subalterns*

She said to one: 'How glows
My heart at the hot thought
Of battle's glorious throes!'
He said: 'For us who fought
Are icy memories
That must for ever freeze
The sunny hours they bought.'

She said to one: 'How light
Must be your freed heart now,
After the heavy fight!'
He said: 'Well, I don't know . . .
The war gave one a shake,
Somehow, knocked one awake . . .
Now, life's so deadly slow.'

MAY WEDDERBURN CANNAN

1893–1973

166   *Rouen*

26 April–25 May 1915

Early morning over Rouen, hopeful, high, courageous morning,
And the laughter of adventure and the steepness of the stair,
And the dawn across the river, and the wind across the bridges,
And the empty littered station and the tired people there.

Can you recall those mornings and the hurry of awakening,
And the long-forgotten wonder if we should miss the way,
And the unfamiliar faces, and the coming of provisions,
And the freshness and the glory of the labour of the day?

Hot noontide over Rouen, and the sun upon the city,
Sun and dust unceasing, and the glare of cloudless skies,
And the voices of the Indians and the endless stream of soldiers,
And the clicking of the tatties, and the buzzing of the flies.

Can you recall those noontides and the reek of steam and coffee,
Heavy-laden noontides with the evening's peace to win,
And the little piles of Woodbines, and the sticky soda bottles,
And the crushes in the 'Parlour', and the letters coming in?

Quiet night-time over Rouen, and the station full of soldiers,
All the youth and pride of England from the ends of all the earth;
And the rifles piled together, and the creaking of the sword-belts,
And the faces bent above them, and the gay, heart-breaking mirth.

Can I forget the passage from the cool white-bedded Aid Post
Past the long sun-blistered coaches of the khaki Red Cross train
To the truck train full of wounded, and the weariness and laughter,
And 'Good-bye, and thank you, Sister', and the empty yards again?

Can you recall the parcels that we made them for the railroad,
Crammed and bulging parcels held together by their string,
And the voices of the sergeants who called the Drafts together,
And the agony and splendour when they stood to save the King?

Can you forget their passing, the cheering and the waving,
The little group of people at the doorway of the shed,
The sudden awful silence when the last train swung to darkness,
And the lonely desolation, and the mocking stars o'erhead?

Can you recall the midnights, and the footsteps of night watchers,
Men who came from darkness and went back to dark again,
And the shadows on the rail-lines and the all-inglorious labour,
And the promise of the daylight firing blue the window-pane?

Can you recall the passing through the kitchen door to morning,
Morning very still and solemn breaking slowly on the town,
And the early coastways engines that had met the ships at daybreak,
And the Drafts just out from England, and the day shift coming down?

Can you forget returning slowly, stumbling on the cobbles,
And the white-decked Red Cross barges dropping seawards for the
     tide,
And the search for English papers, and the blessed cool of water,
And the peace of half-closed shutters that shut out the world outside?

Can I forget the evenings and the sunsets on the island,
And the tall black ships at anchor far below our balcony,
And the distant call of bugles, and the white wine in the glasses,
And the long line of the street lamps, stretching Eastwards to the sea?

. . . When the world slips slow to darkness, when the office fire burns
     lower,
My heart goes out to Rouen, Rouen all the world away;
When other men remember I remember our Adventure
And the trains that go from Rouen at the ending of the day.

167   *MCMXIV*

Those long uneven lines
Standing as patiently
As if they were stretched outside
The Oval or Villa Park,
The crowns of hats, the sun
On moustached archaic faces
Grinning as if it were all
An August Bank Holiday lark;

And the shut shops, the bleached
Established names on the sunblinds,
The farthings and sovereigns,
And dark-clothed children at play
Called after kings and queens,
The tin advertisements
For cocoa and twist, and the pubs
Wide open all day;

And the countryside not caring:
The place-names all hazed over
With flowering grasses, and fields
Shadowing Domesday lines
Under wheat's restless silence;
The differently-dressed servants
With tiny rooms in huge houses,
The dust behind limousines;

Never such innocence,
Never before or since,
As changed itself to past
Without a word—the men
Leaving the gardens tidy,
The thousands of marriages
Lasting a little while longer:
Never such innocence again.

VERNON SCANNELL

1922–

The Great War

Whenever war is spoken of
I find
The war that was called Great invades the mind:
The grey militia marches over land
A darker mood of grey
Where fractured tree-trunks stand
And shells, exploding, open sudden fans
Of smoke and earth.
Blind murders scythe
The deathscape where the iron brambles writhe;
The sky at night
Is honoured with rosettes of fire,
Flares that define the corpses on the wire
As terror ticks on wrists at zero hour.
These things I see,
But they are only part
Of what it is that slyly probes the heart:
Less vivid images and words excite
The sensuous memory
And, even as I write,
Fear and a kind of love collaborate
To call each simple conscript up
For quick inspection:
Trenches' parapets
Paunchy with sandbags; bandoliers, tin-hats,
Candles in dug-outs,
Duckboards, mud and rats.
Then, like patrols, tunes creep into the mind:
A long, long, trail, The Rose of No Man's Land,
Home Fires and *Tipperary*;
And through the misty keening of a band
Of Scottish pipes the proper names are heard
Like fateful commentary of distant guns:
Passchendaele, Bapaume, and Loos, and Mons.
And now,
Whenever the November sky

Quivers with a bugle's hoarse, sweet cry,
The reason darkens; in its evening gleam
Crosses and flares, tormented wire, grey earth
Splattered with crimson flowers,
And I remember,
Not the war I fought in
But the one called Great
Which ended in a sepia November
Four years before my birth.

TED HUGHES

1930–

169   *Six Young Men*

The celluloid of a photograph holds them well,—
Six young men, familiar to their friends.
Four decades that have faded and ochre-tinged
This photograph have not wrinkled the faces or the hands.
Though their cocked hats are not now fashionable,
Their shoes shine. One imparts an intimate smile,
One chews a grass, one lowers his eyes, bashful,
One is ridiculous with cocky pride—
Six months after this picture they were all dead.

All are trimmed for a Sunday jaunt. I know
That bilberried bank, that thick tree, that black wall,
Which are there yet and not changed. From where these sit
You hear the water of seven streams fall
To the roarer in the bottom, and through all
The leafy valley a rumouring of air go.
Pictured here, their expressions listen yet,
And still that valley has not changed its sound
Though their faces are four decades under the ground.

This one was shot in an attack and lay
Calling in the wire, then this one, his best friend,
Went out to bring him in and was shot too;
And this one, the very moment he was warned
From potting at tin-cans in no-man's-land,

Fell back dead with his rifle-sights shot away.
The rest, nobody knows what they came to,
But come to the worst they must have done, and held it
Closer than their hope; all were killed.

Here see a man's photograph,
The locket of a smile, turned overnight
Into the hospital of his mangled last
Agony and hours; see bundled in it
His mightier-than-a-man dead bulk and weight:
And on this one place which keeps him alive
(In his Sunday best) see fall war's worst
Thinkable flash and rending, onto his smile
Forty years rotting into soil.

That man's not more alive whom you confront
And shake by the hand, see hale, hear speak loud,
Than any of these six celluloid smiles are,
Nor prehistoric or fabulous beast more dead;
No thought so vivid as their smoking blood:
To regard this photograph might well dement,
Such contradictory permanent horrors here
Smile from the single exposure and shoulder out
One's own body from its instant and heat.

DOUGLAS DUNN

1942–

170   *War Blinded*

For more than sixty years he has been blind
Behind that wall, these trees, with terrible
Longevity wheeled in the sun and wind
On pathways of the soldiers' hospital.

For half that time his story's troubled me—
That showroom by the ferry, where I saw
His basketwork, a touch-turned filigree
His fingers coaxed from charitable straw;

Or how he felt when young, enlisting at
Recruiting tables on the football pitch,
To end up slumped across a parapet,
His eye-blood running in a molten ditch;

Or how the light looked when I saw two men,
One blind, one in a wheelchair, in that park,
Their dignity, which I have not forgotten,
Which helps me struggle with this lesser dark.

That war's too old for me to understand
How he might think, nursed now in wards of want,
Remembering that day when his right hand
Gripped on the shoulder of the man in front.

LOUIS MacNEICE

1907–1963

171   from *Autumn Journal*

And I remember Spain
   At Easter ripe as an egg for revolt and ruin
Though for a tripper the rain
   Was worse than the surly or the worried or the haunted faces
With writings on the walls—
   Hammer and sickle, Boicot, Viva, Muerra;
With café-au-lait brimming the waterfalls,
   With sherry, shellfish, omelettes.
With fretted stone the Moor
   Had chiselled for effects of sun and shadow;
With shadows of the poor,
   The begging cripples and the children begging.
The churches full of saints
   Tortured on racks of marble—
The old complaints
   Covered with gilt and dimly lit with candles.
With powerful or banal
   Monuments of riches or repression
And the Escorial
   Cold for ever within like the heart of Philip.

With ranks of dominoes
  Deployed on café tables the whole of Sunday;
With cabarets that call the tourist, shows
  Of thighs and eyes and nipples.
With slovenly soldiers, nuns,
  And peeling posters from the last elections
Promising bread or guns
  Or an amnesty or another
Order or else the old
  Glory veneered and varnished
As if veneer could hold
  The rotten guts and crumbled bones together.
And a vulture hung in air
  Below the cliffs of Ronda and below him
His hook-winged shadow wavered like despair
  Across the chequered vineyards.
And the boot-blacks in Madrid
  Kept us half an hour with polish and pincers
And all we did
  In that city was drink and think and loiter.
And in the Prado half-
  wit princes looked from the canvas they had paid for
(Goya had the laugh—
  But can what is corrupt be cured by laughter?)
And the day at Aranjuez
  When the sun came out for once on the yellow river
With Valdepeñas burdening the breath
  We slept a royal sleep in the royal gardens;
And at Toledo walked
  Around the ramparts where they throw the garbage
And glibly talked
  Of how the Spaniards lack all sense of business.
And Avila was cold
  And Segovia was picturesque and smelly
And a goat on the road seemed old
  As the rocks or the Roman arches.
And Easter was wet and full
  In Seville and in the ring on Easter Sunday
A clumsy bull and then a clumsy bull
  Nodding his banderillas died of boredom.
And the standard of living was low
  But that, we thought to ourselves, was not our business;
All that the tripper wants is the *status quo*

Cut and dried for trippers.
And we thought the papers a lark
  With their party politics and blank invective;
And we thought the dark
  Women who dyed their hair should have it dyed more often.
And we sat in trains all night
  With the windows shut among civil guards and peasants
And tried to play piquet by a tiny light
  And tried to sleep bolt upright;
And cursed the Spanish rain
  And cursed their cigarettes which came to pieces
And caught heavy colds in Cordova and in vain
  Waited for the right light for taking photos.
And we met a Cambridge don who said with an air
  'There's going to be trouble shortly in this country,'
And ordered anis, pudgy and debonair,
  Glad to show off his mastery of the language.
But only an inch behind
  This map of olive and ilex, this painted hoarding,
Careless of visitors the people's mind
  Was tunnelling like a mole to day and danger.
And the day before we left
  We saw the mob in flower at Algeciras
Outside a toothless door, a church bereft
  Of its images and its aura.
And at La Linea while
  The night put miles between us and Gibraltar
We heard the blood-lust of a drunkard pile
  His heaven high with curses;
And next day took the boat
  For home, forgetting Spain, not realising
That Spain would soon denote
  Our grief, our aspirations;
Not knowing that our blunt
  Ideals would find their whetstone, that our spirit
Would find its frontier on the Spanish front,
  Its body in a rag-tag army.

JOHN CORNFORD

1915–1936

A Letter from Aragon

This is a quiet sector of a quiet front.

We buried Ruiz in a new pine coffin,
But the shroud was too small and his washed feet stuck out.
The stink of his corpse came through the clean pine boards
And some of the bearers wrapped handkerchiefs round their faces.
Death was not dignified.
We hacked a ragged grave in the unfriendly earth
And fired a ragged volley over the grave.

You could tell from our listlessness, no one much missed him.

This is a quiet sector of a quiet front.
There is no poison gas and no H. E.

But when they shelled the other end of the village
And the streets were choked with dust
Women came screaming out of the crumbling houses,
Clutched under one arm the naked rump of an infant.
I thought: how ugly fear is.

This is a quiet sector of a quiet front.
Our nerves are steady; we all sleep soundly.

In the clean hospital bed, my eyes were so heavy
Sleep easily blotted out one ugly picture,
A wounded militiaman moaning on a stretcher,
Now out of danger, but still crying for water,
Strong against death, but unprepared for such pain.

This on a quiet front.

But when I shook hands to leave, an Anarchist worker
Said: 'Tell the workers of England
This was a war not of our own making
We did not seek it.
But if ever the Fascists again rule Barcelona
It will be as a heap of ruins with us workers beneath it.'

173   *Full Moon at Tierz:*
        Before the Storming of Huesca

I

The past, a glacier, gripped the mountain wall,
And time was inches, dark was all.
But here it scales the end of the range,
The dialectic's point of change,
Crashes in light and minutes to its fall.

Time present is a cataract whose force
Breaks down the banks even at its source
And history forming in our hand's
Not plasticine but roaring sands,
Yet we must swing it to its final course.

The intersecting lines that cross both ways,
Time future, has no image in space,
Crooked as the road that we must tread,
Straight as our bullets fly ahead.
We are the future. The last fight let us face.

II

Where, in the fields by Huesca, the full moon
Throws shadows clear as daylight's, soon
The innocence of this quiet plain
Will fade in sweat and blood, in pain,
As our decisive hold is lost or won.

All round the barren hills of Aragon
Announce our testing has begun.
Here what the Seventh Congress said,
If true, if false, is live or dead,
Speaks in the Oviedo mausers tone.

Three years ago Dimitrov fought alone
And we stood taller when he won.
But now the Leipzig dragon's teeth
Sprout strong and handsome against death
And here an army fights where there was one.

We studied well how to begin this fight,
Our Maurice Thorez held the light.
But now by Monte Aragon
We plunge into the dark alone,
Earth's newest planet wheeling through the night.

III

Though Communism was my waking time,
Always before the lights of home
Shone clear and steady and full in view—
Here, if you fall, there's help for you—
Now, with my Party, I stand quite alone.

Then let my private battle with my nerves,
The fear of pain whose pain survives,
The love that tears me by the roots,
The loneliness that claws my guts,
Fuse in the welded front our fight preserves.

O be invincible as the strong sun,
Hard as the metal of my gun,
O let the mounting tempo of the train
Sweep where my footsteps slipped in vain,
October in the rhythm of its run.

IV

Now the same night falls over Germany
And the impartial beauty of the stars
Lights from the unfeeling sky
Oranienburg and freedom's crooked scars.
We can do nothing to ease that pain
But prove the agony was not in vain.

England is silent under the same moon,
From Clydeside to the gutted pits of Wales.
The innocent mask conceals that soon
Here, too, our freedom's swaying in the scales.
O understand before too late
Freedom was never held without a fight.

Freedom is an easily spoken word
But facts are stubborn things. Here, too, in Spain
Our fight's not won till the workers of all the world
Stand by our guard on Huesca's plain
Swear that our dead fought not in vain,
Raise the red flag triumphantly
For Communism and for liberty.

174   *To Margot Heinemann*

Heart of the heartless world,
Dear heart, the thought of you
Is the pain at my side,
The shadow that chills my view.

The wind rises in the evening,
Reminds that autumn's near.
I am afraid to lose you,
I am afraid of my fear.

On the last mile to Huesca,
The last fence for our pride,
Think so kindly, dear, that I
Sense you at my side.

And if bad luck should lay my strength
Into the shallow grave,
Remember all the good you can;
Don't forget my love.

GEORGE ORWELL

1903–1950

175   The Italian soldier shook my hand
Beside the guard-room table;
The strong hand and the subtle hand
Whose palms are only able

To meet within the sound of guns,
But oh! what peace I knew then
In gazing on his battered face
Purer than any woman's!

For the fly-blown words that make me spew
Still in his ears were holy,
And he was born knowing what I had learned
Out of books and slowly.

The treacherous guns had told their tale
And we both had bought it,
But my gold brick was made of gold—
Oh! who ever would have thought it?

Good luck go with you, Italian soldier!
But luck is not for the brave;
What would the world give back to you?
Always less than you gave.

Between the shadow and the ghost,
Between the white and the red,
Between the bullet and the lie,
Where would you hide your head?

For where is Manuel Gonzalez,
And where is Pedro Aguilar,
And where is Ramon Fenellosa?
The earthworms know where they are.

Your name and your deeds were forgotten
Before your bones were dry,
And the lie that slew you is buried
Under a deeper lie;

But the thing that I saw in your face
No power can disinherit:
No bomb that ever burst
Shatters the crystal spirit.

ANONYMOUS

mid 1930s

176 [*Stanzas found on a leaf of an International Brigader's notebook*]

Eyes of men running, falling, screaming
Eyes of men shouting, sweating, bleeding
The eyes of the fearful, those of the sad
The eyes of exhaustion, and those of the mad.

Eyes of men thinking, hoping, waiting
Eyes of men loving, cursing, hating
The eyes of the wounded sodden in red
The eyes of the dying and those of the dead.

LAURIE LEE

1914–

177 *A Moment of War*

It is night like a red rag
drawn across the eyes

the flesh is bitterly pinned
to desperate vigilance

the blood is stuttering with fear

O praise the security of worms
in cool crumbs of soil,
flatter the hidden sap
and the lost unfertilized spawn of fish!

The hands melt with weakness
into the gun's hot iron

the body melts with pity,

the face is braced for wounds
the odour and the kiss of final pain.

O envy the peace of women
giving birth and love like toys
into the hands of men!

The mouth chatters with pale curses

the bowels struggle like a nest of rats

the feet wish they were grass
spaced quietly.

O Christ and Mother!

But darkness opens like a knife for you
and you are marked down by your pulsing brain

and isolated

and your breathing,

your breathing is the blast, the bullet,
and the final sky.

Spanish Frontier, 1937

SYLVIA TOWNSEND WARNER
1893–1978

178   *Benicasim**

Here for a little we pause.
The air is heavy with sun and salt and colour.
On palm and lemon-tree, on cactus and oleander
a dust of dust and salt and pollen lies.
And the bright villas
sit in a row like perched macaws,
and rigid and immediate yonder
the mountains rise.

* At Benicasim on the east coast of Spain is the Rest Home for the convalescent wounded of the Spanish People's Army, and the Villa dedicated to Ralph Fox, supported by the Spanish Medical Aid. [STW]

And it seems to me we have come
into a bright-painted landscape of Acheron.
For along the strand
in bleached cotton pyjamas, on rope-soled tread,
wander the risen-from-the-dead,
the wounded, the maimed, the halt.
Or they lay bare their hazarded flesh to the salt
air, the recaptured sun,
or bathe in the tideless sea, or sit fingering the sand.

But narrow is this place, narrow is this space
of garlanded sun and leisure and colour, of return
to life and release from living. Turn
(Turn not!) sight inland:
there, rigid as death and unforgiving, stand
the mountains—and close at hand.

W. H. AUDEN

1907–1973

179   *Spain 1937*

Yesterday all the past. The language of size
Spreading to China along the trade-routes; the diffusion
        Of the counting-frame and the cromlech;
Yesterday the shadow-reckoning in the sunny climates.

Yesterday the assessment of insurance by cards,
The divination of water; yesterday the invention
        Of cart-wheels and clocks, the taming of
Horses; yesterday the bustling world of the navigators.

Yesterday the abolition of fairies and giants;
The fortress like a motionless eagle eyeing the valley,
        The chapel built in the forest;
Yesterday the carving of angels and of frightening gargoyles;

The trial of heretics among the columns of stone;
Yesterday the theological feuds in the taverns
        And the miraculous cure at the fountain;
Yesterday the Sabbath of Witches. But today the struggle.

Yesterday the installation of dynamos and turbines;
The construction of railways in the colonial desert;
        Yesterday the classic lecture
On the origin of Mankind. But today the struggle.

Yesterday the belief in the absolute value of Greek;
The fall of the curtain upon the death of a hero;
        Yesterday the prayer to the sunset,
And the adoration of madmen. But today the struggle.

As the poet whispers, startled among the pines
Or, where the loose waterfall sings, compact, or upright
        On the crag by the leaning tower:
'O my vision. O send me the luck of the sailor.'

And the investigator peers through his instruments
At the inhuman provinces, the virile bacillus
        Or enormous Jupiter finished:
'But the lives of my friends. I inquire, I inquire.'

And the poor in their fireless lodgings dropping the sheets
Of the evening paper: 'Our day is our loss. O show us
        History the operator, the
Organiser, Time the refreshing river.'

And the nations combine each cry, invoking the life
That shapes the individual belly and orders
        The private nocturnal terror:
'Did you not found once the city state of the sponge,

'Raise the vast military empires of the shark
And the tiger, establish the robin's plucky canton?
        Intervene. O descend as a dove or
A furious papa or a mild engineer: but descend.'

And the life, if it answers at all, replies from the heart
And the eyes and the lungs, from the shops and squares of the city:
        'O no, I am not the Mover,
Not today, not to you. To you I'm the

'Yes-man, the bar-companion, the easily-duped:
I am whatever you do; I am your vow to be
        Good, your humorous story;
I am your business voice; I am your marriage.

'What's your proposal? To build the Just City? I will.
I agree. Or is it the suicide pact, the romantic
            Death? Very well, I accept, for
I am your choice, your decision: yes, I am Spain.'

Many have heard it on remote peninsulas,
On sleepy plains, in the aberrant fishermen's islands,
            In the corrupt heart of the city;
Have heard and migrated like gulls or the seeds of a flower.

They clung like burrs to the long expresses that lurch
Through the unjust lands, through the night, through the alpine
    tunnel;
            They floated over the oceans;
They walked the passes: they came to present their lives.

On that arid square, that fragment nipped off from hot
Africa, soldered so crudely to inventive Europe,
            On that tableland scored by rivers,
Our fever's menacing shapes are precise and alive.

Tomorrow, perhaps, the future: the research on fatigue
And the movements of packers; the gradual exploring of all the
            Octaves of radiation;
Tomorrow the enlarging of consciousness by diet and breathing.

Tomorrow the rediscovery of romantic love;
The photographing of ravens; all the fun under
            Liberty's masterful shadow;
Tomorrow the hour of the pageant-master and the musician.

Tomorrow, for the young, the poets exploding like bombs,
The walks by the lake, the winter of perfect communion;
            Tomorrow the bicycle races
Through the suburbs on summer evenings: but today the struggle.

Today the inevitable increase in the chances of death;
The conscious acceptance of guilt in the fact of murder;
            Today the expending of powers
On the flat ephemeral pamphlet and the boring meeting.

Today the makeshift consolations; the shared cigarette;
The cards in the candle-lit barn and the scraping concert,
          The masculine jokes; today the
Fumbled and unsatisfactory embrace before hurting.

The stars are dead; the animals will not look:
We are left alone with our day, and the time is short and
          History to the defeated
May say Alas but cannot help or pardon.

STEPHEN SPENDER

1909–

180   *Two Armies*

Deep in the winter plain, two armies
Dig their machinery, to destroy each other.
Men freeze and hunger. No one is given leave
On either side, except the dead and wounded.
These have their leave; while new battalions wait
On time at last to bring them violent peace.

All have become so nervous and so cold
That each man hates the cause and distant words
That brought him here, more terribly than bullets.
Once a boy hummed a popular marching song,
Once a novice hand flapped their salute;
The voice was choked, the lifted hand fell,
Shot through the wrist by those of his own side.

From their numb harvest, all would flee, except
For discipline drilled once in an iron school
Which holds them at the point of the revolver.
Yet when they sleep, the images of home
Ride wishing horses of escape
Which herd the plain in a mass unspoken poem.

Finally, they cease to hate: for although hate
Bursts from the air and whips the earth with hail
Or shoots it up in fountains to marvel at,
And although hundreds fall, who can connect
The inexhaustible anger of the guns
With the dumb patience of those tormented animals?

Clean silence drops at night, when a little walk
Divides the sleeping armies, each
Huddled in linen woven by remote hands.
When the machines are stilled, a common suffering
Whitens the air with breath and makes both one
As though these enemies slept in each other's arms.

Only the lucid friend to aerial raiders
The brilliant pilot moon, stares down
Upon this plain she makes a shining bone
Cut by the shadows of many thousand bones.
Where amber clouds scatter on No Man's Land
She regards death and time throw up
The furious words and minerals which destroy.

181 *Ultima Ratio Regum*

The guns spell money's ultimate reason
In letters of lead on the Spring hillside.
But the boy lying dead under the olive trees
Was too young and too silly
To have been notable to their important eye.
He was a better target for a kiss.

When he lived, tall factory hooters never summoned him
Nor did restaurant plate-glass doors revolve to wave him in.
His name never appeared in the papers.
The world maintained its traditional wall
Round the dead with their gold sunk deep as a well,
Whilst his life, intangible as a Stock Exchange rumour, drifted
    outside.

O too lightly he threw down his cap
One day when the breeze threw petals from the trees.
The unflowering wall sprouted with guns,
Machine-gun anger quickly scythed the grasses;
Flags and leaves fell from hands and branches;
The tweed cap rotted in the nettles.

Consider his life which was valueless
In terms of employment, hotel ledgers, news files.
Consider. One bullet in ten thousand kills a man.
Ask. Was so much expenditure justified
On the death of one so young, and so silly
Lying under the olive trees, O world, O death?

BERNARD SPENCER

1909–1963

182   *A Thousand Killed*

I read of a thousand killed.
And am glad because the scrounging imperial paw
Was there so bitten:
As a man at elections is thrilled
When the results pour in, and the North goes with him
And the West breaks in the thaw.

(That fighting was a long way off.)

Forgetting therefore an election
Being fought with votes and lies and catch-cries
And orator's frowns and flowers and posters' noise,
Is paid for with cheques and toys:
Wars the most glorious
Victory-winged and steeple-uproarious
. . . With the lives, burned-off,
Of young men and boys.

HERBERT READ

1893–1968

183   *To a Conscript of 1940*

> Qui n'a pas une fois désespéré de l'honneur, ne sera
> jamais un héros.
>
> Georges Bernanos

A soldier passed me in the freshly fallen snow
His footsteps muffled, his face unearthly grey;
And my heart gave a sudden leap
As I gazed on a ghost of five-and-twenty years ago.

I shouted Halt! and my voice had the old accustomed ring
And he obeyed it as it was obeyed
In the shrouded days when I too was one
Of an army of young men marching

Into the unknown. He turned towards me and I said:
'I am one of those who went before you
Five-and-twenty years ago: one of the many who never returned,
Of the many who returned and yet were dead.

'We went where you are going, into the rain and the mud;
We fought as you will fight
With death and darkness and despair;
We gave what you will give—our brains and our blood.

'We think we gave in vain. The world was not renewed.
There was hope in the homestead and anger in the streets
But the old world was restored and we returned
To the dreary field and workshop, and the immemorial feud

'Of rich and poor. Our victory was our defeat.
Power was retained where power had been misused
And youth was left to sweep away
The ashes that the fires had strewn beneath our feet.

'But one thing we learned: there is no glory in the deed
Until the soldier wears a badge of tarnished braid;
There are heroes who have heard the rally and have seen
The glitter of a garland round their head.

'Theirs is the hollow victory. They are deceived.
But you, my brother and my ghost, if you can go
Knowing that there is no reward, no certain use
In all your sacrifice, then honour is reprieved.

'To fight without hope is to fight with grace,
The self reconstructed, the false heart repaired.'
Then I turned with a smile, and he answered my salute
As he stood against the fretted hedge, which was like white lace.

LOUIS ARAGON

1897–1983

184   *The Lilacs and the Roses*

O months of blossoming, months of transfigurations,
May without a cloud and June stabbed to the heart,
I shall not ever forget the lilacs or the roses
Nor those the Spring has kept folded away apart.

I shall not ever forget the tragic sleight-of-hand,
The cavalcade, the cries, the crowd, the sun,
The lorries loaded with love, the Belgian gifts,
The road humming with bees, the atmosphere that spun,
The feckless triumphing before the battle,
The scarlet blood the scarlet kiss bespoke
And those about to die bolt upright in the turrets
Smothered in lilac by a drunken folk.

I shall not ever forget the flower-gardens of France—
Illuminated scrolls from eras more than spent—
Nor forget the trouble of dusk, the sphinx-like silence,
The roses all along the way we went;
Flowers that gave the lie to the soldiers passing
On wings of fear, a fear importunate as a breeze,
And gave the lie to the lunatic push-bikes and the ironic
Guns and the sorry rig of the refugees.

But what I do not know is why this whirl
Of memories always comes to the same point and drops
At Sainte-Marthe . . . a general . . . a black pattern . . .
A Norman villa where the forest stops;
All is quiet here, the enemy rests in the night
And Paris has surrendered, so we have just heard—
I shall never forget the lilacs nor the roses
Nor those two loves whose loss we have incurred:

Bouquets of the first day, lilacs, Flanders lilacs,
Soft cheeks of shadow rouged by death—and you,
Bouquets of the Retreat, delicate roses, tinted
Like far-off conflagrations: roses of Anjou.

Translated from the French by Louis MacNeice

C. DAY LEWIS

1904–1972

185   *The Stand-To*

Autumn met me today as I walked over Castle Hill.
The wind that had set our corn by the ears was blowing still:
Autumn, who takes the leaves and the long days, crisped the air
With a tang of action, a taste of death; and the wind blew fair

From the east for men and barges massed on the other side—
Men maddened by numbers or stolid by nature, they have their pride
As we in work and children, but now a contracting will
Crumples their meek petitions and holds them poised to kill.

Last night a Stand-To was ordered. Thirty men of us here
Came out to guard the star-lit village—my men who wear
Unwitting the season's beauty, the received truth of the spade—
Roadmen, farm labourers, masons, turned to another trade.

A dog barked over the fields, the candle stars put a sheen
On the rifles ready, the sandbags fronded with evergreen:
The dawn wind blew, the stars winked out on the posts where we lay,
The order came, Stand Down, and thirty went away.

Since a cold wind from Europe blows back the words in my teeth,
Since autumn shortens the days and the odds against our death,
And the harvest moon is waxing and high tides threaten harm,
Since last night may be the last night all thirty men go home,

I write this verse to record the men who have watched with me—
Spot who is good at darts, Squibby at repartee,
Mark and Cyril, the dead shots, Ralph with a ploughman's gait,
Gibson, Harris and Long, old hands for the barricade,

Whiller the lorry-driver, Francis and Rattlesnake,
Fred and Charl and Stan—these nights I have lain awake
And thought of my thirty men and the autumn wind that blows
The apples down too early and shatters the autumn rose.

Destiny, History, Duty, Fortitude, Honour—all
The words of the politicians seem too big or too small
For the ragtag fighters of lane and shadow, the love that has grown
Familiar as working-clothes, faithful as bone to bone.

Blow, autumn wind, upon orchard and rose! Blow leaves along
Our lanes, but sing through me for the lives that are worth a song!
Narrowing days have darkened the vistas that hurt my eyes,
But pinned to the heart of darkness a tattered fire-flag flies.

September 1940

186   *Where are the War Poets?*

They who in folly or mere greed
Enslaved religion, markets, laws,
Borrow our language now and bid
Us to speak up in freedom's cause.

It is the logic of our times,
No subject for immortal verse—
That we who lived by honest dreams
Defend the bad against the worse.

DAVID GASCOYNE

1916–

Ecce Homo

Whose is this horrifying face,
This putrid flesh, discoloured, flayed,
Fed on by flies, scorched by the sun?
Whose are these hollow red-filmed eyes
And thorn-spiked head and spear-stuck side?
Behold the Man: He is Man's Son.

Forget the legend, tear the decent veil
That cowardice or interest devised
To make their mortal enemy a friend,
To hide the bitter truth all His wounds tell,
Lest the great scandal be no more disguised:
He is in agony till the world's end,

And we must never sleep during that time!
He is suspended on the cross-tree now
And we are onlookers at the crime,
Callous contemporaries of the slow
Torture of God. Here is the hill
Made ghastly by His spattered blood

Whereon He hangs and suffers still:
See, the centurions wear riding-boots,
Black shirts and badges and peaked caps,
Greet one another with raised-arm salutes;
They have cold eyes, unsmiling lips;
Yet these His brothers know not what they do.

And on his either side hang dead
A labourer and a factory hand,
Or one is maybe a lynched Jew
And one a Negro or a Red,
Coolie or Ethiopian, Irishman,
Spaniard or German democrat.

Behind His lolling head the sky
Glares like a fiery cataract
Red with the murders of two thousand years
Committed in His name and by
Crusaders, Christian warriors
Defending faith and property.

Amid the plain beneath His transfixed hands,
Exuding darkness as indelible
As guilty stains, fanned by funereal
And lurid airs, besieged by drifting sands
And clefted landslides our about-to-be
Bombed and abandoned cities stand.

He who wept for Jerusalem
Now sees His prophecy extend
Across the greatest cities of the world
A guilty panic reason cannot stem
Rising to raze them all as He foretold;
And He must watch this drama to the end.

Though often named, He is unknown
To the dark kingdoms at His feet
Where everything disparages His words,
And each man bears the common guilt alone
And goes blindfolded to his fate,
And fear and greed are sovereign lords.

The turning point of history
Must come. Yet the complacent and the proud
And who exploit and kill, may be denied—
Christ of Revolution and of Poetry—
The resurrection and the life
Wrought by your spirit's blood.

Involved in their own sophistry
The black priest and the upright man
Faced by subversive truth shall be struck dumb,
Christ of Revolution and of Poetry,
While the rejected and condemned become
Agents of the divine.

Not from a monstrance silver-wrought
But from the tree of human pain
Redeem our sterile misery,
Christ of Revolution and of Poetry,
That man's long journey through the night
May not have been in vain.

EDITH SITWELL

1887–1964

188   *Still Falls the Rain*

(The raids, 1940. Night and dawn)

Still falls the Rain—
Dark as the world of man, black as our loss—
Blind as the nineteen hundred and forty nails
Upon the Cross.

Still falls the Rain
With a sound like the pulse of the heart that is changed
                     to the hammer-beat
In the Potter's Field, and the sound of the impious feet

On the Tomb:
            Still falls the Rain
In the Field of Blood where the small hopes breed and
                   the human brain
Nurtures its greed, that worm with the brow of Cain.

Still falls the Rain
At the feet of the Starved Man hung upon the Cross.
Christ that each day, each night, nails there,
                 have mercy on us—
On Dives and on Lazarus:
Under the Rain the sore and the gold are as one.

Still falls the Rain—
Still falls the Blood from the Starved Man's wounded Side:
He bears in His Heart all wounds,—those of the light
                 that died,

The last faint spark
In the self-murdered heart, the wounds of the sad
                                    uncomprehending dark,

The wounds of the baited bear,—
The blind and weeping bear whom the keepers beat
On his helpless flesh . . . the tears of the hunted hare.

Still falls the Rain—
Then—O Ile leape up to my God: who pulles me doune—
See, see where Christ's blood streames in the firmament:
It flows from the Brow we nailed upon the tree
Deep to the dying, to the thirsting heart
That holds the fires of the world,—dark-smirched with pain
As Caesar's laurel crown.

Then sounds the voice of One who like the heart of man
Was once a child who among beasts has lain—
'Still do I love, still shed my innocent light, my Blood, for thee.'

H.D. [HILDA DOOLITTLE]

1886–1961

189   from *The Walls Do Not Fall*

An incident here and there,
and rails gone (for guns)
from your (and my) old town square:

mist and mist-grey, no colour,
still the Luxor bee, chick and hare
pursue unalterable purpose

in green, rose-red, lapis;
they continue to prophesy
from the stone papyrus:

there, as here, ruin opens
the tomb, the temple; enter,
there as here, there are no doors:

the shrine lies open to the sky,
the rain falls, here, there
sand drifts; eternity endures:

ruin everywhere, yet as the fallen roof
leaves the sealed room
open to the air,

so, through our desolation,
thoughts stir, inspiration stalks us
through gloom:

unaware, Spirit announces the Presence;
shivering overtakes us,
as of old, Samuel:

trembling at a known street-corner,
we know not nor are known;
the Pythian pronounces—we pass on

to another cellar, to another sliced wall
where poor utensils show
like rare objects in a museum;

Pompeii has nothing to teach us,
we know crack of volcanic fissure,
slow flow of terrible lava,

pressure on heart, lungs, the brain
about to burst its brittle case
(what the skull can endure!):

over us, Apocryphal fire,
under us, the earth sway, dip of a floor,
slope of a pavement

where men roll, drunk
with a new bewilderment,
sorcery, bedevilment:

the bone-frame was made for
no such shock knit within terror,
yet the skeleton stood up to it:

the flesh? it was melted away,
the heart burnt out, dead ember,
tendons, muscles shattered, outer husk dismembered,

yet the frame held:
we passed the flame: we wonder
what saved us? what for?

LOUIS MacNEICE

1907–1963

190   *The Streets of Laredo*

O early one morning I walked out like Agag,
Early one morning to walk through the fire
Dodging the pythons that leaked on the pavements
With tinkle of glasses and tangle of wire;

When grimed to the eyebrows I met an old fireman
Who looked at me wryly and thus did he say:
'The streets of Laredo are closed to all traffic,
We won't never master this joker today.

'O hold the branch tightly and wield the axe brightly,
The bank is in powder, the banker's in hell,
But loot is still free on the streets of Laredo
And when we drive home we drive home on the bell.'

Then out from a doorway there sidled a cockney,
A rocking-chair rocking on top of his head:
'O fifty-five years I been feathering my love-nest
And look at it now—why, you'd sooner be dead.'

At which there arose from a wound in the asphalt,
His big wig a-smoulder, Sir Christopher Wren
Saying: 'Let them make hay of the streets of Laredo;
When your ground-rents expire I will build them again.'

Then twangling their bibles with wrath in their nostrils
From Bonehill Fields came Bunyan and Blake:
'Laredo the golden is fallen, is fallen;
Your flame shall not quench nor your thirst shall not
 slake.'

'I come to Laredo to find me asylum',
Says Tom Dick and Harry the Wandering Jew;
'They tell me report at the first police station
But the station is pancaked—so what can I do?'

Thus eavesdropping sadly I strolled through Laredo
Perplexed by the dicta misfortunes inspire
Till one low last whisper inveigled my earhole—
The voice of the Angel, the voice of the fire:

O late, very late, have I come to Laredo
A whimsical bride in my new scarlet dress
But at last I took pity on those who were waiting
To see my regalia and feel my caress.

Now ring the bells gaily and play the hose daily,
Put splints on your legs, put a gag on your breath;
O you streets of Laredo, you streets of Laredo,
Lay down the red carpet—My dowry is death.

R. N. CURREY

1907–

191   *Unseen Fire*

This is a damned inhuman sort of war.
I have been fighting in a dressing-gown
Most of the night; I cannot see the guns,
The sweating gun-detachments or the planes;

I sweat down here before a symbol thrown
Upon a screen, sift facts, initiate
Swift calculations and swift orders; wait
For the precise split-second to order fire.

We chant our ritual words; beyond the phones
A ghost repeats the orders to the guns:
One Fire ... Two Fire ... ghosts answer: the guns roar
Abruptly; and an aircraft waging war
Inhumanly from nearly five miles height
Meets our bouquet of death—and turns sharp right.

KENNETH ALLOTT

1912–1973

192   *Prize for Good Conduct*

The worn-out voice of the clock breaks on the hour:
The State requires
　　　　　My wedding ring and my apostle spoons,
　　　　　My sons.

There will be a special service in the cathedral
After which the clergy will be disbanded
And the fane profaned and put to immediate service
To manufacture wooden legs for heroes
With a useful sideline in glass-eyes
And employment found for over two hundred widows.

The feverish wounded in the base hospital,
The nurse's coif becomes a phallic symbol,
He hears the red coal drop, and the cistern filling;
And the stripped dead buried in ungainly postures
Their lucky charms sent back with kindly letters,
The invalids sent home with eyesight failing
To sit on a waiting-list for operations
And never to be put off iron rations;
And the nervous shipwrecked bodies in lovely grounds
Set aside by old ladies with unearned incomes;
The cows are eating the shadows off the field,
The wasps buzz angrily in the stoppered bottle,
The devil comes daintily over the stepping-stones
As they sit in the sunshine, crying no rest for the wicked.

HENRY REED
1914–1986

Lessons of the War

To Alan Michell

Vixi duellis nuper idoneus
Et militavi non sine gloria

I. NAMING OF PARTS

Today we have naming of parts. Yesterday,
We had daily cleaning. And tomorrow morning,
We shall have what to do after firing. But today,
Today we have naming of parts. Japonica
Glistens like coral in all of the neighbouring gardens,
     And today we have naming of parts.

This is the lower sling swivel. And this
Is the upper sling swivel, whose use you will see,
When you are given your slings. And this is the piling swivel,
Which in your case you have not got. The branches
Hold in the gardens their silent, eloquent gestures,
     Which in our case we have not got.

This is the safety-catch, which is always released
With an easy flick of the thumb. And please do not let me
See anyone using his finger. You can do it quite easy
If you have any strength in your thumb. The blossoms
Are fragile and motionless, never letting anyone see
     Any of them using their finger.

And this you can see is the bolt. The purpose of this
Is to open the breech, as you see. We can slide it
Rapidly backwards and forwards: we call this
Easing the spring. And rapidly backwards and forwards
The early bees are assaulting and fumbling the flowers:
     They call it easing the Spring.

They call it easing the Spring: it is perfectly easy
If you have any strength in your thumb: like the bolt,

And the breech, and the cocking-piece, and the point of balance,
Which in our case we have not got; and the almond-blossom
Silent in all of the gardens and the bees going backwards and forwards,
> For today we have naming of parts.

II. JUDGING DISTANCES

Not only how far away, but the way that you say it
Is very important. Perhaps you may never get
The knack of judging a distance, but at least you know
How to report on a landscape: the central sector,
The right of arc and that, which we had last Tuesday,
> And at least you know

That maps are of time, not place, so far as the army
Happens to be concerned—the reason being,
Is one which need not delay us. Again, you know
There are three kinds of tree, three only, the fir and the poplar,
And those which have bushy tops to; and lastly
> That things only seem to be things.

A barn is not called a barn, to put it more plainly,
Or a field in the distance, where sheep may be safely grazing.
You must never be over-sure. You must say, when reporting:
At five o'clock in the central sector is a dozen
Of what appear to be animals; whatever you do,
> Don't call the bleeders *sheep*.

I am sure that's quite clear; and suppose, for the sake of example,
The one at the end, asleep, endeavours to tell us
What he sees over there to the west, and how far away,
After first having come to attention. There to the west,
On the fields of summer the sun and the shadows bestow
> Vestments of purple and gold.

The still white dwellings are like a mirage in the heat,
And under the swaying elms a man and a woman
Lie gently together. Which is, perhaps, only to say
That there is a row of houses to the left of arc,
And that under some poplars a pair of what appear to be humans
> Appear to be loving.

Well that, for an answer, is what we might rightly call
Moderately satisfactory only, the reason being,
Is that two things have been omitted, and those are important.
The human beings, now: in what direction are they,
And how far away, would you say? And do not forget
    There may be dead ground in between.

There may be dead ground in between; and I may not have got
The knack of judging a distance; I will only venture
A guess that perhaps between me and the apparent lovers,
(Who, incidentally, appear by now to have finished,)
At seven o'clock from the houses, is roughly a distance
    Of about one year and a half.

III. UNARMED COMBAT

In due course of course you will all be issued with
Your proper issue; but until tomorrow,
You can hardly be said to need it; and until that time,
We shall have unarmed combat. I shall teach you.
The various holds and rolls and throws and breakfalls
    Which you may sometimes meet.

And the various holds and rolls and throws and breakfalls
Do not depend on any sort of weapon,
But only on what I might coin a phrase and call
The ever-important question of human balance,
And the ever-important need to be in a strong
    Position at the start.

There are many kinds of weakness about the body,
Where you would least expect, like the ball of the foot.
But the various holds and rolls and throws and breakfalls
Will always come in useful. And never be frightened
To tackle from behind: it may not be clean to do so,
    But this is global war.

So give them all you have, and always give them
As good as you get; it will always get you somewhere.
(You may not know it, but you can tie a Jerry
Up without rope; it is one of the things I shall teach you.)
Nothing will matter if only you are ready for him.
    The readiness is all.

The readiness is all. How can I help but feel
I have been here before? But somehow then,
I was the tied-up one. How to get out
Was always then my problem. And even if I had
A piece of rope I was always the sort of person
    Who threw the rope aside.

And in my time I have given them all I had,
Which was never as good as I got, and it got me nowhere.
And the various holds and rolls and throws and breakfalls
Somehow or other I always seemed to put
In the wrong place. And as for war, my wars
    Were global from the start.

Perhaps I was never in a strong position,
Or the ball of my foot got hurt, or I had some weakness
Where I had least expected. But I think I see your point.
While awaiting a proper issue, we must learn the lesson
Of the ever-important question of human balance.
    It is courage that counts.

Things may be the same again; and we must fight
Not in the hope of winning but rather of keeping
Something alive: so that when we meet our end,
It may be said that we tackled wherever we could,
That battle-fit we lived, and though defeated,
    Not without glory fought.

ALUN LEWIS

1915–1944

194   *All day it has rained . . .*

All day it has rained, and we on the edge of the moors
Have sprawled in our bell-tents, moody and dull as boors,
Groundsheets and blankets spread on the muddy ground
And from the first grey wakening we have found
No refuge from the skirmishing fine rain
And the wind that made the canvas heave and flap
And the taut wet guy-ropes ravel out and snap.

ALUN LEWIS

All day the rain has glided, wave and mist and dream,
Drenching the gorse and heather, a gossamer stream
Too light to stir the acorns that suddenly
Snatched from their cups by the wild south-westerly
Pattered against the tent and our upturned dreaming faces.
And we stretched out, unbuttoning our braces,
Smoking a Woodbine, darning dirty socks,
Reading the Sunday papers—I saw a fox
And mentioned it in the note I scribbled home;—
And we talked of girls, and dropping bombs on Rome,
And thought of the quiet dead and the loud celebrities
Exhorting us to slaughter, and the herded refugees;
—Yet thought softly, morosely of them, and as indifferently
As of ourselves or those whom we
For years have loved, and will again
Tomorrow maybe love; but now it is the rain
Possesses us entirely, the twilight and the rain.

And I can remember nothing dearer or more to my heart
Than the children I watched in the woods on Saturday
Shaking down burning chestnuts for the schoolyard's merry
    play,
Or the shaggy patient dog who followed me
By Sheet and Steep and up the wooded scree
To the Shoulder o' Mutton where Edward Thomas brooded
    long
On death and beauty—till a bullet stopped his song.

195   *Dawn on the East Coast*

From Orford Ness to Shingle Street
The grey disturbance spreads
Washing the icy seas on Deben Head.

Cock pheasants scratch the frozen fields,
Gulls lift thin horny legs and step
Fastidiously among the rusted mines.

The soldier leaning on the sandbagged wall
Hears in the combers' curling rush and crash
His single self-centred monotonous wish;

And time is a froth of such transparency
His drowning eyes see what they wish to see;
A girl laying his table with a white cloth.

. . .

The light assails him from a flank,
Two carbons touching in his brain
Crumple the cellophane lanterns of his dream.

And then the day, grown feminine and kind,
Stoops with the gulfing motion of the tide
And pours his ashes in a tiny urn.

From Orford Ness to Shingle Street
The grey disturbance lifts its head
And one by one, reluctantly,
The living come back slowly from the dead.

196   *Goodbye*

So we must say Goodbye, my darling,
And go, as lovers go, for ever;
Tonight remains, to pack and fix on labels
And make an end of lying down together.

I put a final shilling in the gas,
And watch you slip your dress below your knees
And lie so still I hear your rustling comb
Modulate the autumn in the trees.

And all the countless things I shall remember
Lay mummy-cloths of silence round my head;
I fill the carafe with a drink of water;
You say 'We paid a guinea for this bed,'

And then, 'We'll leave some gas, a little warmth
For the next resident, and these dry flowers,'
And turn your face away, afraid to speak
The big word, that Eternity is ours.

Your kisses close my eyes and yet you stare
As though God struck a child with nameless fears;
Perhaps the water glitters and discloses
Time's chalice and its limpid useless tears.

Everything we renounce except our selves;
Selfishness is the last of all to go;
Our sighs are exhalations of the earth,
Our footprints leave a track across the snow.

We made the universe to be our home,
Our nostrils took the wind to be our breath,
Our hearts are massive towers of delight,
We stride across the seven seas of death.

Yet when all's done you'll keep the emerald
I placed upon your finger in the street;
And I will keep the patches that you sewed
On my old battledress tonight, my sweet.

197   *Song*

(On seeing dead bodies floating off the Cape)

The first month of his absence
I was numb and sick
And where he'd left his promise
Life did not turn or kick.
The seed, the seed of love was sick.

The second month my eyes were sunk
In the darkness of despair,
And my bed was like a grave
And his ghost was lying there.
And my heart was sick with care.

The third month of his going
I thought I heard him say
'Our course deflected slightly
On the thirty-second day—'
The tempest blew his words away.

And he was lost among the waves,
His ship rolled helpless in the sea,
The fourth month of his voyage
He shouted grievously
'Beloved, do not think of me.'

The flying fish like kingfishers
Skim the sea's bewildered crests,
The whales blow steaming fountains,
The seagulls have no nests
Where my lover sways and rests.

We never thought to buy and sell
This life that blooms or withers in the leaf,
And I'll not stir, so he sleeps well,
Though cell by cell the coral reef
Builds an eternity of grief.

But oh! the drag and dullness of my Self;
The turning seasons wither in my head;
All this slowness, all this hardness,
The nearness that is waiting in my bed,
The gradual self-effacement of the dead.

SIDNEY KEYES

1922–1943

198   from *The Foreign Gate*

The moon is a poor woman.
The moon returns to weep with us. The crosses
Burn raw and white upon the night's stiff banners.
The wooden crosses and the marble trees
Shrink from the foreign moon.
The iron gate glitters. Here the soldiers lie.
Fold up the flags, muffle the soldier's drum;
Silence the calling fife. O drape
The soldier's drum with heavy crêpe;

With mourning weeds muffle the soldier's girl.
It's a long way and a long march
To the returning moon and to the soil
No time at all.
          O call
The soldier's glory by another name:
Shroud up the soldier's common shame
And drape the soldier's drum, but spare
The steel-caged brain, the feet that walk to war.

Once striding under a horsehair plume
Once beating the taut drums for war
The sunlight rang from brass and iron;
History was an angry play—
The boy grew tall and rode away;
The door hung slack; the pale girl wept
And cursed the company he kept.
And dumb men spoke
Through the glib mouths of smoke;
The servile learned to strike
The proud to shriek;
And strangled in their lovers' lips
The young fell short of glory in the sand
Raking for graves among the scattered sand;
The tattered flags strained at the wind
Scaring the thrifty kite, mocking the dead.
But muffle the soldier's drum, hide his pale head,
His face a spider's web of blood. O fold
The hands that grip a splintered gun.
          The glittering gate
Baffles him still, his starvecrow soul. O drape
The soldier's drum and cry, who never dare
Defy the ironbound brain, the feet that walk to war.

The cold hand clenches. The stupid mouth
Writhes like a ripple. Now the field is full
Of noises and dead voices . . .
          'My rags flap
Though the great flags are trampled . . .'
          'My mouth speaks
Terror and truth, instead of hard command.'
'Remember the torn lace, the fine coats slashed

With steel instead of velvet. Künersdorf
Fought in the shallow sand was my relief.'
'I rode to Naseby' . . . 'And the barren land
Of Tannenberg drank me. Remember now
The grey and jointed corpses in the snow,
The struggle in the drift, the numb hands freezing
Into the bitter iron . . .'
                                    'At Dunkirk I
Rolled in the shallows, and the living trod
Across me for a bridge . . .'
                                    'Let me speak out
Against this sham of policy, for pain
Alone is true. I was a general
Who fought the cunning Africans, returned
Crowned with harsh laurel, frantically cheered
Through Roman streets. I spoke of fame and glory.
Women grabbed at my robe. Great poets praised me.
I died of cancer, screaming, in a year.'
'I fell on a black Spanish hillside
Under the thorn-hedge, fighting for a dream
That troubled me in Paris; vomited
My faith and courage out among the stones . . .'
'I was a barb of light, a burning cross
Of wood and canvas, falling through the night.'
'I was shot down at morning, in a yard.'

The moon regards them without shame. The wind
Rises and twitters through the wreck of bone . . .
                                    'It is so hard to be alone
Continually, watching the great stars march
Their circular unending route; sharp sand
Straying about the eyes, blinding the quick-eyed spirit.'
A soldier's death is hard;
There's no prescribed or easy word
For dissolution in the Army books.
The uniform of pain with pain put on is straiter
Than any lover's garment; yet the death
Of these is different, and their glory greater.
Once men, then moving figures on a map,
Patiently giving time and strength and vision
Even identity
Into the future's keeping;
Nourished on wounds and weeping

Faces and laughing flags and pointed laurels,
Their pain cries down the noise of poetry.

So muffle the soldier's drum, forget the battles;
Remember only fame's a way of living:
The writing may be greater than the speaking
And every death for something different
From time's compulsion, is a written word.
Whatever gift, it is the giving
Remains significant: whatever death
It is the dying matters.
                    Emblematic
Bronze eagle or bright banner or carved name
Of fighting ancestor; these never pardon
The pain and sorrow. It is the dying pardons,
For something different from man or emblem.
Then drape the soldier's drum
And carry him down
Beyond the moon's inspection, and the noise
Of bands and banners and the striking sun.
Scatter the soldier's emblems and his fame:
Shroud up the shattered face, the empty name;
Speak out the word and drape the drum and spare
The captive brain, the feet that walk to war
The ironbound brain, the hand unskilled in war
The shrinking brain, sick of an inner war.

199   *Timoshenko**

Hour ten he rose, ten-sworded, every finger
A weighted blade, and strapping round his loins
The courage of attack, he threw the window
Open to look on his appointed night.

Where lay, beneath the winds and creaking flares
Tangled like lovers or alone assuming
The wanton postures of the drunk with sleep,
An army of twisted limbs and hollow faces
Thrown to and fro between the winds and shadows.

* In June 1940, the Russian Marshal Semyon Konstantinovich Timoshenko was
appointed commissar for defence. He achieved renown in the Second World War for
recapturing Rostov from the Germans (November 1941), and for his command on the
north-west front (1942), in the Caucasus (1942), and in Bessarabia (1944).

O hear the wind, the wind that shakes the dawn.
And there before the night, he was aware
Of the flayed fields of home, and black with ruin
The helpful earth under the tracks of tanks.
His bladed hand, in pity falling, mimicked
The crumpled hand lamenting the broken plow;
And the oracular metal lips in anger
Squared to the shape of the raped girl's yelling mouth.
He heard the wind explaining nature's sorrow
And humming in the wire hair of the dead.

He turned, and his great shadow on the wall
Swayed like a tree. His eyes grew cold as lead.
Then, in a rage of love and grief and pity,
He made the pencilled map alive with war.

September 1942

200   from *The Wilderness*

The red rock wilderness
Shall be my dwelling-place.

Where the wind saws at the bluffs
And the pebble falls like thunder
I shall watch the clawed sun
Tear the rocks asunder.

The seven-branched cactus
Will never sweat wine:
My own bleeding feet
Shall furnish the sign.

The rock says 'Endure.'
The wind says 'Pursue.'
The sun says 'I will suck your bones
And afterwards bury you.'

Here where the horned skulls mark the limit
Of instinct and intransigent desire
I beat against the rough-tongued wind
Towards the heart of fire.

So knowing my youth, which was yesterday,
And my pride which shall be gone tomorrow,
I turn my face to the sun, remembering gardens
Planted by others—Longinus, Guillaume de Lorris
And all love's gardeners, in an early May.
O sing, small ancient bird, for I am going
Into the sun's garden, the red rock desert
I have dreamt of and desired more than the lilac's promise.
The flowers of the rock shall never fall.

O speak no more of love and death
And speak no word of sorrow:
My anger's eaten up my pride
And both shall die tomorrow.

Knowing I am no lover, but destroyer,
I am content to face the destroying sun.
There shall be no more journeys, nor the anguish
Of meeting and parting, after the last great parting
From the images of dancing and the gardens
Where the brown bird chokes in its song:
Until that last great meeting among mountains
Where the metal bird sings madly from the fire.

O speak no more of ceremony,
Speak no more of fame:
My heart must seek a burning land
To bury its foolish pain.

By the dry river at the desert edge
I regret the speaking rivers I have known;
The sunlight shattered under the dark bridge
And many tongues of rivers in the past.
Rivers and gardens, singing under the willows,
The glowing moon. . . .
                              And all the poets of summer
Must lament another spirit's passing over.

O never weep for me, my love,
Or seek me in this land:
But light a candle for my luck
And bear it in your hand.

KEITH DOUGLAS

1920–1944

201   *Gallantry*

The Colonel in a casual voice
spoke into the microphone a joke
which through a hundred earphones broke
into the ears of a doomed race.

Into the ears of the doomed boy, the fool
whose perfectly mannered flesh fell
in opening the door for a shell
as he had learnt to do at school.

Conrad luckily survived the winter:
he wrote a letter to welcome
the auspicious spring: only his silken
intentions severed with a single splinter.

Was George fond of little boys?
We always suspected it,
but who will say: since George was hit
we never mention our surmise.

It was a brave thing the Colonel said,
but the whole sky turned too hot
and the three heroes never heard what
it was, gone deaf with steel and lead.

But the bullets cried with laughter,
the shells were overcome with mirth,
plunging their heads in steel and earth—
(the air commented in a whisper).

202   *Vergissmeinnicht*

Three weeks gone and the combatants gone
returning over the nightmare ground
we found the place again, and found
the soldier sprawling in the sun.

267

The frowning barrel of his gun
overshadowing. As we came on
that day, he hit my tank with one
like the entry of a demon.

Look. Here in the gunpit spoil
the dishonoured picture of his girl
who has put: *Steffi. Vergissmeinnicht*
in a copybook gothic script.

We see him almost with content,
abased, and seeming to have paid
and mocked at by his own equipment
that's hard and good when he's decayed.

But she would weep to see today
how on his skin the swart flies move;
the dust upon the paper eye
and the burst stomach like a cave.

For here the lover and killer are mingled
who had one body and one heart.
And death who had the soldier singled
has done the lover mortal hurt.

203   *Aristocrats*

'I think I am becoming a God'

The noble horse with courage in, his eye
clean in the bone, looks up at a shellburst:
away fly the images of the shires
but he puts the pipe back in his mouth.

Peter was unfortunately killed by an 88:
it took his leg away, he died in the ambulance.
I saw him crawling on the sand, he said
It's most unfair, they've shot my foot off.

How can I live among this gentle
obsolescent breed of heroes, and not weep?
Unicorns, almost,
for they are fading into two legends
in which their stupidity and chivalry
are celebrated. Each, fool and hero, will be an immortal.

These plains were their cricket pitch
and in the mountains the tremendous drop fences
brought down some of the runners. Here then
under the stones and earth they dispose themselves,
I think with their famous unconcern.
It is not gunfire I hear, but a hunting horn.

Enfidaville, Tunisia, 1943

NORMAN CAMERON

1905–1953

204   *Green, Green is El Aghir*

Sprawled on the crates and sacks in the rear of the truck,
I was gummy-mouthed from the sun and the dust of the track,
And the two Arab soldiers I'd taken on as hitch-hikers
At a torrid petrol-dump, had been there on their hunkers
Since early morning. I said, in a kind of French
'On m'a dit, qu'il y a une belle source d'eau fraîche,
Plus loin, à El Aghir' . . .

It was eighty more kilometres
Until round a corner we heard a splashing of waters,
And there, in a green, dark street, was a fountain with two faces
Discharging both ways, from full-throated faucets
Into basins, thence into troughs and thence into brooks.
Our negro corporal driver slammed his brakes,
And we yelped and leapt from the truck and went at the double
To fill our bidons and bottles and drink and dabble.
Then, swollen with water, we went to an inn for wine.
The Arabs came, too, though their faith might have stood between.

'After all,' they said, 'it's a boisson,' without contrition.
Green, green is El Aghir. It has a railway-station,
And the wealth of its soil has borne many another fruit,
A mairie, a school and an elegant Salle de Fêtes.
Such blessings, as I remarked, in effect, to the waiter,
Are added unto them that have plenty of water.

F. T. PRINCE

1912–

205   *Soldiers Bathing*

The sea at evening moves across the sand.
Under a reddening sky I watch the freedom of a band
Of soldiers who belong to me. Stripped bare
For bathing in the sea, they shout and run in the warm air;
Their flesh worn by the trade of war, revives
And my mind towards the meaning of it strives.

All's pathos now. The body that was gross,
Rank, ravenous, disgusting in the act or in repose,
All fever, filth and sweat, its bestial strength
And bestial decay, by pain and labour grows at length
Fragile and luminous. 'Poor bare forked animal,'
Conscious of his desires and needs and flesh that rise and fall,
Stands in the soft air, tasting after toil
The sweetness of his nakedness: letting the sea-waves coil
Their frothy tongues about his feet, forgets
His hatred of the war, its terrible pressure that begets
A machinery of death and slavery,
Each being a slave and making slaves of others: finds that he
Remembers his old freedom in a game
Mocking himself, and comically mimics fear and shame.

He plays with death and animality;
And reading in the shadows of his pallid flesh, I see
The idea of Michelangelo's cartoon
Of soldiers bathing, breaking off before they were half done
At some sortie of the enemy, an episode
Of the Pisan wars with Florence. I remember how he showed
Their muscular limbs that clamber from the water,

And heads that turn across the shoulder, eager for the slaughter,
Forgetful of their bodies that are bare,
And hot to buckle on and use the weapons lying there.
—And I think too of the theme another found
When, shadowing men's bodies on a sinister red ground,
Another Florentine, Pollaiuolo,
Painted a naked battle: warriors, straddled, hacked the foe,
Dug their bare toes into the ground and slew
The brother-naked man who lay between their feet and drew
His lips back from his teeth in a grimace.

They were Italians who knew war's sorrow and disgrace
And showed the thing suspended, stripped: a theme
Born out of the experience of war's horrible extreme
Beneath a sky where even the air flows
With lacrimae Christi. For that rage, that bitterness, those blows,
That hatred of the slain, what could they be
But indirectly or directly a commentary
On the Crucifixion? And the picture burns
With indignation and pity and despair by turns,
Because it is the obverse of the scene
Where Christ hangs murdered, stripped, upon the Cross. I mean,
That is the explanation of its rage.

And we too have our bitterness and pity that engage
Blood, spirit, in this war. But night begins,
Night of the mind: who nowadays is conscious of our sins?
Though every human deed concerns our blood,
And even we must know, what nobody has understood,
That some great love is over all we do,
And that is what has driven us to this fury, for so few
Can suffer all the terror of that love:
The terror of that love has set us spinning in this groove
Greased with our blood.

                    These dry themselves and dress,
Combing their hair, forget the fear and shame of nakedness.
Because to love is frightening we prefer
The freedom of our crimes. Yet, as I drink the dusky air,
I feel a strange delight that fills me full,
Strange gratitude, as if evil itself were beautiful,
And kiss the wound in thought, while in the west
I watch a streak of red that might have issued from Christ's breast.

ROY FULLER

1912–

206   *The Middle of a War*

My photograph already looks historic.
The promising youthful face, the matelot's collar,
Say 'This one is remembered for a lyric.
His place and period—nothing could be duller.'

Its position is already indicated—
The son or brother in the album; pained
The expression and the garments dated,
His fate so obviously pre-ordained.

The original turns away; as horrible thoughts,
Loud fluttering aircraft slope above his head
At dusk. The ridiculous empires break like biscuits.

Ah, life has been abandoned by the boats—
Only the trodden island and the dead
Remain, and the once inestimable caskets.

GAVIN EWART

1916–

207   *When a Beau Goes In*

When a Beau goes in,
Into the drink,
It makes you think,
Because, you see, they always sink
But nobody says 'Poor lad'
Or goes about looking sad
Because, you see, it's war,
It's the unalterable law.

Although it's perfectly certain
The pilot's gone for a Burton
And the observer too
It's nothing to do with you
And if they both should go
To a land where falls no rain nor hail nor driven snow—
Here, there or anywhere
Do you suppose *they* care?

You shouldn't cry
Or say a prayer or sigh.
In the cold sea, in the dark,
It isn't a lark
But it isn't Original Sin—
It's just a Beau going in.

MARIANNE MOORE

1887–1972

208   *In Distrust of Merits*

Strengthened to live, strengthened to die for
    medals and positioned victories?
They're fighting, fighting, fighting the blind
    man who thinks he sees,—
who cannot see that the enslaver is
enslaved; the hater, harmed. O shining O
      firm star, O tumultuous
        ocean lashed till small things go
    as they will, the mountainous
      wave makes us who look, know

depth. Lost at sea before they fought! O
    star of David, star of Bethlehem,
O black imperial lion
    of the Lord—emblem
of a risen world—be joined at last, be
joined. There is hate's crown beneath which all is
      death; there's love's without which none
        is king; the blessed deeds bless
    the halo. As contagion
      of sickness makes sickness,

contagion of trust can make trust. They're
    fighting in deserts and caves, one by
one, in battalions and squadrons;
    they're fighting that I
may yet recover from the disease, My
Self; some have it lightly; some will die. 'Man
        wolf to man' and we devour
           ourselves. The enemy could not
        have made a greater breach in our
        defences. One pilot-

ing a blind man can escape him, but
    Job disheartened by false comfort knew
that nothing can be so defeating
    as a blind man who
can see. O alive who are dead, who are
proud not to see, O small dust of the earth
        that walks so arrogantly,
           trust begets power and faith is
        an affectionate thing. We
        vow, we make this promise

to the fighting—it's a promise—'We'll
    never hate black, white, red, yellow, Jew,
Gentile, Untouchable.' We are
    not competent to
make our vows. With set jaw they are fighting,
fighting, fighting,—some we love whom we know,
        some we love but know not—that
           hearts may feel and not be numb.
        It cures me; or am I what
        I can't believe in? Some

in snow, some on crags, some in quicksands,
    little by little, much by much, they
are fighting fighting fighting that where
    there was death there may
be life. 'When a man is prey to anger,
he is moved by outside things; when he holds
        his ground in patience patience
           patience, that is action or
        beauty', the soldier's defence
        and hardest armour for

the fight. The world's an orphans' home. Shall
    we never have peace without sorrow?
without pleas of the dying for
    help that won't come? O
quiet form upon the dust, I cannot
look and yet I must. If these great patient
        dyings—all these agonies
            and woundbearings and bloodshed—
        can teach us how to live, these
        dyings were not wasted.

Hate-hardened heart, O heart of iron,
    iron is iron till it is rust.
There never was a war that was
    not inward; I must
fight till I have conquered in myself what
causes war, but I would not believe it.
        I inwardly did nothing.
            O Iscariotlike crime!
        Beauty is everlasting
        and dust is for a time.

RICHARD EBERHART

1904–

209   *The Fury of Aerial Bombardment*

You would think the fury of aerial bombardment
Would rouse God to relent; the infinite spaces
Are still silent. He looks on shock-pried faces.
History, even, does not know what is meant.

You would feel that after so many centuries
God would give man to repent; yet he can kill
As Cain could, but with multitudinous will,
No farther advanced than in his ancient furies.

Was man made stupid to see his own stupidity?
Is God by definition indifferent, beyond us all?
Is the eternal truth man's fighting soul
Wherein the Beast ravens in its own avidity?

Of Van Wettering I speak, and Averill,
Names on a list, whose faces I do not recall
But they are gone to early death, who late in school
Distinguished the belt feed lever from the belt holding pawl.

RANDALL JARRELL

1914–1965

210   *Eighth Air Force*

If, in an odd angle of the hutment,
A puppy laps the water from a can
Of flowers, and the drunk sergeant shaving
Whistles O *Paradiso!*—shall I say that man
Is not as men have said: a wolf to man?

The other murderers troop in yawning;
Three of them play Pitch, one sleeps, and one
Lies counting missions, lies there sweating
Till even his heart beats: One; One; One.
O *murderers!* . . . Still, this is how it's done:

This is a war. . . . But since these play, before they die,
Like puppies with their puppy; since, a man,
I did as these have done, but did not die—
I will content the people as I can
And give up these to them: Behold the man!

I have suffered, in a dream, because of him,
Many things; for this last saviour, man,
I have lied as I lie now. But what is lying?
Men wash their hands, in blood, as best they can:
I find no fault in this just man.

211   *The Death of the Ball Turret Gunner*

From my mother's sleep I fell into the State,
And I hunched in its belly till my wet fur froze.
Six miles from earth, loosed from its dream of life,
I woke to black flak and the nightmare fighters.
When I died they washed me out of the turret with a hose.

212   *A Camp in the Prussian Forest*

I walk beside the prisoners to the road.
Load on puffed load,
Their corpses, stacked like sodden wood,
Lie barred or galled with blood

By the charred warehouse. No one comes today
In the old way
To knock the fillings from their teeth;
The dark, coned, common wreath

Is plaited for their grave—a kind of grief.
The living leaf
Clings to the planted profitable
Pine if it is able;

The boughs sigh, mile on green, calm, breathing mile,
From this dead file
The planners ruled for them. . . . One year
They sent a million here:

Here men were drunk like water, burnt like wood.
The fat of good
And evil, the breast's star of hope
Were rendered into soap.

I paint the star I sawed from yellow pine—
And plant the sign
In soil that does not yet refuse
Its usual Jews

Their first asylum. But the white, dwarfed star—
This dead white star—
Hides nothing, pays for nothing; smoke
Fouls it, a yellow joke,

The needles of the wreath are chalked with ash,
A filmy trash
Litters the black woods with the death
Of men; and one last breath

Curls from the monstrous chimney. . . . I laugh aloud
Again and again;
The star laughs from its rotting shroud
Of flesh. O star of men!

213   *A Front*

Fog over the base: the beams ranging
From the five towers pull home from the night
The crews cold in fur, the bombers banging
Like lost trucks down the levels of the ice.
A glow drifts in like mist (how many tons of it?),
Bounces to a roll, turns suddenly to steel
And tires and turrets, huge in the trembling light.
The next is high, and pulls up with a wail,
Comes round again—no use. And no use for the rest
In drifting circles out along the range;
Holding no longer, changed to a kinder course,
The flights drone southward through the steady rain.
The base is closed. . . . But one voice keeps on calling,
The lowering pattern of the engines grows;
The roar gropes downward in its shaky orbit
For the lives the season quenches. Here below
They beg, order, are not heard; and hear the darker
Voice rising: *Can't you hear me? Over. Over—*
All the air quivers, and the east sky glows.

W. D. SNODGRASS

1926–

'After Experience Taught Me . . .'

After experience taught me that all the ordinary
Surroundings of social life are futile and vain;

> I'm going to show you something very
> Ugly: someday, it might save your life.

Seeing that none of the things I feared contain
In themselves anything either good or bad

> What if you get caught without a knife;
> Nothing—even a loop of piano wire;

Excepting only in the effect they had
Upon my mind, I resolved to inquire

> Take the first two fingers of this hand;
> Fork them out—kind of a 'V for Victory'—

Whether there might be something whose discovery
Would grant me supreme, unending happiness.

> And jam them into the eyes of your enemy.
> You have to do this hard. Very hard. Then press

No virtue can be thought to have priority
Over this endeavor to preserve one's being.

> Both fingers down around the cheekbone
> And setting your foot high into the chest

No man can desire to act rightly, to be blessed,
To live rightly, without simultaneously

> You must call up every strength you own
> And you can rip off the whole facial mask.

Wishing to be, to act, to live. He must ask
First, in other words, to actually exist.

> And you, whiner, who wastes your time
> Dawdling over the remorseless earth,
> What evil, what unspeakable crime
> Have you made your life worth?

LOUIS SIMPSON

1923–

215

*Carentan O Carentan**

Trees in the old days used to stand
And shape a shady lane
Where lovers wandered hand in hand
Who came from Carentan.

This was the shining green canal
Where we came two by two
Walking at combat-interval.
Such trees we never knew.

The day was early June, the ground
Was soft and bright with dew.
Far away the guns did sound,
But here the sky was blue.

The sky was blue, but there a smoke
Hung still above the sea
Where the ships together spoke
To towns we could not see.

Could you have seen us through a glass
You would have said a walk
Of farmers out to turn the grass,
Each with his own hay-fork.

---

* Carentan was the site of a battle in the invasion of Normandy in June 1944.

The watchers in their leopard suits
Waited till it was time,
And aimed between the belt and boot
And let the barrel climb.

I must lie down at once, there is
A hammer at my knee.
And call it death or cowardice,
Don't count again on me.

Everything's all right, Mother,
Everyone gets the same
At one time or another.
It's all in the game.

I never strolled, nor ever shall,
Down such a leafy lane.
I never drank in a canal,
Nor ever shall again.

There is a whistling in the leaves
And it is not the wind,
The twigs are falling from the knives
That cut men to the ground.

Tell me, Master-Sergeant,
The way to turn and shoot.
But the Sergeant's silent
That taught me how to do it.

O Captain, show us quickly
Our place upon the map.
But the Captain's sickly
And taking a long nap.

Lieutenant, what's my duty,
My place in the platoon?
He too's a sleeping beauty,
Charmed by that strange tune.

Carentan O Carentan
Before we met with you
We never yet had lost a man
Or known what death could do.

LOUIS SIMPSON

Memories of a Lost War

The guns know what is what, but underneath
In fearful file
We go around burst boots and packs and teeth
That seem to smile.

The scene jags like a strip of celluloid,
A mortar fires,
Cinzano falls, Michelin is destroyed,
The man of tires.

As darkness drifts like fog in from the sea
Somebody says
'We're digging in.' Look well, for this may be
The last of days.

Hot lightnings stitch the blind eye of the moon,
The thunder's blunt.
We sleep. Our dreams pass in a faint platoon
Toward the front.

Sleep well, for you are young. Each tree and bush
Drips with sweet dew,
And earlier than morning June's cool hush
Will waken you.

The riflemen will wake and hold their breath.
Though they may bleed
They will be proud a while of something death
Still seems to need.

The Battle

Helmet and rifle, pack and overcoat
Marched through a forest. Somewhere up ahead
Guns thudded. Like the circle of a throat
The night on every side was turning red.

They halted and they dug. They sank like moles
Into the clammy earth between the trees.
And soon the sentries, standing in their holes,
Felt the first snow. Their feet began to freeze.

At dawn the first shell landed with a crack.
Then shells and bullets swept the icy woods.
This lasted many days. The snow was black.
The corpses stiffened in their scarlet hoods.

Most clearly of that battle I remember
The tiredness in eyes, how hands looked thin
Around a cigarette, and the bright ember
Would pulse with all the life there was within.

218   *The Heroes*

I dreamed of war-heroes, of wounded war-heroes
With just enough of their charms shot away
To make them more handsome. The women moved nearer
To touch their brave wounds and their hair streaked with gray.

I saw them in long ranks ascending the gang-planks;
The girls with the doughnuts were cheerful and gay.
They minded their manners and muttered their thanks;
The Chaplain advised them to watch and to pray.

They shipped these rapscallions, these sea-sick battalions
To a patriotic and picturesque spot;
They gave them new bibles and marksmen's medallions,
Compasses, maps, and committed the lot.

A fine dust has settled on all that scrap metal.
The heroes were packaged and sent home in parts
To pluck at a poppy and sew on a petal
And count the long night by the stroke of their hearts.

RICHARD WILBUR

1921–

219   *First Snow in Alsace*

The snow came down last night like moths
Burned on the moon; it fell till dawn,
Covered the town with simple cloths.

Absolute snow lies rumpled on
What shellbursts scattered and deranged,
Entangled railings, crevassed lawn.

As if it did not know they'd changed,
Snow smoothly clasps the roofs of homes
Fear-gutted, trustless and estranged.

The ration stacks are milky domes;
Across the ammunition pile
The snow has climbed in sparkling combs.

You think: beyond the town a mile
Or two, this snowfall fills the eyes
Of soldiers dead a little while.

Persons and persons in disguise,
Walking the new air white and fine,
Trade glances quick with shared surprise.

At children's windows, heaped, benign,
As always, winter shines the most,
And frost makes marvellous designs.

The night guard coming from his post,
Ten first-snows back in thought, walks slow
And warms him with a boyish boast:

He was the first to see the snow.

LINCOLN KIRSTEIN

1907–

220 *Rank*

Differences between rich and poor, king and queen,
Cat and dog, hot and cold, day and night, now and then,
Are less clearly distinct than all those between
Officers and us: enlisted men.

Not by brass may you guess nor their private latrine
Since distinctions obtain in any real well-run war;
It's when off duty, drunk, one acts nice or mean
In a sawdust-strewn bistro-type bar.

Ours was on a short street near the small market square;
Farmers dropped by for some beer or oftener to tease
The Gargantuan bartender Jean-Pierre
About his sweet wife, Marie-Louise.

GI's got the habit who liked French movies or books,
Tried to talk French or were happy to be left alone;
It was our kinda club; we played chess in nooks
With the farmers. We made it our own.

To this haven one night came an officer bold;
Crocked and ugly, he'd had it in five bars before.
A lurid luster glazed his eye which foretold
He'd better stay out of our shut door,

But did not. He barged in, slung his cap on the zinc:
'Dewbelle veesky,' knowing well there was little but beer.
Jean-Pierre showed the list of what one could drink:
'What sorta jerk joint you running here?'

Jean-Pierre had wine but no whisky to sell.
Wine loves the soul. Hard liquor hots up bloody fun,
And it's our rule noncommissioned personnel
Must keep by them their piece called a gun.

As well we are taught, enlisted soldiers may never
Ever surrender this piece—M1, carbine, or rifle—
With which no mere officer whomsoever
May freely or foolishly trifle.

A porcelain stove glowed in its niche, white and warm.
Jean-Pierre made jokes with us French-speaking boys.
Marie-Louise lay warm in bed far from harm;
Upstairs, snored through the ensuing noise.

This captain swilled beer with minimal grace. He began:
'Shit. What you-all are drinkin's not liquor. It's piss.'
Two privates (first class) now consider some plan
To avoid what may result from this.

Captain Stearnes is an Old Army joe. Eighteen years
In the ranks, man and boy; bad luck, small promotion;
Without brains or cash, not the cream of careers.
Frustration makes plenty emotion.

'Now, Mac,' Stearnes grins (Buster's name is not Mac; it is Jack),
'Toss me your gun an' I'll show you an old army trick;
At forty feet, with one hand, I'll crack that stove, smack.'
'Let's not,' drawls Jack back, scared of this prick.

'You young punk,' Stearnes now storms, growing moody but mean,
'Do you dream I daren't pull my superior rank?'
His hand snatches Jack's light clean bright carbine.
What riddles the roof is no blank.

The rifle is loaded as combat zones ever require.
His arm kicks back without hurt to a porcelain stove.
Steel drilling plaster and plank, thin paths of fire
Plug Marie-Louise sleeping above.

Formal enquiry subsequent to this shootin'
Had truth and justice separately demanded.
Was Stearnes found guilty? You are darned tootin':
Fined, demoted. More: reprimanded.

The charge was not murder, mayhem, mischief malicious,
Yet something worse, and this they brought out time and again:
Clearly criminal and caddishly vicious
Was his: Drinking With Enlisted Men.

I'm serious. It's what the Judge Advocate said:
Strict maintenance of rank or our system is sunk.
Stearnes saluted. Jean-Pierre wept his dead.
Jack and I got see-double drunk.

221   *Foresight*

Previsioning death in advance, our doom is delayed.
I guess mine:
I'm driving for some dumb officer on this raid:

I can't doubt his sense of direction, his perfect right.
Still, he's wrong.
I hint we're too far front. Been warned plenty about this before.

Base far off. No lights may be shown. He starts to get sore.
Lost, our road.
He feels he's failed. Abruptly down drops night.

Anticipate panic: his, mine, contagions fear takes.
THIS IS IT.
Not good. I invoke calm plus prayer for both our sakes.

Calm makes sense. Prayer is less useful than gin or a smoke.
Where are we?
If this ass hadn't tried to crack his great big joke,

Pushing beyond where he knew well we were told to go,
We'd be safe.
Checking my estimate, my unvoiced I Told You So,

Granite bang-bangs blossom all over hell and gone.
Let me Out!
My foreseen fright swells, a warm swarm and we're sure done

In by Mistake, including his fright, faking him brave;
Me the same,
Making me clam tight when I oughta had the brains to save

Our skins, sparing official pride by baring my fear:
(Please, sir. *Turn.*)
Sharing his shame with me, who, also, deserve some. Oh dear,

It's too late. The end of two nervous careers,
Of dear me,
And him, dear doubtless to someone, worth her dear tears.

VERNON SCANNELL

1922–

222   *Walking Wounded*

A mammoth morning moved grey flanks and groaned.
In the rusty hedges pale rags of mist hung;
The gruel of mud and leaves in the mauled lane
Smelled sweet, like blood. Birds had died or flown,
Their green and silent attics sprouting now

With branches of leafed steel, hiding round eyes
And ripe grenades ready to drop and burst.
In the ditch at the cross-roads the fallen rider lay
Hugging his dead machine and did not stir
At crunch of mortar, tantrum of a Bren
Answering a Spandau's manic jabber.
Then into sight the ambulances came,
Stumbling and churning past the broken farm,
The amputated sign-post and smashed trees,
Slow wagonloads of bandaged cries, square trucks
That rolled on ominous wheels, vehicles
Made mythopoeic by their mortal freight
And crimson crosses on the dirty white.
This grave procession passed, though, for a while,
The grinding of their engines could be heard,
A dark noise on the pallor of the morning,
Dark as dried blood; and then it faded, died.
The road was empty, but it seemed to wait—
Like a stage which knows the cast is in the wings—
Wait for a different traffic to appear.
The mist still hung in snags from dripping thorns;
Absent-minded guns still sighed and thumped.
And then they came, the walking wounded,
Straggling the road like convicts loosely chained,
Dragging at ankles exhaustion and despair.
Their heads were weighted down by last night's lead,
And eyes still drank the dark. They trailed the night
Along the morning road. Some limped on sticks;
Others wore rough dressings, splints and slings;
A few had turbanned heads, the dirty cloth
Brown-badged with blood. A humble brotherhood,
Not one was suffering from a lethal hurt,
They were not magnified by noble wounds,
There was no splendour in that company.
And yet, remembering after eighteen years,
In the heart's throat a sour sadness stirs;
Imagination pauses and returns
To see them walking still, but multiplied
In thousands now. And when heroic corpses
Turn slowly in their decorated sleep
And every ambulance has disappeared
The walking wounded still trudge down that lane,
And when recalled they must bear arms again.

PAUL DEHN

1912–1976

223 *St Aubin D'Aubigné*

It was only a small place and they had cheered us too much,
A couple of allies, chance symbol of Freedom new-found.
They were eager to beckon, to back-slap, even to touch;
They put flowers in my helmet and corn-coloured wine in my hand.

The boy from Dakota and I, we had suffered too little
To deserve all the flowers, the kisses, the wine and the thanks.
We both felt ashamed; till the kettledrum clangour of metal
On cobble and kerbstone proclaimed the arrival of tanks.

Who saw them first, the exiles returning, the fighters,
The Croix de Lorraine and the Tricolour flown from the hull?
Who saw us moving more fitly to join the spectators,
The crazy, the crying, the silent whose hearts were full?

It was only a small place, but a bugle was blowing.
I remember the Mayor performing an intricate dance
And the boy from Dakota most gravely, most quietly, throwing
The flowers from his helmet toward the deserving of France.

August 1944

DYLAN THOMAS

1914–1953

224 *The hand that signed the paper*

The hand that signed the paper felled a city;
Five sovereign fingers taxed the breath,
Doubled the globe of dead and halved a country;
These five kings did a king to death.

The mighty hand leads to a sloping shoulder,
The finger joints are cramped with chalk;
A goose's quill has put an end to murder
That put an end to talk.

The hand that signed the treaty bred a fever,
And famine grew, and locusts came;
Great is the hand that holds dominion over
Man by a scribbled name.

The five kings count the dead but do not soften
The crusted wound nor stroke the brow;
A hand rules pity as a hand rules heaven;
Hands have no tears to flow.

JAMES DICKEY

1923–

225   *The Firebombing*

Denke daran, dass nach den grossen Zerstörungen
Jedermann beweisen wird, dass er unschuldig war.
Günter Eich

Or hast thou an arm like God?
The Book of Job

Homeowners unite.

All families lie together, though some are burned alive.
The others try to feel
For them. Some can, it is often said.

Starve and take off

Twenty years in the suburbs, and the palm trees willingly leap
Into the flashlights,
And there is beneath them also
A booted crackling of snailshells and coral sticks.
There are cowl flaps and the tilt cross of propellers,
The shovel-marked clouds' far sides against the moon,
The enemy filling up the hills
With ceremonial graves. At my somewhere among these,

Snap, a bulb is tricked on in the cockpit

And some technical-minded stranger with my hands
Is sitting in a glass treasure-hole of blue light,
Having potential fire under the undeodorized arms
Of his wings, on thin bomb-shackles,
The 'tear-drop-shaped' 300-gallon drop-tanks
Filled with napalm and gasoline.

Thinking forward ten minutes
From that, there is also the burst straight out
Of the overcast into the moon; there is now
The moon-metal-shine of propellers, the quarter-
moonstone, aimed at the waves,
Stopped on the cumulus.

There is then this re-entry
Into cloud, for the engines to ponder their sound.
In white dark the aircraft shrinks; Japan

Dilates around it like a thought.
Coming out, the one who is here is over
Land, passing over the all-night grainfields,
In dark paint over
The woods with one silver side,
Rice-water calm at all levels
Of the terraced hill.

                              Enemy rivers and trees
Sliding off me like snakeskin,
Strips of vapor spooled from the wingtips
Going   invisible   passing   over   on
Over   bridges   roads for nightwalkers
Sunday night in the enemy's country   absolute
Calm   the moon's face   coming   slowly
About
        the inland sea
Slants   is woven with wire thread
Levels out   holds together like a quilt
Off the starboard wing   cloud flickers
At my glassed-off forehead   the moon's now and again
Uninterrupted face going forward
Over the waves in a glide-path
Lost into land.

Going: going with it

Combat booze by my side in a cratered canteen,
Bourbon frighteningly mixed
With GI pineapple juice,
Dogs trembling under me for hundreds of miles, on many
Islands, sleep-smelling that ungodly mixture
Of napalm and high-octane fuel,
Good bourbon and GI juice.

Rivers circling behind me around
Come to the fore, and bring
A town with everyone darkened.
Five thousand people are sleeping off
An all-day American drone.
Twenty years in the suburbs have not shown me
Which ones were hit and which not.

Haul on the wheel   racking slowly
The aircraft blackly around
In a dark dream   that   that is
That is like flying inside someone's head

Think of this   think of this

I did not think of my house
But think of my house now

Where the lawn mower rests on its laurels
Where the diet exists
For my own good   where I try to drop
Twenty years, eating figs in the pantry
Blinded by each and all
Of the eye-catching cans that gladly have caught my wife's eye
Until I cannot say
Where the screwdriver is   where the children
Get off the bus   where the new
Scoutmaster lives   where the fly
Hones his front legs   where the hammock folds
Its erotic daydreams   where the Sunday
School text for the day has been put   where the fire
Wood is   where the payments
For everything under the sun
Pile peacefully up,

But in this half-paid-for pantry
Among the red lids that screw off
With an easy half-twist to the left
And the long drawers crammed with dim spoons,
I still have charge—secret charge—
Of the fire developed to cling
To everything: to golf carts and fingernail
Scissors as yet unborn   tennis shoes
Grocery baskets   toy fire engines
New Buicks stalled by the half-moon
Shining at midnight on crossroads   green paint
Of jolly garden tools   red Christmas ribbons:

Not atoms, these, but glue inspired
By love of country to burn,
The apotheosis of gelatin.

Behind me having risen the Southern Cross
Set up by chaplains in the Ryukyus—
Orion, Scorpio, the immortal silver
Like the myths of king-
insects at swarming time—
One mosquito, dead drunk
On altitude, drones on, far under the engines,
And bites between
The oxygen mask and the eye.
The enemy-colored skin of families
Determines to hold its color
In sleep, as my hand turns whiter
Than ever, clutching the toggle—
The ship shakes   bucks
Fire hangs   not yet fire
In the air above Beppu
For I am fulfilling

An 'anti-morale' raid upon it.
All leashes of dogs
Break under the first bomb, around those
In bed, or late in the public baths: around those
Who inch forward on their hands
Into medicinal waters.
Their heads come up with a roar
Of Chicago fire:

Come up with the carp pond showing
The bathhouse upside down,
Standing stiller to show it more
As I sail artistically over
The resort town followed by farms,
Singing and twisting
All the handles in heaven   kicking
The small cattle off their feet
In a red costly blast
Flinging jelly over the walls
As in a chemical war-
fare field demonstration.
With fire of mine like a cat

Holding onto another man's walls,
My hat should crawl on my head
In streetcars, thinking of it,
The fat on my body should pale.

Gun down
The engines, the eight blades sighing
For the moment when the roofs will connect
Their flames, and make a town burning with all
American fire.
                    Reflections of houses catch;
Fire shuttles from pond to pond
In every direction, till hundreds flash with one death.
With this in the dark of the mind,
Death will not be what it should;
Will not, even now, even when
My exhaled face in the mirror
Of bars, dilates in a cloud like Japan.
The death of children is ponds
Shutter-flashing; responding mirrors; it climbs
The terraces of hills
Smaller and smaller, a mote of red dust
At a hundred feet; at a hundred and one it goes out.
That is what should have got in
To my eye
And shown the insides of houses, the low tables
Catch fire from the floor mats,
Blaze up in gas around their heads
Like a dream of suddenly growing

Too intense for war. Ah, under one's dark arms
Something strange-scented falls—when those on earth
Die, there is not even sound;
One is cool and enthralled in the cockpit,
Turned blue by the power of beauty,
In a pale treasure-hole of soft light
Deep in aesthetic contemplation,
Seeing the ponds catch fire
And cast it through ring after ring
Of land: O death in the middle
Of acres of inch-deep water!   Useless

Firing   small arms
Speckles   from the river
Bank   one ninety-millimeter
Misses   far down   wrong petals   gone

It is this detachment,
The honored aesthetic evil,
The greatest sense of power in one's life,
That must be shed in bars, or by whatever
Means, by starvation
Visions in well-stocked pantries:
The moment when the moon sails in between
The tail-booms   the rudders nod   I swing
Over   directly over the heart
The *heart* of the fire. A mosquito burns out on my cheek
With the cold of my face   there are the eyes
In blue light   bar light
All masked but them   the moon
Crossing from left to right   in the streams below
Oriental fish form quickly
In the chemical shine,
In their eyes one tiny seed
Of deranged, Old Testament light.
Letting go   letting go
The plane rises gently   dark forms
Glide off me   long water   pales
In safe zones   a new cry enters
The voice box of chained family dogs

We buck   leap over something
Not there   settle back

Leave it   leave it clinging and crying
It consumes them in a hot
Body-flash, old age or menopause
Of children, clings and burns

                     eating through
And when a reed mat catches fire
From me, it explodes through field after field
Bearing its sleeper   another

Bomb finds a home
And clings to it like a child. And so

Goodbye to the grassy mountains
To cloud streaming from the night engines
Flags   pennons   curved silks
Of air   myself streaming also
My body covered
With flags, the air of flags
Between the engines.
Forever I do sleep in that position,
Forever in a turn
For home that breaks out streaming banners
From my wingtips,
Wholly in position to admire.

O then I knock it off
And turn for home over the black complex thread worked through
The silver night-sea,
Following the huge, moon-washed steppingstones
Of the Ryukyus south,
The nightgrass of mountains billowing softly
In my rising heat.
                  Turn and tread down
The yellow stones of the islands
To where Okinawa burns,
Pure gold, on the radar screen,
Beholding, beneath, the actual island form
In the vast water-silver poured just above solid ground,
An inch of water extending for thousands of miles
Above flat ploughland. Say 'down,' and it is done.

All this, and I am still hungry,
Still twenty years overweight, still unable

To get down there or see
What really happened.

But it may be that I could not,
If I tried, say to any
Who lived there, deep in my flames: say, in cold
Grinning sweat, as to another
Of these homeowners who are always curving
Near me down the different-grassed street: say
As though to the neighbor
I borrowed the hedge-clippers from
On the darker-grassed side of the two,
Come in, my house is yours, come in
If you can, if you
Can pass this unfired door. It is that I can imagine
At the threshold nothing
With its ears crackling off
Like powdery leaves,
Nothing with children of ashes, nothing not
Amiable, gentle, well-meaning,
A little nervous for no
Reason   a little worried   a little too loud
Or too easygoing   nothing I haven't lived with
For twenty years, still nothing not as
American as I am, and proud of it.

Absolution? Sentence? No matter;
The thing itself is in that.

KARL SHAPIRO

1913–

226   *Elegy for a Dead Soldier*

I

A white sheet on the tail-gate of a truck
Becomes an altar; two small candlesticks
Sputter at each side of the crucifix
Laid round with flowers brighter than the blood,

Red as the red of our apocalypse,
Hibiscus that a marching man will pluck
To stick into his rifle or his hat,
And great blue morning-glories pale as lips
That shall no longer taste or kiss or swear.
The wind begins a low magnificat,
The chaplain chats, the palmtrees swirl their hair,
The columns come together through the mud.

II

We too are ashes as we watch and hear
The psalm, the sorrow, and the simple praise
Of one whose promised thoughts of other days
Were such as ours, but now wholly destroyed,
The service record of his youth wiped out,
His dream dispersed by shot, must disappear.
What can we feel but wonder at a loss
That seems to point at nothing but the doubt
Which flirts our sense of luck into the ditch?
Reader of Paul who prays beside this fosse,
Shall we believe our eyes or legends rich
With glory and rebirth beyond the void?

III

For this comrade is dead, dead in the war,
A young man out of millions yet to live,
One cut away from all that war can give,
Freedom of self and peace to wander free.
Who mourns in all this sober multitude
Who did not feel the bite of it before
The bullet found its aim? This worthy flesh,
This boy laid in a coffin and reviewed—
Who has not wrapped himself in this same flag,
Heard the light fall of dirt, his wound still fresh,
Felt his eyes closed, and heard the distant brag
Of the last volley of humanity?

IV

By chance I saw him die, stretched on the ground,
A tattooed arm lifted to take the blood
Of someone else sealed in a tin. I stood
During the last delirium that stays

The intelligence a tiny moment more,
And then the strangulation, the last sound.
The end was sudden, like a foolish play,
A stupid fool slamming a foolish door,
The absurd catastrophe, half-prearranged,
And all the decisive things still left to say.
So we disbanded, angrier and unchanged,
Sick with the utter silence of dispraise.

V

We ask for no statistics of the killed,
For nothing political impinges on
This single casualty, or all those gone,
Missing or healing, sinking or dispersed,
Hundreds of thousands counted, millions lost.
More than an accident and less than willed
Is every fall, and this one like the rest.
However others calculate the cost,
To us the final aggregate is *one*,
One with a name, one transferred to the blest;
And though another stoops and takes the gun,
We cannot add the second to the first.

VI

I would not speak for him who could not speak
Unless my fear were true: he was not wronged,
He knew to which decision he belonged
But let it choose itself. Ripe in instinct,
Neither the victim nor the volunteer,
He followed, and the leaders could not seek
Beyond the followers. Much of this he knew;
The journey was a detour that would steer
Into the Lincoln Highway of a land
Remorselessly improved, excited, new,
And that was what he wanted. He had planned
To earn and drive. He and the world had winked.

VII

No history deceived him, for he knew
Little of times and armies not his own;
He never felt that peace was but a loan,
Had never questioned the idea of gain.

Beyond the headlines once or twice he saw
The gathering of a power by the few
But could not tell their names; he cast his vote,
Distrusting all the elected but not law.
He laughed at socialism; *on mourrait*
Pour les industriels? He shed his coat
And not for brotherhood, but for his pay.
To him the red flag marked the sewer main.

VIII

Above all else he loathed the homily,
The slogan and the ad. He paid his bill,
But not for Congressmen at Bunker Hill.
Ideals were few and those there were not made
For conversation. He belonged to church
But never spoke of God. The Christmas tree,
The Easter egg, baptism, he observed,
Never denied the preacher on his perch,
And would not sign Resolved That or Whereas.
Softness he had and hours and nights reserved
For thinking, dressing, dancing to the jazz.
His laugh was real, his manners were homemade.

IX

Of all men poverty pursued him least;
He was ashamed of all the down and out,
Spurned the panhandler like an uneasy doubt,
And saw the unemployed as a vague mass
Incapable of hunger or revolt.
He hated other races, south or east,
And shoved them to the margin of his mind.
He could recall the justice of the Colt,
Take interest in a gang-war like a game.
His ancestry was somewhere far behind
And left him only his peculiar name.
Doors opened, and he recognized no class.

X

His children would have known a heritage,
Just or unjust, the richest in the world,
The quantum of all art and science curled
In the horn of plenty, bursting from the horn,

A people bathed in honey, Paris come,
Vienna transferred with the highest wage,
A World's Fair spread to Phoenix, Jacksonville,
Earth's capital, the new Byzantium,
Kingdom of man—who knows? Hollow or firm,
No man can ever prophesy until
Out of our death some undiscovered germ,
Whole toleration or pure peace is born.

XI

The time to mourn is short that best becomes
The military dead. We lift and fold the flag,
Lay bare the coffin with its written tag,
And march away. Behind, four others wait
To lift the box, the heaviest of loads.
The anesthetic afternoon benumbs,
Sickens our senses, forces back our talk.
We know that others on tomorrow's roads
Will fall, ourselves perhaps, the man beside,
Over the world the threatened, all who walk:
And could we mark the grave of him who died
We would write this beneath his name and date:

EPITAPH

Underneath this wooden cross there lies
A Christian killed in battle. You who read,
Remember that this stranger died in pain;
And passing here, if you can lift your eyes
Upon a peace kept by a human creed,
Know that one soldier has not died in vain.

EPHIM FOGEL

1920–

227   *Shipment to Maidanek*

Arrived from scattered cities, several lands,
intact from sea land, mountain land, and plain.
Item: six surgeons, slightly mangled hands.
Item: three poets, hopelessly insane.

Item: a Russian mother and her child,
the former with five gold teeth and usable shoes,
the latter with seven dresses, peasant-styled.

Item: another hundred thousand Jews.

Item: a crippled Czech with a handmade crutch.
Item: a Spaniard with a subversive laugh;
seventeen dozen Danes, nine gross of Dutch.

Total: precisely a million and a half.

They are sorted and marked—the method is up to you.
The books must be balanced, the disposition stated.
Take care that all accounts are neat and true.

Make sure that they are thoroughly cremated.

W. H. AUDEN

1907–1973

228   from *Sonnets from China*

Here war is harmless like a monument:
A telephone is talking to a man;
Flags on a map declare that troops were sent;
A boy brings milk in bowls. There is a plan

For living men in terror of their lives,
Who thirst at nine who were to thirst at noon,
Who can be lost and are, who miss their wives
And, unlike an idea, can die too soon.

Yet ideas can be true, although men die:
For we have seen a myriad faces
Ecstatic from one lie,

And maps can really point to places
Where life is evil now.
Nanking. Dachau.

ANTHONY HECHT

1923–

229

'More Light! More Light!'

for Heinrich Blücher and Hannah Arendt

Composed in the Tower before his execution
These moving verses, and being brought at that time
Painfully to the stake, submitted, declaring thus:
'I implore my God to witness that I have made no crime.'

Nor was he forsaken of courage, but the death was horrible,
The sack of gunpowder failing to ignite.
His legs were blistered sticks on which the black sap
Bubbled and burst as he howled for the Kindly Light.

And that was but one, and by no means one of the worst;
Permitted at least his pitiful dignity;
And such as were by made prayers in the name of Christ,
That shall judge all men, for his soul's tranquillity.

We move now to outside a German wood.
Three men are there commanded to dig a hole
In which the two Jews are ordered to lie down
And be buried alive by the third, who is a Pole.

Not light from the shrine at Weimar beyond the hill
Nor light from heaven appeared. But he did refuse.
A Lüger settled back deeply in its glove.
He was ordered to change places with the Jews.

Much casual death had drained away their souls.
The thick dirt mounted toward the quivering chin.
When only the head was exposed the order came
To dig him out again and to get back in.

No light, no light in the blue Polish eye.
When he finished a riding boot packed down the earth.
The Lüger hovered lightly in its glove.
He was shot in the belly and in three hours bled to death.

No prayers or incense rose up in those hours
Which grew to be years, and every day came mute
Ghosts from the ovens, sifting through crisp air,
And settled upon his eyes in a black soot.

THOM GUNN

1929–

230

Claus Von Stauffenberg

of the bomb-plot on Hitler, 1944

What made the place a landscape of despair,
History stunned beneath, the emblems cracked?
Smell of approaching snow hangs on the air;
The frost meanwhile can be the only fact.

They chose the unknown, and the bounded terror,
As a corrective, who corrected live
Surveying without choice the bounding error:
An unsanctioned present must be primitive.

A few still have the vigour to deny
Fear is a natural state; their motives neither
Of doctrinaire, of turncoat, nor of spy.
Lucidity of thought draws them together.

The maimed young Colonel who can calculate
On two remaining fingers and a will,
Takes lessons from the past, to detonate
A bomb that Brutus rendered possible.

Over the maps a moment, face to face:
Across from Hitler, whose grey eyes have filled
A nation with the illogic of their gaze,
The rational man is poised, to break, to build.

And though he fails, honour personified
In a cold time where honour cannot grow,
He stiffens, like a statue, in mid-stride
—Falling toward history, and under snow.

CHARLES CAUSLEY

1917–

231   *Armistice Day*

I stood with three comrades in Parliament Square
November her freights of grey fire unloading,
No sound from the city upon the pale air
Above us the sea-bell eleven exploding.

Down by the bands and the burning memorial
Beats all the brass in a royal array,
But at our end we are not so sartorial:
Out of (as usual) the rig of the day.

Starry is wearing a split pusser's flannel
Rubbed, as he is, by the regular tide;
Oxo the ducks that he ditched in the Channel
In June, 1940 (when he was inside).

Kitty recalls his abandon-ship station,
Running below at the Old Man's salute
And (with a deck-watch) going down for duration
Wearing his oppoe's pneumonia-suit.

Comrades, for you the black captain of carracks
Writes in Whitehall his appalling decisions,
But as was often the case in the Barracks
Several ratings are not at Divisions.

Into my eyes the stiff sea-horses stare,
Over my head sweeps the sun like a swan.
As I stand alone in Parliament Square
A cold bugle calls, and the city moves on.

232   *At the British War Cemetery, Bayeux*

I walked where in their talking graves
And shirts of earth five thousand lay,
When history with ten feasts of fire
Had eaten the red air away.

I am Christ's boy, I cried, I bear
In iron hands the bread, the fishes.
I hang with honey and with rose
This tidy wreck of all your wishes.

On your geometry of sleep
The chestnut and the fir-tree fly,
And lavender and marguerite
Forge with their flowers an English sky.

Turn now towards the belling town
Your jigsaws of impossible bone,
And rising read your rank of snow
Accurate as death upon the stone.

About your easy heads my prayers
I said with syllables of clay.
What gift, I asked, shall I bring now
Before I weep and walk away?

Take, they replied, the oak and laurel.
Take our fortune of tears and live
Like a spendthrift lover. All we ask
Is the one gift you cannot give.

SIR JOHN BETJEMAN

1906–1984

233

In Memory of Basil, Marquess of Dufferin and Ava

On such a morning as this
  with birds ricocheting their music
Out of the whelming elms
  to a copper beech's embrace
And a sifting sound of leaves
  from multitudinous branches
Running across the park
  to a chequer of light on the lake,
On such a morning as this
  with *The Times* for June the eleventh
Left with coffee and toast
  you opened the breakfast-room window
And, sprawled on the southward terrace,
  Said: 'That means war in September.'

Friend of my youth, you are dead!
  and the long peal pours from the steeple
Over this sunlit quad
  in our University city
And soaks in Headington stone.
  Motionless stand the pinnacles
Under a flying sky
  as though they too listened and waited
Like me for your dear return
  with a Bullingdon noise of an evening
In a Sports-Bugatti from Thame
  that belonged to a man in Magdalen.
Friend of my youth, you are dead!
  and the quads are empty without you.

Then there were people about.
  Each hour, like an Oxford archway,
Opened on long green lawns
  and distant unvisited buildings

And you my friend were explorer
   and so you remained to me always
Humorous, reckless, loyal—
   my kind, heavy-lidded companion.
Stop, oh many bells, stop
   pouring on roses and creeper
Your unremembering peal
   this hollow, unhallowed V.E. day,—
I am deaf to your notes and dead
   by a soldier's body in Burma.

HOWARD NEMEROV

1920–

234

A Fable of the War

The full moon is partly hidden by cloud,
The snow that fell when we came off the boat
Has stopped by now, and it is turning colder.
I pace the platform under the blue lights,
Under a frame of glass and emptiness
In a station whose name I do not know.

Suddenly, passing the known and unknown
Bowed faces of my company, the sad
And potent outfit of the armed, I see
That we are dead. By stormless Acheron
We stand easy, and the occasional moon
Strikes terribly from steel and bone alike.

Our flesh, I see, was too corruptible
For the huge work of death. Only the blind
Crater of the eye can suffer well
The midnight cold of stations in no place,
And hold the tears of pity frozen that
They will implacably reflect on war.

But I have read that God let Solomon
Stand upright, although dead, until the temple
Should be raised up, that demons forced to the work
Might not revolt before the thing was done.
And the king stood, until a little worm
Had eaten through the stick he leaned upon.

So, gentlemen—by greatcoat, cartridge belt
And helmet held together for the time—
In honorably enduring here we seek
The second death. Until the worm shall bite
To betray us, lean each man on his gun
That the great work not falter but go on.

235   *Redeployment*

They say the war is over. But water still
Comes bloody from the taps, and my pet cat
In his disorder vomits worms which crawl
Swiftly away. Maybe they leave the house.
These worms are white, and flecked with the cat's blood.

The war may be over. I know a man
Who keeps a pleasant souvenir, he keeps
A soldier's dead blue eyeballs that he found
Somewhere—hard as chalk, and blue as slate.
He clicks them in his pocket while he talks.

And now there are cockroaches in the house,
They get slightly drunk on DDT,
Are fast, hard, shifty—can be drowned but not
Without you hold them under quite some time.
People say the Mexican kind can fly.

The end of the war. I took it quietly
Enough. I tried to wash the dirt out of
My hair and from under my fingernails,
I dressed in clean white clothes and went to bed.
I heard the dust falling between the walls.

ARCHIBALD MacLEISH

1892–1982

for Kenneth MacLeish

Ambassador Puser the ambassador
Reminds himself in French, felicitous tongue,
What these (young men no longer) lie here for
In rows that once, and somewhere else, were young . . .

All night in Brussels the wind had tugged at my door:
I had heard the wind at my door and the trees strung
Taut, and to me who had never been before
In that country it was a strange wind, blowing
Steadily, stiffening the walls, the floor,
The roof of my room. I had not slept for knowing
He too, dead, was a stranger in that land
And felt beneath the earth in the wind's flowing
A tightening of roots and would not understand,
Remembering lake winds in Illinois,
That strange wind. I had felt his bones in the sand
Listening.

> *. . . Reflects that these enjoy*
Their country's gratitude, that deep repose,
That peace no pain can break, no hurt destroy,
That rest, that sleep . . .

At Ghent the wind rose.
There was a smell of rain and a heavy drag
Of wind in the hedges but not as the wind blows
Over fresh water when the waves lag
Foaming and the willows huddle and it will rain:
I felt him waiting.

> *. . . Indicates the flag*
Which (may he say) enisles in Flanders plain
This little field these happy, happy dead
Have made America . . .

                              In the ripe grain
The wind coiled glistening, darted, fled,
Dragging its heavy body: at Waereghem
The wind coiled in the grass above his head:
Waiting—listening . . .

       . . . Dedicates to them
This earth their bones have hallowed, this last gift
A grateful country . . .

                              Under the dry grass stem
The words are blurred, are thickened, the words sift
Confused by the rasp of the wind, by the thin grating
Of ants under the grass, the minute shift
And tumble of dusty sand separating
From dusty sand. The roots of the grass strain,
Tighten, the earth is rigid, waits—he is waiting—

And suddenly, and all at once, the rain!

JOHN PUDNEY

1909–1977

237   *For Johnny*

Do not despair
For Johnny-head-in-air;
He sleeps as sound
As Johnny underground.

Fetch out no shroud
For Johnny-in-the-cloud;
And keep your tears
For him in after years.

Better by far
For Johnny-the-bright-star,
To keep your head,
And see his children fed.

1943–

238

The Lost Pilot

for my father, 1922–1944

Your face did not rot
like the others—the co-pilot,
for example, I saw him

yesterday. His face is corn-
mush: his wife and daughter,
the poor ignorant people, stare

as if he will compose soon.
He was more wronged than Job.
But your face did not rot

like the others—it grew dark,
and hard like ebony;
the features progressed in their

distinction. If I could cajole
you to come back for an evening,
down from your compulsive

orbiting, I would touch you,
read your face as Dallas,
your hoodlum gunner, now,

with the blistered eyes, reads
his braille editions. I would
touch your face as a disinterested

scholar touches an original page.
However frightening, I would
discover you, and I would not

turn you in; I would not make
you face your wife, or Dallas,
or the co-pilot, Jim. You

could return to your crazy
orbiting, and I would not try
to fully understand what

it means to you. All I know
is this: when I see you,
as I have seen you at least

once every year of my life,
spin across the wilds of the sky
like a tiny, African god,

I feel dead. I feel as if I were
the residue of a stranger's life,
that I should pursue you.

My head cocked toward the sky,
I cannot get off the ground,
and, you, passing over again,

fast, perfect, and unwilling
to tell me that you are doing
well, or that it was mistake

that placed you in that world,
and me in this; or that misfortune
placed these worlds in us.

GEORGE MACBETH

1932–

239 *The Land-Mine*

It fell when I was sleeping. In my dream
  It brought the garden to the house
And let it in. I heard no parrot scream
  Or lion roar, but there were flowers
And water flowing where the cellared mouse
Was all before. And air moved as in bowers

Of cedar with a scented breath of smoke
    And fire. I rubbed scales from my eyes
And white with brushed stone in my hair half-woke
    In fear. I saw my father kneel
On glass that scarred the ground. And there were flies
Thick on that water, weeds around his heel

Where he was praying. And I knew that night
    Had cataracted through the wall
And loosed fine doors whose hinges had been tight
    And made each window weep glass tears
That clawed my hands. I climbed through holes. My hall
Where I had lain asleep with stoppered ears

Was all in ruins, planted thick with grime
    Of war. I walked as if in greaves
Through fire, lay down in gutters choked with lime
    And spoke for help. Alas, those birds
That dived in light above me in the leaves
Were birds of prey, and paid no heed to words.

Now I was walking, wearing on my brow
    What moved before through fireless coal
And held my father's head. I touch it now
    And feel my dream go. And no sound
That flying birds can make, or burrowing mole,
Will bring my garden back, or break new ground.

The war is over and the mine has gone
    That filled the air with whinnying fire
And no more nights will I lie waiting on
    Cold metal or cold stone to freeze
Before it comes again. That day of ire,
If it shall come, will find me on my knees.

ALAN ROSS

1922–

Off Brighton Pier

I saw him a squat man with red hair,
Grown into sideburns, fishing off Brighton pier:
Suddenly he bent, and in a lumpy bag
Rummaged for bait, letting his line dangle,
And I noticed the stiffness of his leg
That thrust out, like a tripod, at an angle.
Then I remembered: the sideburns, that gloss
Of slicked-down ginger on a skin like candy floss.
He was there, not having moved, as last,
On a windless night, leaning against the mast,
I saw him, groping a bag for numbers.
And the date was the 17th of September,
15 years back, and we were playing Tombola
During the last Dog, someone beginning to holler
'Here you are' for a full card, and I remember
He'd just called 'Seven and six, she was worth it,'
When—without contacts or warning—we were hit.
Some got away with it, a few bought it.
And I recall now, when they carried him ashore,
Fishing gear lashed to his hammock, wishing
Him luck, and his faint smile, more
To himself than to me, when he saluted
From the stretcher, and, cadging a fag,
Cracked 'I'm quids in, it's only one leg,
They'll pension me off to go fishing.'

JON STALLWORTHY

1935–

A Letter from Berlin

My dear,
    Today a letter from Berlin
where snow—the first of '38—flew in,

settled and shrivelled on the lamp last night,
broke moth wings mobbing the window. Light
woke me early, but the trams were late:
I had to run from the Brandenburg Gate
skidding, groaning like a tram, and sodden
to the knees. Von Neumann operates at 10
and would do if the sky fell in. They lock
his theatre doors on the stroke of the clock—
but today I was lucky: found a gap
in the gallery next to a chap
I knew just as the doors were closing. Last,
as expected, on Von Showmann's list
the new vaginal hysterectomy
that brought me to Berlin.
$\qquad\qquad\qquad$ *Delicately*
he went to work, making from right to left
a semi-circular incision. Deft
dissection of the fascia. The blood-
blossoming arteries nipped in the bud.
Speculum, scissors, clamps—the uterus
cleanly delivered, the pouch of Douglas
stripped to the rectum, and the cavity
closed. Never have I seen such masterly
technique. 'And so little bleeding!' I said
half to myself, half to my neighbour.
$\qquad\qquad\qquad\qquad$ *'Dead',*
came his whisper. 'Don't be a fool'
I said, for still below us in the pool
of light the marvellous unhurried hands
were stitching, tying the double strands
of catgut, stitching, tying. It was like
a concert, watching those hands unlock
the music from their score. And at the end
one half expected him to turn and bend
stiffly towards us. Stiffly he walked out
and his audience shuffled after. But
finishing my notes in the gallery
I saw them uncover the patient: she
was dead.
$\qquad\qquad$ *I met my neighbour in the street*
waiting for the same tram, stamping his feet
on the pavement's broken snow, and said:
'I have to apologize. She was dead,

but how did you know?' Back came his voice
like a bullet '—saw it last month, twice.'

Returning your letter to an envelope
yellower by years than when you sealed it up,
darkly the omens emerge. A ritual wound
yellow at the lip yawns in my hand;
a turbulent crater; a trench, filled
not with snow only, east of Buchenwald.

GEOFFREY HILL

1932–

242   *September Song*

born 19.6.32–deported 24.9.42

Undesirable you may have been, untouchable
you were not. Not forgotten
or passed over at the proper time.

As estimated, you died. Things marched,
sufficient, to that end.
Just so much Zyklon and leather, patented
terror, so many routine cries.

(I have made
an elegy for myself it
is true)

September fattens on vines. Roses
flake from the wall. The smoke
of harmless fires drifts to my eyes.

This is plenty. This is more than enough.

ANDREI VOZNESENSKY

1933–

I am Goya

I am Goya
of the bare field, by the enemy's beak gouged
till the craters of my eyes gape
I am grief

I am the tongue
of war, the embers of cities
on the snows of the year 1941
I am hunger

I am the gullet
of a woman hanged whose body like a bell
tolled over a blank square
I am Goya

O grapes of wrath!
I have hurled westward

                     the ashes of the uninvited guest!
and hammered stars into the unforgetting sky—like nails
I am Goya

Translated from the Russian by Stanley Kunitz

ROBERT LOWELL

1917–1977

Fall 1961

Back and forth, back and forth
goes the tock, tock, tock
of the orange, bland, ambassadorial
face of the moon
on the grandfather clock.

All autumn, the chafe and jar
of nuclear war;
we have talked our extinction to death.
I swim like a minnow
behind my studio window.

Our end drifts nearer,
the moon lifts,
radiant with terror.
The state
is a diver under a glass bell.

A father's no shield
for his child.
We are like a lot of wild
spiders crying together,
but without tears.

Nature holds up a mirror.
One swallow makes a summer.
It's easy to tick
off the minutes,
but the clockhands stick.

Back and forth!
Back and forth, back and forth—
my one point of rest
is the orange and black
oriole's swinging nest!

245   *For the Union Dead*

'Relinquunt Omnia Servare Rem Publicam.'

The old South Boston Aquarium stands
in a Sahara of snow now. Its broken windows are boarded.
The bronze weathervane cod has lost half its scales.
The airy tanks are dry.

Once my nose crawled like a snail on the glass;
my hand tingled
to burst the bubbles
drifting from the noses of the cowed, compliant fish.

My hand draws back. I often sigh still
for the dark downward and vegetating kingdom
of the fish and reptile. One morning last March,
I pressed against the new barbed and galvanized

fence on the Boston Common. Behind their cage,
yellow dinosaur steamshovels were grunting
as they cropped up tons of mush and grass
to gouge their underworld garage.

Parking spaces luxuriate like civic
sandpiles in the heart of Boston.
A girdle of orange, Puritan-pumpkin colored girders
braces the tingling Statehouse,

shaking over the excavations, as it faces Colonel Shaw
and his bell-cheeked Negro infantry
on St. Gaudens' shaking Civil War relief,
propped by a plank splint against the garage's earthquake.

Two months after marching through Boston,
half the regiment was dead;
at the dedication,
William James could almost hear the bronze Negroes breathe.

Their monument sticks like a fishbone
in the city's throat.
Its Colonel is as lean
as a compass-needle.

He has an angry wrenlike vigilance,
a greyhound's gentle tautness;
he seems to wince at pleasure,
and suffocate for privacy.

He is out of bounds now. He rejoices in man's lovely,
peculiar power to choose life and die—
when he leads his black soldiers to death,
he cannot bend his back.

On a thousand small town New England greens,
the old white churches hold their air
of sparse, sincere rebellion; frayed flags
quilt the graveyards of the Grand Army of the Republic.

The stone statues of the abstract Union Soldier
grow slimmer and younger each year—
wasp-waisted, they doze over muskets
and muse through their sideburns . . .

Shaw's father wanted no monument
except the ditch,
where his son's body was thrown
and lost with his 'niggers.'

The ditch is nearer.
There are no statues for the last war here;
on Boylston Street, a commercial photograph
shows Hiroshima boiling

over a Mosler Safe, the 'Rock of Ages'
that survived the blast. Space is nearer.
When I crouch to my television set,
the drained faces of Negro school-children rise like balloons.

Colonel Shaw
is riding on his bubble,
he waits
for the blessèd break.

The Aquarium is gone. Everywhere,
giant finned cars nose forward like fish;
a savage servility
slides by on grease.

ALLEN GINSBERG

1926–

246   *A Vow*

I will haunt these States
        with beard bald head
        eyes staring out plane window,
        hair hanging in Greyhound bus midnight

leaning over taxicab seat to admonish
      an angry cursing driver
      hand lifted to calm
      his outraged vehicle
that I pass with the Green Light of common law.

Common Sense, Common law, common tenderness
      & common tranquillity
our means in America to control the money munching
      war machine, bright lit industry
everywhere digesting forests & excreting soft pyramids
    of newsprint, Redwood and Ponderosa patriarchs
    silent in Meditation murdered & regurgitated as smoke,
      sawdust, screaming ceilings of Soap Opera,
      thick dead Lifes, slick Advertisements
          for Gubernatorial big guns
      burping Napalm on palm rice tropic greenery.

Dynamite in forests,
    boughs fly slow motion
      thunder down ravine,
    Helicopters roar over National Park, Mekong Swamp,
      Dynamite fire blasts thru Model Villages,
Violence screams at Police, Mayors get mad over radio,
      Drop the Bomb on Niggers!
          drop Fire on the gook China
          Frankenstein Dragon
      waving its tail over Bayonne's domed Aluminum
                    oil reservoir!

I'll haunt these States all year
    gazing bleakly out train windows, blue airfield
      red TV network on evening plains,
    decoding radar Provincial editorial paper message,
      deciphering Iron Pipe laborers' curses as
        clanging hammers they raise steamshovel claws
    over Puerto Rican agony lawyers' screams in slums.

October 11, 1966

DENISE LEVERTOV

1923–

What Were They Like?

1) Did the people of Vietnam
   use lanterns of stone?
2) Did they hold ceremonies
   to reverence the opening of buds?
3) Were they inclined to quiet laughter?
4) Did they use bone and ivory,
   jade and silver, for ornament?
5) Had they an epic poem?
6) Did they distinguish between speech and singing?

1) Sir, their light hearts turned to stone.
   It is not remembered whether in gardens
   stone lanterns illumined pleasant ways.
2) Perhaps they gathered once to delight in blossom,
   but after the children were killed
   there were no more buds.
3) Sir, laughter is bitter to the burned mouth.
4) A dream ago, perhaps. Ornament is for joy.
   All the bones were charred.
5) It is not remembered. Remember,
   most were peasants; their life
   was in rice and bamboo.
   When peaceful clouds were reflected in the paddies
   and the water buffalo stepped surely along terraces,
   maybe fathers told their sons old tales.
   When bombs smashed those mirrors
   there was time only to scream.
6) There is an echo yet
   of their speech which was like a song.
   It was reported their singing resembled
   the flight of moths in moonlight.
   Who can say? It is silent now.

GALWAY KINNELL

1927–

248   *Vapor Trail Reflected in the Frog Pond*

I

The old watch: their
thick eyes
puff and foreclose by the moon. The young, heads
trailed by the beginnings of necks,
shiver,
in the guarantee they shall be bodies.

In the frog pond
the vapor trail of a SAC bomber creeps,

I hear its drone, drifting, high up
in immaculate ozone.

II

And I hear,
coming over the hills, America singing,
her varied carols I hear:
crack of deputies' rifles practicing their aim on stray dogs at
     night,
sput of cattleprod,
TV groaning at the smells of the human body,
curses of the soldier as he poisons, burns, grinds, and stabs
the rice of the world,
with open mouth, crying strong, hysterical curses.

III

And by rice paddies in Asia
bones
wearing a few shadows
walk down a dirt road, smashed
bloodsuckers on their heel, knowing
the flesh a man throws down in the sunshine
dogs shall eat
and the flesh that is upthrown in the air

shall be seized by birds,
shoulder blades smooth, unmarked by old feather-holes,
hands rivered
by blue, erratic wanderings of the blood,
eyes crinkled up
as they gaze up at the drifting sun that gives us our lives,
seed dazzled over the footbattered blaze of the earth.

ROBERT MEZEY

1935–

249   *How Much Longer?*

Day after day after day it goes on
and no one knows how to stop it or escape.
Friends come bearing impersonal agonies,
I hear our hopeless laughter, I watch us drink.
War is in everyone's eyes, war is made
in the kitchen, in the bedroom, in the car at stoplights.
A marriage collapses like a burning house
and the other houses smolder. Old friends
make their way in silence. Students stare
at their teachers, and suddenly feel afraid.
The old people are terrified like cattle
rolling their eyes and bellowing, while the young
wander in darkness, dazed, half-believing
some half-forgotten poem, or else come out
with their hearts on fire, alive in the last days.
Small children roam the neighborhoods armed
with submachineguns, gas masks and riot sticks.
Excavations are made in us and slowly
we are filled in with used-up things: knives
too dull to cut bread with, bombs that failed to go off,
cats smashed on the highway, broken pencils,
slivers of soap, hair, gristle, old TV sets
that hum and stare out blindly like the insane.
Bridges kneel down, the cities billow and plunge
like horses in their smoke, the tall buildings
open their hysterical burning eyes at night,
the leafy suburbs look up at the clouds and tremble—

and my wife leaves her bed before dawn, walking
the icy pasture, shrieking her grief to the cows,
praying in tears to the softening blackness. I hear her
outside the window, crazed, inconsolable,
and go out to fetch her. Yesterday she saw
a photograph, Naomi our little girl
in a ditch in Viet Nam, half in the water,
the rest of her, beached on the mud, was horribly burned.

MARGARET ATWOOD

1939–

250   *It is Dangerous to Read Newspapers*

While I was building neat
castles in the sandbox,
the hasty pits were
filling with bulldozed corpses

and as I walked to the school
washed and combed, my feet
stepping on the cracks in the cement
detonated red bombs.

Now I am grownup
and literate, and I sit in my chair
as quietly as a fuse

and the jungles are flaming, the under-
brush is charged with soldiers,
the names on the difficult
maps go up in smokè.

I am the cause, I am a stockpile of chemical
toys, my body
is a deadly gadget,
I reach out in love, my hands are guns,
my good intentions are completely lethal.

Even my
passive eyes transmute
everything I look at to the pocked
black and white of a war photo,
how
can I stop myself

It is dangerous to read newspapers.

Each time I hit a key
on my electric typewriter,
speaking of peaceful trees

another village explodes.

ADRIAN MITCHELL

1932–

251 *To Whom It May Concern*

I was run over by the truth one day.
Ever since the accident I've walked this way
    So stick my legs in plaster
    Tell me lies about Vietnam.

Heard the alarm clock screaming with pain,
Couldn't find myself so I went back to sleep again
    So fill my ears with silver
    Stick my legs in plaster
    Tell me lies about Vietnam.

Every time I shut my eyes all I see is flames.
Made a marble phone book and I carved all the names
    So coat my eyes with butter
    Fill my ears with silver
    Stick my legs in plaster
    Tell me lies about Vietnam.

I smell something burning, hope it's just my brains.
They're only dropping peppermints and daisy-chains
    So stuff my nose with garlic
    Coat my eyes with butter
    Fill my ears with silver
    Stick my legs in plaster
    Tell me lies about Vietnam.

Where were you at the time of the crime?
Down by the Cenotaph drinking slime
    So chain my tongue with whisky
    Stuff my nose with garlic
    Coat my eyes with butter
    Fill my ears with silver
    Stick my legs in plaster
    Tell me lies about Vietnam.

You put your bombers in, you put your conscience out,
You take the human being and you twist it all about
    So scrub my skin with women
    Chain my tongue with whisky
    Stuff my nose with garlic
    Coat my eyes with butter
    Fill my ears with silver
    Stick my legs in plaster
    Tell me lies about Vietnam.

JAMES FENTON

1949–

252

Dead Soldiers

When His Excellency Prince Norodom Chantaraingsey
Invited me to lunch on the battlefield
I was glad of my white suit for the first time that day.
They lived well, the mad Norodoms, they had style.
The brandy and the soda arrived in crates.
Bricks of ice, tied around with raffia,
Dripped from the orderlies' handlebars.

And I remember the dazzling tablecloth
As the APCs fanned out along the road,
The dishes piled high with frogs' legs,
Pregnant turtles, their eggs boiled in the carapace,
Marsh irises in fish sauce
And inflorescence of a banana salad.

On every bottle, Napoleon Bonaparte
Pleaded for the authenticity of the spirit.
They called the empties Dead Soldiers
And rejoiced to see them pile up at our feet.

Each diner was attended by one of the other ranks
Whirling a table-napkin to keep off the flies.
It was like eating between rows of morris dancers—
Only they didn't kick.

On my left sat the prince;
On my right, his drunken aide.
The frogs' thighs leapt into the sad purple face
Like fish to the sound of a Chinese flute.
I wanted to talk to the prince. I wish now
I had collared his aide, who was Saloth Sar's brother.
We treated him as the club bore. He was always
Boasting of his connections, boasting with a head-shake
Or by pronouncing of some doubtful phrase.
And well might he boast. Saloth Sar, for instance,
Was Pol Pot's real name. The APCs
Fired into the sugar palms but met no resistance.

In a diary, I refer to Pol Pot's brother as the Jockey Cap.
A few weeks later, I find him 'in good form
And very skeptical about Chantaraingsey.'
'But one eats well there,' I remark.
'So one should,' says the Jockey Cap:
'The tiger always eats well,
It eats the raw flesh of the deer,
And Chantaraingsey was born in the year of the tiger.
So, did they show you the things they do
With the young refugee girls?'

And he tells me how he will one day give me the gen.
He will tell me how the prince financed the casino
And how the casino brought Lon Nol to power.
He will tell me this.
He will tell me all these things.
All I must do is drink and listen.

In those days, I thought that when the game was up
The prince would be far, far away—
In a limestone faubourg, on the promenade at Nice,
Reduced in circumstances but well enough provided for.
In Paris, he would hardly require his private army.
The Jockey Cap might suffice for café warfare,
And matchboxes for APCs.

But we were always wrong in these predictions.
It was a family war. Whatever happened,
The principals were obliged to attend its issue.
A few were cajoled into leaving, a few were expelled,
And there were villains enough, but none of them
Slipped away with the swag.

For the prince was fighting Sihanouk, his nephew,
And the Jockey Cap was ranged against his brother
Of whom I remember nothing more
Than an obscure reputation for virtue.
I have been told that the prince is still fighting
Somewhere in the Cardamoms or the Elephant Mountains.
But I doubt that the Jockey Cap would have survived his good
    connections.
I think the lunches would have done for him—
Either the lunches or the dead soldiers.

SEAMUS HEANEY

1939-

253   *Requiem for the Croppies*

The pockets of our great coats full of barley—
No kitchens on the run, no striking camp—
We moved quick and sudden in our own country.
The priest lay behind ditches with the tramp.
A people, hardly marching—on the hike—
We found new tactics happening each day:
We'd cut through reins and rider with the pike
And stampede cattle into infantry,
Then retreat through hedges where cavalry must be thrown.
Until, on Vinegar Hill, the fatal conclave.
Terraced thousands died, shaking scythes at cannon.
The hillside blushed, soaked in our broken wave.
They buried us without shroud or coffin
And in August the barley grew up out of the grave.

254   *Whatever You Say Say Nothing*

I

I'm writing just after an encounter
With an English journalist in search of 'views
On the Irish thing'. I'm back in winter
Quarters where bad news is no longer news,

Where media-men and stringers sniff and point,
Where zoom lenses, recorders and coiled leads
Litter the hotels. The times are out of joint
But I incline as much to rosary beads

As to the jottings and analyses
Of politicians and newspapermen
Who've scribbled down the long campaign from gas
And protest to gelignite and sten,

Who proved upon their pulses 'escalate',
'Backlash' and 'crack down', 'the provisional wing',
'Polarization' and 'long-standing hate'.
Yet I live here, I live here too, I sing,

Expertly civil tongued with civil neighbours
On the high wires of first wireless reports,
Sucking the fake taste, the stony flavours
Of those sanctioned, old, elaborate retorts:

'Oh, it's disgraceful, surely, I agree,'
'Where's it going to end?' 'It's getting worse.'
'They're murderers.' 'Internment, understandably . . .'
The 'voice of sanity' is getting hoarse.

II

Men die at hand. In blasted street and home
The gelignite's a common sound effect:
As the man said when Celtic won, 'The Pope of Rome
's a happy man this night.' His flock suspect

In their deepest heart of hearts the heretic
Has come at last to heel and to the stake.
We tremble near the flames but want no truck
With the actual firing. We're on the make

As ever. Long sucking the hind tit
Cold as a witch's and as hard to swallow
Still leaves us fork-tongued on the border bit:
The liberal papist note sounds hollow

When amplified and mixed in with the bangs
That shake all hearts and windows day and night.
(It's tempting here to rhyme on 'labour pangs'
And diagnose a rebirth in our plight

But that would be to ignore other symptoms.
Last night you didn't need a stethoscope
To hear the eructation of Orange drums
Allergic equally to Pearse and Pope.)

On all sides 'little platoons' are mustering—
The phrase is Cruise O'Brien's via that great
Backlash, Burke—while I sit here with a pestering
Drouth for words at once both gaff and bait

To lure the tribal shoals to epigram
And order. I believe any of us
Could draw the line through bigotry and sham
Given the right line, *aere perennius.*

III

'Religion's never mentioned here,' of course.
'You know them by their eyes,' and hold your tongue.
'One side's as bad as the other,' never worse.
Christ, it's near time that some small leak was sprung

In the great dykes the Dutchman made
To dam the dangerous tide that followed Seamus.
Yet for all this art and sedentary trade
I am incapable. The famous

Northern reticence, the tight gag of place
And times: yes, yes. Of the 'wee six' I sing
Where to be saved you only must save face
And whatever you say, you say nothing.

Smoke-signals are loud-mouthed compared with us:
Manoeuvrings to find out name and school,
Subtle discrimination by addresses
With hardly an exception to the rule

That Norman, Ken and Sidney signalled Prod
And Seamus (call me Sean) was sure-fire Pape.
O land of password, handgrip, wink and nod,
Of open minds as open as a trap,

Where tongues lie coiled, as under flames lie wicks,
Where half of us, as in a wooden horse
Were cabin'd and confined like wily Greeks,
Besieged within the siege, whispering morse.

IV

This morning from a dewy motorway
I saw the new camp for the internees:
A bomb had left a crater of fresh clay
In the roadside, and over in the trees

Machine-gun posts defined a real stockade.
There was that white mist you get on a low ground
And it was déjà-vu, some film made
Of Stalag 17, a bad dream with no sound.

Is there a life before death? That's chalked up
In Ballymurphy. Competence with pain,
Coherent miseries, a bit and sup,
We hug our little destiny again.

255   *The Strand at Lough Beg*

*In memory of Colum McCartney**

> All round this little island, on the strand
> Far down below there, where the breakers strive,
> Grow the tall rushes from the oozy sand.
> > Dante, *Purgatorio*, i. 100–3

Leaving the white glow of filling stations
And a few lonely streetlamps among fields
You climbed the hills towards Newtownhamilton
Past the Fews Forest, out beneath the stars—
Along that road, a high, bare pilgrim's track
Where Sweeney fled before the bloodied heads,
Goat-beards and dogs' eyes in a demon pack
Blazing out of the ground, snapping and squealing.
What blazed ahead of you? A faked road block?
The red lamp swung, the sudden brakes and stalling
Engine, voices, heads hooded and the cold-nosed gun?
Or in your driving mirror, tailing headlights

* Colum McCartney, a relative of the author, was the victim of a random sectarian killing in the late summer of 1975.
Sweeney is the hero of a Middle Irish prose and poem sequence, one part of which takes place in Fews in Co. Armagh. [SH]

That pulled out suddenly and flagged you down
Where you weren't known and far from what you knew:
The lowland clays and waters of Lough Beg,
Church Island's spire, its soft treeline of yew.

There you used hear guns fired behind the house
Long before rising time, when duck shooters
Haunted the marigolds and bulrushes,
But still were scared to find spent cartridges,
Acrid, brassy, genital, ejected,
On your way across the strand to fetch the cows.
For you and yours and yours and mine fought shy,
Spoke an old language of conspirators
And could not crack the whip or seize the day:
Big-voiced scullions, herders, feelers round
Haycocks and hindquarters, talkers in byres,
Slow arbitrators of the burial ground.
Across that strand of yours the cattle graze
Up to their bellies in an early mist
And now they turn their unbewildered gaze
To where we work our way through squeaking sedge
Drowning in dew. Like a dull blade with its edge
Honed bright, Lough Beg half shines under the haze.
I turn because the sweeping of your feet
Has stopped behind me, to find you on your knees
With blood and roadside muck in your hair and eyes,
Then kneel in front of you in brimming grass
And gather up cold handfuls of the dew
To wash you, cousin. I dab you clean with moss
Fine as the drizzle out of a low cloud.
I lift you under the arms and lay you flat.
With rushes that shoot green again, I plait
Green scapulars to wear over your shroud.

CAROLYN FORCHÉ

1951–

256 *The Colonel*

What you have heard is true. I was in his house. His wife carried a tray of coffee and sugar. His daughter filed her nails, his son went out for the night. There were daily papers, pet dogs, a pistol on the cushion beside him. The moon swung bare on its black cord over the house. On the television was a cop show. It was in English. Broken bottles were embedded in the walls around the house to scoop the kneecaps from a man's legs or cut his hands to lace. On the windows there were gratings like those in liquor stores. We had dinner, rack of lamb, good wine, a gold bell was on the table for calling the maid. The maid brought green mangoes, salt, a type of bread. I was asked how I enjoyed the country. There was a brief commercial in Spanish. His wife took everything away. There was some talk then of how difficult it had become to govern. The parrot said hello on the terrace. The colonel told it to shut up, and pushed himself from the table. My friend said to me with his eyes: say nothing. The colonel returned with a sack used to bring groceries home. He spilled many human ears on the table. They were like dried peach halves. There is no other way to say this. He took one of them in his hands, shook it in our faces, dropped it into a water glass. It came alive there. I am tired of fooling around he said. As for the rights of anyone, tell your people they can go fuck themselves. He swept the ears to the floor with his arm and held the last of his wine in the air. Something for your poetry, no? he said. Some of the ears on the floor caught this scrap of his voice. Some of the ears on the floor were pressed to the ground.

May 1978

RICHARD WILBUR

1921–

257   *Advice to a Prophet*

When you come, as you soon must, to the streets of our city,
Mad-eyed from stating the obvious,
Not proclaiming our fall but begging us
In God's name to have self-pity,

Spare us all word of the weapons, their force and range,
The long numbers that rocket the mind;
Our slow, unreckoning hearts will be left behind,
Unable to fear what is too strange.

Nor shall you scare us with talk of the death of the race.
How should we dream of this place without us?—
The sun mere fire, the leaves untroubled about us,
A stone look on the stone's face?

Speak of the world's own change. Though we cannot conceive
Of an undreamt thing, we know to our cost
How the dreamt cloud crumbles, the vines are blackened by frost,
How the view alters. We could believe,

If you told us so, that the white-tailed deer will slip
Into perfect shade, grown perfectly shy,
The lark avoid the reaches of our eye,
The jack-pine lose its knuckled grip

On the cold ledge, and every torrent burn
As Xanthus once, its gliding trout
Stunned in a twinkling. What should we be without
The dolphin's arc, the dove's return,

These things in which we have seen ourselves and spoken?
Ask us, prophet, how we shall call
Our natures forth when that live tongue is all
Dispelled, that glass obscured or broken

In which we have said the rose of our love and the clean
Horse of our courage, in which beheld
The singing locust of the soul unshelled,
And all we mean or wish to mean.

Ask us, ask us whether with the worldless rose
Our hearts shall fail us; come demanding
Whether there shall be lofty or long standing
When the bronze annals of the oak-tree close.

WILLIAM STAFFORD

1914–

258 *At the Bomb Testing Site*

At noon in the desert a panting lizard
waited for history, its elbows tense,
watching the curve of a particular road
as if something might happen.

It was looking at something farther off
than people could see, an important scene
acted in stone for little selves
at the flute end of consequences.

There was just a continent without much on it
under a sky that never cared less.
Ready for a change, the elbows waited.
The hands gripped hard on the desert.

PETER PORTER

1929–

Your Attention Please

The Polar DEW has just warned that
A nuclear rocket strike of
At least one thousand megatons
Has been launched by the enemy
Directly at our major cities.
This announcement will take
Two and a quarter minutes to make,
You therefore have a further
Eight and a quarter minutes
To comply with the shelter
Requirements published in the Civil
Defence Code—section Atomic Attack.
A specially shortened Mass
Will be broadcast at the end
Of this announcement—
Protestant and Jewish services
Will begin simultaneously—
Select your wavelength immediately
According to instructions
In the Defence Code. Do not
Take well-loved pets (including birds)
Into your shelter—they will consume
Fresh air. Leave the old and bed-
ridden, you can do nothing for them.
Remember to press the sealing
Switch when everyone is in
The shelter. Set the radiation
Aerial, turn on the geiger barometer.
Turn off your Television now.
Turn off your radio immediately
The Services end. At the same time
Secure explosion plugs in the ears
Of each member of your family. Take
Down your plasma flasks. Give your children
The pills marked one and two
In the C.D. green container, then put

339

Them to bed. Do not break
The inside airlock seals until
The radiation All Clear shows
(Watch for the cuckoo in your
Perspex panel), or your District
Touring Doctor rings your bell.
If before this, your air becomes
Exhausted or if any of your family
Is critically injured, administer
The capsules marked 'Valley Forge'
(Red pocket in No. 1 Survival Kit)
For painless death. (Catholics
Will have been instructed by their priests
What to do in this eventuality.)
This announcement is ending. Our President
Has already given order for
Massive retaliation—it will be
Decisive. Some of us may die.
Remember, statistically
It is not likely to be you.
All flags are flying fully dressed
On Government buildings—the sun is shining.
Death is the least we have to fear.
We are all in the hands of God,
Whatever happens happens by His Will.
Now go quickly to your shelters.

NOTES AND REFERENCES

TEXTS are based on the author's final version, with a few exceptions noted below. Spelling and punctuation have been modernized except for the extract from Spenser's *Astrophel*, whose spelling is part of its deliberate archaism.

The sources of passages excerpted from longer works are set out below. No references are given for poems by authors whose collected poems are easily available, since these can be found by consulting first-line indexes. The sources of poems in copyright may be found in the section of Acknowledgements (pp. 344–50).

1, 2. The Book of Exodus, 15: 1–18, and the Second Book of Samuel, 1: 19–27.

3. Homer. *The Iliad*, trans. Robert Fitzgerald (1974), xxii. 309–515.

4. Simonides. 'Thermopylae', William Tirebuck, ed., *The Poetical Works of Bowles, Lamb and Hartley Coleridge* (1887).

5. Anonymous. 'Hymn to the Fallen', trans. Arthur Waley, *Chinese Poems* (1946, fifth impression 1976).

6. Virgil. *The Aeneid*, trans. Allen Mandelbaum (1971), xii. 1178–1271.

7. Horace. *The Odes*, trans. James Michie (1963), ii. 7 and iii. 2.

8. Aneirin. 'The Gododdin', trans. Joseph P. Clancy, *The Earliest Welsh Poetry* (1970), stanzas vi–xi and xxi.

9. Rihaku. 'Lament of the Frontier Guard', trans. Ezra Pound, *Personae: Collected Poems* (1926, rev. 1949).

10, 12. Anonymous. 'The Finnesburh Fragment' and 'The Battle of Maldon', trans., Kevin Crossley-Holland and Bruce Mitchell, *The Battle of Maldon and other Old English Poems* (1965).

13. Anonymous. *The Song of Roland*, trans. Dorothy L. Sayers (1957), sections 161–3.

14. Anonymous. 'The Lament of Maev Leith-Dherg', Stopford A. Brook and T. W. Rolleston, eds., *A Treasury of Irish Poetry in the English Tongue* (1932).

15. Geoffrey Chaucer. 'The Knight's Tale', trans. John Dryden, *Fables, Ancient and Modern* (1700), ll. 1967–2038.

17. Edmund Spenser. *Astrophel, A Pastorall Elegie Upon the Death of the Most Noble and Valorous Knight, Sir Philip Sidney*, ll. 85–138.

18. Samuel Daniel. *The Civil Wars between the Two Houses of Lancaster and York*, bk. 8, stanzas 14–22.

20. George Gascoigne. 'The Fruits of War', stanzas 155–72.

21. George Peele. 'Farewell to Arms', *Polyhymnia* (1590).

27. John Milton. *Paradise Lost*, bk. 6, ll. 296–353.

28. Charles Sackville, Earl of Dorset. 'Song. Written at Sea in the First Dutch War (1665), the night before an Engagement', *Works* (1749).

29. John Dryden. 'Annus Mirabilis', stanzas 186–202.

30. Daniel Defoe. 'The Spanish Descent'. Text from Frank H. Ellis, ed., *Anthology of Poems on Affairs of State: Augustan Satirical Verse, 1660–1714*, vol. 6 (1970), ll. 269–344.

31. Joseph Addison. 'The Campaign: A Poem to His Grace the Duke of Marlborough', ll. 283–302.

33. James Thomson. 'Rule Brittania!' From the masque, *Alfred* (1740) by James Thomson and David Mallet. This song is probably, but not certainly, by Thomson.

34. Samuel Johnson. 'The Vanity of Human Wishes', ll. 191–222.

35. John Scott of Amwell. 'The Drum', *Poetical Works* (1782).

43. Percy Bysshe Shelley. *The Revolt of Islam*, canto 5, stanzas i–xiii.

44. Charles Wolfe. 'The Burial of Sir John Moore after Corunna'. Text from *Newry Telegraph*, 19 April 1817.

45. Joel Barlow. 'Advice to a Raven in Russia'. Text from Leon Howard, 'Joel Barlow and Napoleon', *The Huntington Library Quarterly*, vol. 2, no. 1, October 1938, pp. 37–51.

46. Adam Mickiewicz. 'The Year 1812', trans. Donald Davie, *The Forests of Lithuania* (1959).

47. Victor Hugo. 'Russia 1812', trans. Robert Lowell, *Imitations* (1961).

48. Fyodor Tyutchev. 'At Vshchizh', trans. Charles Tomlinson, *Selected Poems 1951–1974* (1978).

50. Thomas Hardy. *The Dynasts*, part 3, act VI, scene viii.

52, 53. Lord Byron. *Childe Harold's Pilgrimage*, canto 3, stanzas xxi–xxviii; and *Don Juan*, canto 7, stanzas xli and lxxix–lxxxvii.

55. Lord Macaulay. 'Horatius', stanzas xlii–lxiv.

56. William Edmonstoune Aytoun. 'Edinburgh after Flodden', sections x and xi.

57. Matthew Arnold. 'Sohrab and Rustum', ll. 495–539 and 827–92.

60. Alfred, Lord Tennyson. 'Maud', part III, vi.

61. William Makepeace Thackeray. 'The Due of the Dead'. Text from *Punch*, vol. xxvii (July–December 1854), p. 173.

75. James Russell Lowell. 'Ode Recited at the Harvard Commemoration', sections i and x–xi.

78. Rainer Maria Rilke. 'Last Evening', trans. J. B. Leishman: R. M. Rilke, *Selected Works*, vol. ii (1960).

79. Arthur Rimbaud. 'Eighteen-Seventy', trans. Robert Lowell, *Imitations* (1961), sections i–iii, vii–viii.

95. T. W. H. Crosland. 'Slain'. Text from M. van Wyk Smith, *Drummer Hodge. The Poetry of the Anglo-Boer War, 1899–1902* (1978), pp. 113–14.

96. Edgar Wallace. 'War', *Writ in Barracks* (1900).

104. Herbert Asquith. 'The Volunteer', *Poems 1912–33* (1933).

105. Julian Grenfell. 'Into Battle'. Text from *The Times*, 27 May 1915.

106. John McCrae. 'In Flanders Fields', *In Flanders Fields and other poems*. With an essay in character by Sir Andrew Macphail (1919).

114. Guillaume Apollinaire. 'Calligram, 15 May 1915', trans. O. Bernard, *Guillaume Apollinaire: Selected Poems* (1965).

115. Benjamin Péret. 'Little Song of the Maimed', trans. David Gascoyne, *Collected Verse Translations* (1970).

120. W. B. Yeats. 'Reprisals'. Text from Peter Allt and Russell K. Alspach, eds., *The Variorium Edition of the Poems of W. B. Yeats* (1957).

159. David Jones. *In Parenthesis*, part 7, pp. 162–6.

161. Ezra Pound. 'Hugh Selwyn Mauberley', sections iv and v.

171. Louis MacNeice. *Autumn Journal*, section vi.

176. Anonymous. 'Eyes of men running, falling, screaming'. Text from Valentine Cunningham, ed., *The Penguin Book of Spanish Civil War Verse* (1980).

178. Sylvia Townsend Warner. 'Benicasim'. Text from Valentine Cunningham, ed., *The Penguin Book of Spanish Civil War Verse* (1980).

184. Louis Aragon. 'The Lilacs and the Roses', trans. Louis MacNeice, *The Collected Poems of Louis MacNeice* (1966).

198, 200. Sidney Keyes. 'The Foreign Gate', section iv; 'The Wilderness', sections i–ii.

203. Keith Douglas. 'Aristocrats'. I prefer this title and text, from Desmond Graham, ed., *The Complete Poems of Keith Douglas* (1978), p. 139, to the later version, entitled 'Sportsmen', on p. 110.

227. Ephim Fogel. 'Shipment to Maidanek'. Text from Edwin Seaver, ed., *Cross Section 1945. A Collection of New American Writings* (1945).

228. W. H. Auden. 'Sonnets from China', xii.

243. Andrei Voznesensky. 'I am Goya', trans. Stanley Kunitz. Text from Patricia Blake and Max Hayward, eds., *Antiworlds and the Fifth Ace. Poetry by Andrei Voznesensky* (1966).

ACKNOWLEDGEMENTS

THE editor and publishers gratefully acknowledge permission to use copyright material in this book as follows:

Richard Aldington: 'Battlefield'. Copyright © Madame Catherine Guillaume. Reprinted by permission of Rosica Colin Ltd.

Kenneth Allott: 'Prize for Good Conduct' from *Collected Poems* (1975). Reprinted by permission of Secker & Warburg Ltd.

Aneirin, 6th century: stanzas vi, vii, viii, ix, x, xi and xxi from 'The Gododdin', trans. Joseph P. Clancy, from *The Earliest Welsh Poems* (Macmillan, 1970). Copyright © 1970 by Joseph Clancy. Reprinted by permission of the translator.

Anonymous, 4th century BC: 'Hymn to the Fallen' from *Chinese Poems*, trans. Arthur Waley (1946). Reprinted by permission of George Allen & Unwin (Publishers) Ltd.

Anonymous, 8th and 11th centuries: 'The Finnesburh Fragment' and 'The Battle of Maldon', trans. Kevin Crossley-Holland, from *The Battle of Maldon and Other Old English Poems* (Macmillan, 1965). Copyright © Kevin Crossley-Holland and Bruce Mitchell 1965. Reprinted by permission of Deborah Rogers Ltd.

Anonymous, 12th century: stanzas 161, 162 and 163 from *The Song of Roland*, trans. Dorothy L. Sayers. Reprinted by permission of David Higham Associates Ltd.

Anonymous, ?1937: an International Brigader's poem, 'Eyes of men running . . .' from *The Penguin Book of Spanish Civil War Verse*, ed. Valentine Cunningham (Penguin Poets, 1980), p. 57. Copyright © Valentine Cunningham, 1980. By permission of Penguin Books Ltd.

Guillaume Apollinaire: 'Calligram, 15 May 1915' from Apollinaire: *Selected Poems* trans. Oliver Bernard (Penguin Modern European Poets, 1965), p. 77. Translation copyright © Oliver Bernard, 1965. First published in *Calligrammes de Guillaume Apollinaire.* copyright Editions Gallimard, 1925. Reprinted by permission of Penguin Books Ltd.

Louis Aragon: see Louis MacNeice.

Herbert Asquith: 'The Volunteer' from *Poems 1912–33* (1934). Reprinted by permission of Sidgwick & Jackson Ltd.

Margaret Atwood: 'It is Dangerous to Read Newspapers' from *Selected Poems*, copyright Margaret Atwood, published by Oxford University Press, Canada, 1976. Used by permission of the publisher.

W. H. Auden: 'Spain 1937 from *The English Auden: Poems, Essays and Domestic Writings*; and stanza xii from 'Sonnets from China' from *Collected Poems*. Reprinted by permission of Faber & Faber Ltd.

Sir John Betjeman: 'In Memory of Basil, Marquess of Dufferin and Ava' from *Collected Poems* (4th revised edn. 1979). Reprinted by permission of John Murray (Publishers) Ltd.

Laurence Binyon: 'For the Fallen (September 1914)'. Reprinted by permission of Mrs Nicolete Gray and The Society of Authors on behalf of the Laurence Binyon Estate.

John Peale Bishop: 'In the Dordogne', in *Now With His Love*. Copyright 1933 Charles Scribner's Sons; copyright renewed 1961 Margaret G. H. Bronson. Reprinted with the permission of Charles Scribner's Sons from *Selected Poems*. Copyright 1941 John Peale Bishop, copyright renewed 1969 Margaret G. H. Bronson.

Edmund Blunden: 'Two Voices', 'The Zonnebeke Road', 'Report on Experience', 'Vlamertinghe', all from *Poems of Many Years* (Wm Collins Sons & Co. Ltd.). Reprinted by permission of A. D. Peters & Co., Ltd.

ACKNOWLEDGEMENTS

Norman Cameron: 'Green, Green is El Aghir' from *Collected Poems*. Reprinted by permission of The Hogarth Press and the author's literary estate.

May Wedderburn Cannan: 'Rouen' from *In War Time* (B. H. Blackwell, 1917).

Charles Causley: 'Armistice Day' and 'At the British War Cemetery, Bayeux' from *Union Street* (Rupert Hart-Davis, 1957). Reprinted by permission of David Higham Associates Ltd.

John Cornford: 'Full Moon at Tierz', 'To Margot Heinemann' and 'A Letter from Aragon' from *Understand the Weapon, Understand the Wound: Selected Writings of John Cornford* (1976). Copyright © 1976 Jonathan Galassi. Reprinted by permission of the Carcanet Press.

E. E. Cummings: 'my sweet old etcetera' and 'next to of course god america i', and 'i sing of Olaf glad and big' from *Complete Poems 1913–1935* (Granada Publishing Ltd., 1968). Reprinted by permission of Grafton Books Ltd.

R. N. Currey: 'Unseen Fire', from *This Other Planet* (1945). Reprinted by permission of Routledge & Kegan Paul Ltd.

Elizabeth Daryush: 'Subalterns'. Reprinted by permission of Mr A. A. Daryush.

Donald Davie: 'The Year 1812' from *The Forests of Lithuania* (Marvell Press, 1959). Reprinted by permission of the author.

C. Day-Lewis: 'The Stand-To' and 'Where are the War Poets?' from *Collected Poems 1954* (Hogarth Press). Reprinted by permission of Jonathan Cape Ltd., on behalf of the Executors of the Estate of C. Day-Lewis.

Paul Dehn: 'St Aubin D'Aubigné' from *The Day's Alarm*. Copyright © 1965, 1976 Dehn Enterprises Ltd. Reprinted by permission of James Bernard.

James Dickey: 'The Firebombing' from *Poems 1957–1967*. Copyright © 1964 by James Dickey. Reprinted by permission of Rapp & Whiting Ltd., and Wesleyan University Press. This poem first appeared in *Poetry*.

Emily Dickinson: 'My Portion is Defeat—today—' (#639), copyright 1929 by Martha Dickinson Bianchi, copyright renewed 1957 by Mary L. Hampson; 'My Triumph lasted till the Drums' (#1227), copyright 1935 by Martha Dickinson Bianchi, copyright © renewed 1963 by Mary L. Hampson. Reprinted from *The Complete Poems of Emily Dickinson*, ed. Thomas H. Johnson, by permission of Little, Brown & Company and by permission of the publishers and the Trustees of Amherst College from *The Poems of Emily Dickinson*, ed. Thomas H. Johnson, Cambridge, Mass.; The Belknap Press of Harvard University Press, copyright 1951, © 1955, 1973, 1983 by the President and Fellows of Harvard College.

Hilda Doolittle: extract from 'The Walls Do Not Fall' from *Collected Poems of H.D. 1912–1944*, copyright © 1973 by Norman Holmes Pearson. Reprinted by permission of Carcanet Press.

Keith Douglas: 'Gallantry'; 'Vergissmeinnicht' and 'Aristocrats' ('Sportsmen') from *The Complete Poems of Keith Douglas*, ed. Desmond Graham (1978), copyright © Marie J. Douglas 1978. Reprinted by permission of Oxford University Press.

Douglas Dunn: 'War Blinded' from *St Kilder's Parliament* (1981). Reprinted by permission of Faber & Faber.

Richard Eberhart: 'The Fury of Aerial Bombardment' from *Collected Poems 1930–1976*. Reprinted by permission of Chatto & Windus Ltd.

T. S. Eliot: 'Triumphal March' from *Collected Poems 1909–1962*. Reprinted by permission of Faber and Faber Ltd.

Gavin Ewart: 'When a Beau Goes In' from *Collected Ewart 1933–80*. Reprinted by permission of Hutchinson Publishing Group Ltd.

James Fenton: 'Dead Soldiers' from *The Memory of War* (Salamander Press, 1982). Reprinted by permission of the author and A. D. Peters & Co. Ltd.

Ephim Fogel: 'Shipment to Maidanek'. Reprinted by permission of the author.

345

ACKNOWLEDGEMENTS

Carolyn Forché: 'The Colonel' from *The Country Between Us*. Reprinted by permission of Jonathan Cape Ltd.

Robert Frost: 'Range Finding' from *The Poetry of Robert Frost*, ed. Edward Connery Lathem. Reprinted by permission of Jonathan Cape Ltd., on behalf of the Estate of Robert Frost.

Roy Fuller: 'The Middle of a War' from *Collected Poems 1968*. Reprinted by permission of André Deutsch.

David Gascoyne: 'Ecce Homo' from *Collected Poems*, copyright © OUP 1965. Reprinted by permission of Oxford University Press.

Allen Ginsberg: 'A Vow' from *Collected Poems 1947–1980* (Viking Books, 1985). Copyright © Allen Ginsberg 1984. Reprinted by permission of Penguin Books Limited.

Robert Graves: 'Sergeant-Major Money', 'Recalling War' from *Collected Poems 1959* and 'The Persian Version' from *Collected Poems 1975*. Reprinted by permission of A. P. Watt Ltd. on behalf of the Executors of the Estate of Robert Graves.

Thom Gunn: 'Claus Von Stauffenberg' from *My Sad Captains*, copyright © 1961, 1973 by Thom Gunn. Reprinted by permission of Faber & Faber Ltd., and Farrar, Straus & Giroux, Inc.

Ivor Gurney: 'To His Love', 'Ballad of the Three Spectres', and 'The Silent One' from *Collected Poems of Ivor Gurney*, ed. P. J. Kavanagh (1982), copyright © Robin Haines, Sole Trustee of the Gurney Estate, 1982. Reprinted by permission of OUP.

Thomas Hardy: from *The Complete Poems of Thomas Hardy*, ed. James Gibson (Macmillan:London/New York, 1978).

Seamus Heaney: 'Requiem for the Croppies' and 'Whatever You Say Say Nothing' from *Poems 1965–1975*. 'The Strand at Lough Beg' from *Field Work*. Reprinted by permission of Faber & Faber Ltd.

Anthony Hecht: 'More Light! More Light!' from *The Hard Hours*, copyright © 1967 by Anthony Hecht. Reprinted by permission of Oxford University Press.

Geoffrey Hill: 'September Song' from *King Log* (1968). Reprinted by permission of André Deutsch.

Homer: 'Book 22' from Homer, *The Iliad*, trans. Robert Fitzgerald, copyright © 1974 by Robert Fitzgerald. Reprinted by permission of Doubleday & Company, Inc., a division of Bantam, Doubleday, Dell Publishing Group, Inc.

Horace: Odes ii. 7, and iii. 2, from *Horace: The Odes*, trans. James Michie. Reprinted by permission of the translator.

Ted Hughes: 'Six Young Men' from *The Hawk in the Rain* (Faber). Reprinted by permission of Faber & Faber Ltd.

Victor Hugo: see Robert Lowell.

Randall Jarrell: 'Eighth Air Force', 'The Death of the Ball Turret Gunner', 'A Camp in the Prussian Forest' and 'A Front', all from *Randall Jarrell: The Complete Poems*. Reprinted by permission of Faber & Faber Ltd.

David Jones: extract from part 7, plus notes 15, 16 & 17, from *In Parenthesis*. Reprinted by permission of Faber & Faber Ltd.

Sidney Keyes: from 'The Foreign Gate', part iv, pp. 72–4, 'Timoshenko', p. 98 and from 'The Wilderness', parts i & ii, pp. 110–13, from *The Collected Poems of Sidney Keyes*, ed. Michael Meyer (1945). Reprinted by permission of Routledge & Kegan Paul Ltd.

Galway Kinnell: 'Vapor Trail Reflected in the Frog Pond' from *Body Rags*. Copyright © 1967 by Galway Kinnell. Reprinted by permission of Rapp & Whiting Ltd.

Lincoln Kirstein: 'Rank' and 'Foresight' from *Rhymes and More Rhymes of a PFC* (New Directions). Reprinted by permission of the author.

Philip Larkin: 'MCMXIV' from *The Whitsun Weddings*. Reprinted by permission of Faber & Faber Ltd.

ACKNOWLEDGEMENTS

Laurie Lee: 'A Moment of War' from *Selected Poems* (1983). Reprinted by permission of André Deutsch.

Denise Levertov: 'What Were They Like?' from *To Stay Alive*. Copyright © 1966 by Denise Levertov Goodman. Reprinted by permission of New Directions Publishing Corporation.

Alun Lewis: 'Dawn on the East Coast', 'Goodbye' and 'Song' from *Ha! Ha! Among the Trumpets* (1945); 'All day it has rained' from *Raiders Dawn*. Reprinted by permission of Unwyn Hyman Ltd.

Robert Lowell: 'For the Union Dead' and 'Fall 1961' from *For the Union Dead*; translations: Hugo, 'Russia 1812' and extract from Rimbaud, 'Eighteen-Seventy' from *Imitations*. Reprinted by permission of Faber & Faber Ltd.

George MacBeth: 'The Land-Mine', copyright © 1965 by George MacBeth, from *Collected Poems 1958-1970* (Macmillan, London). Reprinted by permission of Anthony Sheil Associates Ltd.

Hugh MacDiarmid: 'Another Epitaph on an Army of Mercenaries' from *The Complete Poems of Hugh MacDiarmid 1920-1976*. Reprinted by permission of the publishers, Martin Brian & O'Keeffe Ltd., and Mrs Valda Grieve.

Archibald MacLeish: 'Memorial Rain' from *New and Collected Poems 1917-1982* by Archibald MacLeish. Copyright © 1985 by the Estate of Archibald MacLeish. Reprinted by permission of Houghton Mifflin Co.

Louis MacNeice: 'And I remember Spain . . .' from *Autumn Journal* (2nd edn. Faber, 1964); 'The Streets of Laredo' and trans. of Aragon, 'The Lilacs and the Roses' from *Collected Poems* (2nd revised edn. Faber, 1979). Reprinted by permission of David Higham Associates Ltd.

Robert Mezey: 'How Much Longer?' from *The Door Standing Open*, copyright © OUP 1970. Reprinted by permission of Oxford University Press and the author.

Adrian Mitchell: 'To Whom It May Concern' from *Out Loud* (1964). Reprinted by permission of Jonathan Cape Ltd., on behalf of the author.

Marianne Moore: 'In Distrust of Merits' published in the UK in *The Complete Poems of Marianne Moore*. Reprinted by permission of Faber & Faber Ltd.

Howard Nemerov: 'A Fable of the War' and 'Redeployment' from *The Collected Poems of Howard Nemerov* (The University of Chicago Press, 1977). Reprinted by permission of the author.

Sir Henry Newbolt: 'He Fell among Thieves' and 'Vitaï Lampada' from *Selected Poems of Henry Newbolt* (Hodder & Stoughton, 1981). Reprinted by permission of Peter Newbolt.

George Orwell: 'The Italian soldier shook my hand', reprinted by permission of A. M. Heath & Company Ltd., on behalf of the Estate of the late Sonia Brownwell Orwell.

Wilfred Owen: 'Anthem for Doomed Youth', 'Dulce et Decorum Est', 'Futility', 'Strange Meeting', 'Exposure', 'Insensibility' and 'The Send-Off' from *The Complete Poems and Fragments*, ed. Jon Stallworthy, 1983. Reprinted by permission of the Owen Estate and Chatto & Windus.

Benjamin Péret: 'Little Song of the Maimed', trans. David Gascoyne in *Collected Verse Translations* by David Gascoyne, ed. Alan Clodd and Robin Skelton (1970), © OUP 1970. Reprinted by permission of Oxford University Press.

Peter Porter: 'Your Attention Please' from *Collected Poems* (1983) © Peter Porter 1983. Reprinted by permission of Oxford University Press.

Ezra Pound: extracts from 'Hugh Selwyn Mauberley' and from trans. of Rihaku, 'Lament of the Frontier Guard' from *Collected Shorter Poems*. Reprinted by permission of Faber & Faber Ltd.

ACKNOWLEDGEMENTS

F. T. Prince: 'Soldiers Bathing' from *Collected Poems* (1979). Reprinted by permission of Anvil Press Poetry Ltd.

John Pudney: 'For Johnny' from *Collected Poems* (Putnam, 1957). Reprinted by permission of David Higham Associates Ltd.

Herbert Read: 'To a Conscript of 1940' from *Collected Poems* (Faber, 1946). Reprinted by permission of David Higham Associates Ltd.

Henry Reed: 'Naming of Parts', 'Judging Distances' and 'Unarmed Combat' from 'Lessons of War', from *A Map of Verona* (1946). Reprinted by permission of Jonathan Cape Ltd., on behalf of the Estate of Henry Reed.

Edgell Rickword: 'Winter Warfare' from *Behind the Eyes: Collected Poems and Translations* (1976), © 1976. Reprinted by permission of the Carcanet Press on behalf of the Estate of Edgell Rickword.

R. M. Rilke: 'Last Evening' from R. M. Rilke: *Selected Works*, vol. ii, Poetry, trans. J. B. Leishman. Reprinted by permission of St John's College, Oxford, and The Hogarth Press.

Arthur Rimbaud: see Robert Lowell.

Isaac Rosenberg: 'August 1914' from *The Collected Works of Isaac Rosenberg*, ed. Ian Parsons. Reprinted by permission of Chatto & Windus Ltd., and the author's literary estate.

Alan Ross: 'Off Brighton Pier' from *Open Sea* (London Magazine Editions). Reprinted by permission of the author.

Carl Sandburg: 'Grass' from *Cornhuskers*. Copyright 1918 by Holt, Rinehart & Winston, Inc; copyright 1946 by Carl Sandburg. Reprinted by permission of Harcourt Brace Jovanovich, Inc.

Siegfried Sassoon: 'They', 'The Hero', 'The Rear-Guard', 'The General', 'Glory of Women' and 'Everyone Sang' from *Collected Poems*. Copyright 1918, 1920 by E. P. Dutton & Co. Copyright 1936, 1946, 1947, 1948 by Siegfried Sassoon. All rights reserved. Reprinted by permission of George Sassoon and of Viking Penguin, Inc.

Vernon Scannell: 'Walking Wounded' and 'The Great War' from *New and Collected Poems 1950–1980* (1980). Reprinted by permission of Robson Books.

Karl Shapiro: 'Elegy for a Dead Soldier'. Copyright 1944 by Karl Shapiro, from *Collected Poems 1940–1978*. Reprinted by permission of Random House, Inc.

Louis Simpson: 'Memories of a Lost War', 'The Battle', and 'The Heroes' first published in *Good News of Death and Other Poems* (Scribners). Reprinted by permission of the author; 'Carentan O Carentan', copyright 1949 by Louis Simpson, from *A Dream of Governors* by permission of Wesleyan University Press. This poem first appeared in *The Arrivistes*.

Edith Sitwell: 'Still Falls the Rain' from *Street Songs* (Macmillan, 1942). Reprinted by permission of David Higham Associates Ltd.

W. D. Snodgrass: 'After Experience Taught Me . . .' from *After Experience*, © W. D. Snodgrass 1964, 1968. Reprinted by permission of Oxford University Press. & Row, Inc.

Bernard Spencer: 'A Thousand Killed' from *Collected Poems*, ed. Roger Bowen (1981), © Mrs Anne Humphreys 1981. Reprinted by permission of Oxford University Press.

Stephen Spender: 'Two Armies'. Copyright 1942 by Stephen Spender; 'Ultima Ratio Regum', copyright 1942 and renewed 1970 by Stephen Spender, both from *Collected Poems 1928–1953*. Reprinted by permission of Faber & Faber Ltd., and Random House, Inc.

William Stafford: 'At the Bomb Testing Site' from *Stories That Could be True*. Copyright © 1960 by William Stafford. Reprinted by permission of Harper & Row, Publishers, Inc.

Jon Stallworthy: 'A Letter from Berlin' from *Root and Branch*. Reprinted by permission of Chatto & Windus Ltd.

ACKNOWLEDGEMENTS

Wallace Stevens: 'The Death of a Soldier', copyright 1923 and renewed 1951 by Wallace Stevens, from *The Collected Poems of Wallace Stevens*. Reprinted by permission of Faber & Faber Ltd., and Alfred A. Knopf, Inc.

Allen Tate: 'Ode to the Confederate Dead' from *Collected Poems 1919–1976*. Reprinted by permission of Faber & Faber Ltd.

James Tate: 'The Lost Pilot' from *The Lost Pilot* (Ecco Press, 1982). Copyright 1978, 1982 by James Tate. Reprinted by permission of the publisher.

Dylan Thomas: 'The hand that signed the paper' from *Collected Poems* (J. M. Dent, 1952). Reprinted by permission of David Higham Associates Ltd.

Fyodor Tyutchev: 'At Vshchizh', trans. Charles Tomlinson, from *Selected Poems 1951–1974*, © Charles Tomlinson 1978. Reprinted by permission of Oxford University Press.

Andrei Voznesensky: 'I am Goya' from *Antiworlds and the Fifth Ace: A Bilingual Edition*, by Andrei Voznesensky, edited by Patricia Blake and Max Hayward. © 1966, 1967 by Basic Books, Inc. © 1963 by Encounter Ltd. Reprinted by permission of Basic Books, Inc., Publishers.

Sylvia Townsend Warner: 'Benicasim', from *Collected Poems* ed. and with an intro. by Claire Harman (1982). Reprinted by permission of Carcanet Press Ltd.

Richard Wilbur: 'First Snow in Alsace' from *Poems 1943–56*; 'Advice to a Prophet' from *Advice to a Prophet*. Reprinted by permission of Faber & Faber Ltd.

W. B. Yeats: 'An Irish Airman Foresees His Death', and 'On Being Asked for a War Poem', 'Easter 1916', and 'Sixteen Dead Men', all from *Collected Poems*; 'Reprisals' from *The Variorum Edition of the Poems of W. B. Yeats* (eds. Peter Allt and Russell K. Alspach). All reprinted by permission of A. P. Watt Ltd., on behalf of Michael B. Yeats, and Macmillan, London Ltd.

INDEX OF FIRST LINES

The references are to the numbers of the poems

INDEX OF POETS AND TRANSLATORS

The references are to the numbers of the poems

INDEX OF POETS AND TRANSLATORS